FROM ANCIENT ULSTER TO THE FIRES OF A NEW WORLD

The Story of the Connecticut Monagans and their Kin

By David Monagan

Also by the Author:

Jaywalking with the Irish
Journey Into the Heart
Ireland Unhinged

From Ancient Ulster to the Fires of a New World
– The Story of the Connecticut Monagans
and their Kin
Copyright ©2022 David Monagan
ALL RIGHTS RESERVED
ISBN: 978 1-7391001-0-0

For the Generations to Come:

There was White Johnny,
Black Johnny,
Peter and Pat
And twice as many more –
Now how many's that?

From Kelly's Cross, Prince Edward Island, Canada, circa 1850
– from an immigrant's ballad of the Monaghans.

CONTENTS

Descendants of Thomas Mulry Monagan and Margaret Kehoe
Descendants of Helen Monagan and Frederick Marks
Lineage of William Butler – Sarah McKeon
Descendants of Walter Monagan and Mary Elizabeth Butler
Descendants of Bernice Monagan and Arthur Owen Nelson

INTRODUCTION

Growing up in a place called Waterbury, Connecticut, it was inevitable that I would become fascinated by thoughts of where we all come from. That town, once proud enough to call itself "the Brass Capitol of the World," was a magnet to thousands of immigrants from a number of lands, each with their stories of striving and transformation to tell. But for a century and more, Waterbury had a particularly strong Irish American identity. In fact, it was one of the most Irish saturated cities in the entire United States.

There were a number of Italian-speaking Sicilians who lived in a multi-family house at the bottom of the hill, and around one corner resided an extended Albanian family, with a son who was only occasionally allowed to play with us. But mostly this was an Irish Catholic world in the 1950s. Nearly all my parents' friends, three quarters of my teachers, all the priests and nuns, all of Waterbury's mayors (in an unbroken continuum from 1921-1981), the doctor, the dentist, and the guy who cleared our driveway of snow – everyone seemed to have an Irish last name. Possibly to make sense of all this, I developed a taste for Irish literature and later studied at Trinity College in Dublin – in an Ireland that feels like far, far back in time now.

I married a Jane Marie Donnelly of Roscommon origins and in 2000 we moved from Cornwall, Connecticut with our three children for a brief "sabbatical" to Cork City. But here we've remained ever since. Countless opportunities have led us to explore the hidden nooks of Ireland – including County Monaghan – in our family travels and through my writings. As to pursuing the larger history of my clan, the impulse was first prompted by my daughter Laura's wedding to a Rohan Geraghty (from Australia) in 2015. Back then I just wanted to give a well-turned toast. Of course, I ended up prowling for thousands of new facts afterwards, leading to this text.

What follows then is the story of a particular family, which though a story of Ireland, begins with ancient seafaring Celts fleeing Roman legions in Belgium.

The tribe that led from there to these typewriting fingers now was called by Julius Caesar the *Menapii*. After his conquest, they inched their way along the British coast and set off on rickety boats to the remote and shadowy land that was Ireland, a place where no Roman dared to tread. There their names began to change again from the *Manach* to the *Mhuineacháin*. After hundreds of years of living around Wexford and then along the upper reaches of the River Shannon, remnants of this group made their way to that area of brooding drumlins and misty lakes in the south of the Province of Ulster that eventually became known as County Monaghan (though first called by the English "the realm of the MacMahons"). The *Uí' Mhuineacháin* became the O'Monaghans, and their name became conjoint with what the English declared to be a county holding that Monaghan name. Only many generations later did the name of "Monagan" arise, chiefly via my family's agitation in Waterbury, Connecticut.

Some caveats are in order from the start. Namely, trying to reconstruct a family's history is a daunting task anywhere, but especially in Ireland, where in the Civil War in 1922 half the country's historical records went up in flames. A more fundamental problem is that the ancient and even medieval Irish lived in a bardic world where history was primarily passed on via the incantations of poets, rather than in writing. Further, for centuries the native Irish did not speak English at all. Worse for the historian, in County Monaghan there is something like a hundred-year black hole into which vanished the Catholic records of baptism and marriage that have so bountifully materialized on-line from most everywhere else in Ireland from the late 1700s onwards. Finally, both the English and American authorities struggled to write down the name Monaghan the same way twice, mainly since it was delivered to them with a strange accent and often pronounced as Mhuineacháin (mon-a-che-aw-in). The genealogy supercomputers of this era still cannot properly track all these variations in spelling – often for the same person – out of the convoluted jumble of time. Nor are the great historic newspaper search engines equal to the task.

Also, it has become apparent that this particular Irish family managed to forget so much of its past than that was passed on to my father's generation was a myopic vision of a solo wayfarer making his way to Massachusetts almost entirely on his own. Not by a long shot was this so. What has become ever clearer is that my great-great grandfather Andrew Monaghan was but one of a number of brothers, sisters and cousins who were making their way to the Americas (and Antipodes) in multiple salients and with several destinations in mind. These included the "Monaghan Settlement" at Canada's Prince Edward Island; the thrumming textile mills around North Andover and Lowell, Massachusetts; and the remote North Country of upstate New York that had been peddled shamelessly to the Irish by the slave and opium trader Michael Hogan. Ever more thorough genetic profiling suggests that certain individuals or clusters of this family's closest ancestry also proceeded directly to Brooklyn, New York, as well as to the farmlands of Pennsylvania, and in one case Quebec. Other DNA links point to an Australian connection, possibly via the "assisted emigration" of both an Edward and Francis Monaghan from the townland of Rafferagh on the Shirley Estate in County Monaghan in the late 1840s. The great communications difficulties still extent in those years likely had much to do with the family fragmenting and losing touch with each other so irrevocably. Then again, a suggestion has recently emerged that a common great-great-great grandfather named John perhaps had two or even three wives (due to deaths in childbirth). This would help explain possible schisms in age groups and allegiances from the start.

This genealogy will attempt to reshape some of these scattered fragments back together into a much larger whole, but in so doing it will not follow an entirely conventional format. For one thing, many side-tracks or tangents are probed at some length, intentionally. Plus, my paternal ancestors of course married in with numerous other families, each with their own fascination. Their names included Castle and Clark, Nolan and McNamara, Henry, Gregg, Marks, Mulry, McKeon, Butler, Clinton, Lerner, and Cetta, too. A few were "all Irish," but others well mixed with Norman, Scottish, English,

3

and even Viking blood, and then later Italian, Polish, and Jewish and African, too. Some of these people faced terrible trials – for example, children lost at sea or to disease – but somehow still soldiered on and even prevailed.

Along the way this human kaleidoscope inevitably became caught up in the great movements of their times. This narrative would be incomplete without exploring some of those profound historical turns. We are speaking of things like the Irish Famine, the Industrial Revolution, and World War. But let's not forget the splendid times of the 1950s either, with the endless supply of Wiffle Balls and Hula Hoops for all.

The core story here concerns a long continuum of huge struggle and suffering all right, but also some human magic. For what my great-grandfather John Stephen Monaghan achieved within Connecticut's Naugatuck Valley was astonishing. He somehow found a way to conjure an entirely new family destiny out of the molten fires involved in creating brass. It happened that young John became a maestro in the forging or "casting" of this alloy of copper and zinc that had become the Connecticut equivalent of gold – and as word of his talents spread, so did his income and authority grow.

This man, who had been a child laborer in the heaving mills of pre-Civil War Massachusetts, mastered the infernos of Connecticut's heavy industry as if he were born with a wand in his hand. With incredible dedication and with his remarkable wife Anna, John Stephen saw to it that the next generations – with its doctors, nurses, pianists, teachers, accountants, and lawyers – could realize almost anything from grabbing the Yale Law Prize to landing in the United States Congress with that most iconic Irish-American of all times, John Fitzgerald Kennedy, as a friend, and even – with thousands of the people of Waterbury involved – arguably helping him into the White House. So, dear reader, think back through the generations as the pages turn, and think of that famous closing line from Walt Whitman in his *Song of Myself,* "I am large, I contain multitudes." Because we all do.

I.

ANCIENT ANCESTRY

The Manaig, the Monach and the Monaghans

People named Monaghan or its many etymological relations – such as Manning, Meany, Mooney and Mongan – all hail from an early seafaring Belgic tribe that Julius Caesar called the *Menapii*. In their ancient Gaelic they said they were a *Manaig* people. They were most concentrated along the coast of what became modern Flanders but had scattered settlements throughout much of the Rhine delta as it filters out into the North Sea.

By the third century B.C. some of the Manaig had crossed the channel and established outposts along the south coast of "Albion," today's England. Their name is cited a number of times by Julius Caesar in the **Gallic Wars** (58-49 B.C.). His accounts in Latin honor the Menapii as being among the most formidable of all the Belgic tribes or *Belgae*, with a knack for both fierce resistance and repeatedly vanishing – a very Irish trait - when necessary, into their region's great forests and deep coastal marshes. They were among the last of the Belgae to surrender to Rome's might, only doing so when Caesar with five legions laid waste to their territory in 54 B.C.

However, a great diaspora ensued with significant bands of the Menapii making it down the Belgian coast and across the channel toward Britannia or modern southeast England, a.k.a. Kent and Sussex. From there they gradually headland-hopped westward along the coast and then north after Cornwall toward Wales and Scotland. These migrations may have spanned many generations. The diaspora clearly took some of these wandering Celts to the Isle of Man and from there the next stop was "Hibernia" (as it was called by the Romans), that thinly inhabited island that was undoubtedly the subject of many scarifying and exotic tales in those ancient times. Some others of the Manaig people eventually undertook a more northerly direct crossing to Ireland from Scotland. Ultimately, this tribe regathered around today's south Wicklow and Wexford in the east of Ireland, below modern Dublin. Here, in the Province of Leinster, the pronunciation of their name began evolving into Monaig and later Manach.

A map projecting the Menapii's ancient migrations.

6

Ptolemy's map of Ireland.

On the first crude map ever made of Ireland in 140 A.D., the ancient Greek mathematician and geographer Ptolemy identified their dominion in Leinster as the "Kingdom of the Menapia." These were the only tribe he so strongly singled out, although other Celtic groups from the continent were well established elsewhere.

The Manaig were linked to one of Ireland's most celebrated foundation myths through a figure known as *Forgail Manac*h or "Manach of the six fortresses," who was the father of the beautiful Emer. It was she who entranced the legendary demigod and protector of the northern province of Ulster, Cuchulainn, as he searched for the most fetching female in the land to be his bride. Approaching the arch-protective Manach's main fortress, Cuchulainn (of the many shifting shapes and spellings) assumed a salmon's mystical powers and performed a spiraling, gravity-defying, triple-leap to land inside its walls and steal away Emer forever.

For unknown reasons, in the sixth century many of the Manaig moved west toward modern County Roscommon and resettled in the lush lands below Lough Erne. This is one of the most entrancing, serpentine lakes in Ireland with scores of jeweled islands, upon some of which arose early monasteries and oratories to celebrate the new Christian religion. Here the ancestors of anyone bearing the name Monaghan or its variants became known as the *Fir Manach* – "the men of the Manach." In these years the Manach name somehow became cognate with the Irish word for monk: Mhuineacháin. A leader in this area named Manachain – "he of the Manach," was identified

7

in the 866 **Annals of the Four Masters** as being the "Lord of the Three Tuathes" (territories), these comprising a great swath of rich grazing lands fanning out from the upper Shannon basin. The Fir Manach grew in wealth and power and ruled over these lands for the next 400 years.

Ultimately, this domain was upended by constant cattle raiding and pillages by the pests of the O'Beirn clan beginning around 1249. The Uí Manacháin (O'Monaghans) scattered in the following decades, with the largest numbers heading west to Galway and Mayo. But others moved slightly to the northeast to Fermanagh, and that county was most definitely named after them, the "Fir Manach." In time, a handful of these Fermanagh families wove their way a few miles southeasterly into the neighboring lands of what is now County Monaghan. A few historians have argued that this county, created by the English in 1585 after the surrender of a major chief named Rossa MacMahon, may in fact be named after them – with Manacháin ("mon-a-che-aw-in") coming across as "Monaghan" to the English ear. But a much larger cabal of linguists argue that the county name comes from a nearly identical Gaelic word of Mhuineacháin for "place of the little hills," which County Monaghan admittedly has in abundance.

The medieval name for the area was in fact *Oirghiala* (Oriel to the English) and for several hundred years it had been under the control of a number of MacMahon chiefs – not Monaghans – who often warred with each other. But this clan is thought to have spread south from Fermanagh as well. Certain of the Ui Manachain or O'Monaghans may have intermarried with them, explaining the likes of Owen and Cormac O'Monaghan living within their midst in that shadowy border region adjoining Fermanagh and Monaghan.

County Monaghan Then and Now

Today's County Monaghan is a landlocked region in the very south of the **Province of Ulster**, the northernmost of the four ancient kingdoms of Ireland. It borders current Northern Ireland, and thus the United Kingdom, but is firmly part of the independent Republic of Ireland (as are the Ulster counties of Cavan and Donegal). At only 500 square miles, or a tenth the size of one of the smallest American states that is Connecticut, Monaghan is one of the tinier of the entire island's 32 counties (with 26 of them within the Republic). Yet it remains a very distinctive and atmospheric hinterland with countless small lakes furled between steep low ridges called drumlins, which are often shrouded in mist.

Until late in the 1500s, primordial forests cloaked its dark valleys and were only intersected with meanderings trails so narrow in places that intruders could be ambushed at will. The Vikings' terrifying incursions across Ireland scarcely penetrated this region, as it remained an ominous place apart, even for those accomplished marauders. The next wave of Anglo-Norman invaders in the late 12th century, financed by England's Henry II and principally led by Richard "Strongbow" de Clare, never stayed long in the eerie Oirghiala back country either, while otherwise carving up most of Ireland for Henry. Cattle raids from rival septs were a continuing menace, however, and both the McGuire and O'Neill clans were capable of pulverizing a Monaghan castle whenever it suited them.

Until yet one more failed uprising against the British in the 1640s, in County Monaghan and other remote places like Fermanagh and Donegal the ancient Celtic ways sometimes held on with fervor. The social order in such places continued to be organized around extended septs or clans ruled by chieftains who typically operated in confederation with extended family groups. Cattle, the main source of wealth and sustenance, grazed in a clan commonage. Children were in some cases taken away from their mothers and fostered by a succession of kin from their first year on, the goal being to assure the continuing supremacy of their unique tribal identity. Many pagan rituals and beliefs never quite disappeared.

Certain later records indicate that there were still reigning in the north of County Monaghan in the mid-1660s a succession of headmen who were named Owen O'Monaghan, and that their territories were bordered by family lines run by a Cormac and an Art and a Hugh O'Monaghan. Each would have had to work out ways of co-existing with the ruling but constantly squabbling MacMahon tribe of the area and may possibly have had to cut other deals, such as paying tribute in cattle, with the powerful O'Neill's or even the warlord Hugh O'Donnell of "Tyrconnell," as County Donegal was then called.

It was through this system of interlocking alignments that the northern chieftains were able to fight off a major invasion under Queen Elizabeth that sought to subjugate the entire Province of Ulster in 1573-1574. This assault was led by two extremely wealthy and land-lusting English adventurers named Walter Devereux, the 1st Earl of Essex, and Thomas Smith. Despite committing terrible atrocities along the way, they failed to gain much new ground. Nonetheless, Queen Elizabeth in 1576 bequeathed, as if with a magisterial wave of her hand, to Devereux the entire Barony of Farney - essentially the southern third of County Monaghan. The English crown in this era handed out 273 of these "baronies" across the island to their own favored aristocrats or generals, with each of these tracts normally being the holdings of some prior Irish great chieftain or regional king who the English were now emasculating. But little County Monaghan had less space to bandy about – all the English could do there was to divide it into five baronies in 1591.

In the 1590s, Queen Elizabeth made Walter's swashbuckling but half-inept son Robert Deveraux, the 2nd Earl of Essex, her "Lord Lieutenant" of all of Ireland. Perhaps the "Virgin Queen" found him handsome. In 1599 she dispatched him with 17,000 infantry and 2,000 horse to vanquish a fresh island-wide rebellion led by Red Hugh O'Donnell and a new generation Hugh O'Neill from Donegal. Devereux's forces had some success in the south but were soundly defeated in the former Monaghan clan stronghold of Roscommon. Far worse for his reputation, the remaining column of troops were stopped dead in their tracks at the southern border of County Monaghan. The reason was that just across the River Langan and sauntering around on Deveraux's own lands in the Barony of Farney the great Hugh O'Neill stood firm with more than 3,000 native Irish troops, yelling out catcalls and banging on their war drums and bellowing at the English to dare set foot into County Monaghan. Some of my ancestors (who became expert at catcalls) had to have stood on that Langan river bank and helped defeat a great English army with the power of ridicule, rather than of bayonet.

The next year Queen Elizabeth, understandably, had Devereux's head chopped off in London. Yet fate is fickle. Devereux's son, the 3rd Earl of Essex, somehow regained the Crown's favor and eventually assumed firm control of the Barony of Farney. But he had no male heir. So at this Robert's death in 1646, half of these Farney lands – roughly 26,000 acres – were consigned to a Robert Shirley, his daughter's spouse. The resultant "**Shirley Estate**" still exists and its voluminous if moldering archives may tell more of the Monaghan/Monagans of County Monaghan family story than anyone reading this may ever guess. After all, it was the Shirley Estate that for some reason paid for my great-great-grandfather Andrew Monagan to go away forever to America in 1844.

The Four Provinces of Ireland.

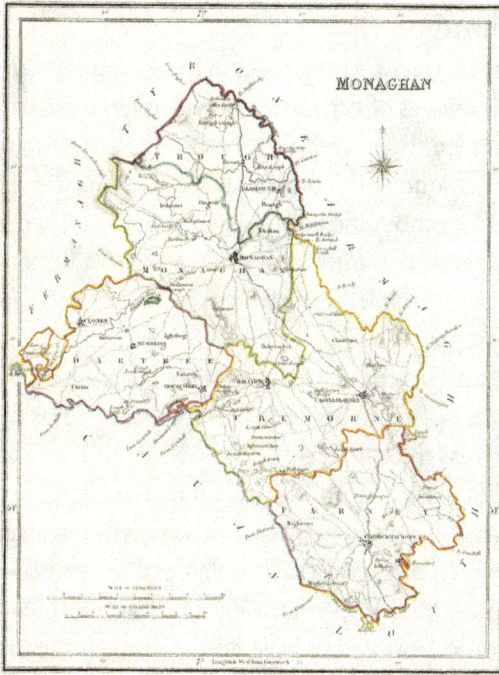

The Baronies of County Monaghan.

Monaghan and its surrounding counties.

Owen the Blond

Following the first Devereux's botched northern campaign, the English launched successive waves of further invasions of Ireland over the next century, so determined they were to wrest absolute control from the ever rebellious populace. Among the most notable conflicts was the **Battle of Kinsale** in 1601 when thousands of Ulstermen fast-marched in the dead of winter to Cork far to the south. But the battle was a fiasco, and the Irish troops were so cut to pieces that the native chieftains' capability for organized rebellion was severely debilitated for generations to follow. To smash resistance further, a particularly ruthless Scots-English campaign was unleashed across Ulster in 1605. But more locally devastating in the Monaghan region was the failed rebellion of 1641. At the siege of Drogheda they said the bodies of men from Monaghan had to be piled in heaps. Even more notorious was Oliver Cromwell's scorched earth campaign across Ireland in 1649, which broke the back of that era's resistance– at least for another generation until the "Glorious Revolution" of 1688-1691. Many of my Monaghan ancestors had to have been present at the nearby **Battle of the Boyne** in 1690 that crushed the Catholic forces in Ireland and effectively put the death knell to the entire region's capacity for any more meaningful resistance for another hundred years.

These waves of English incursions into Ireland inevitably led to further eradication of my ancestors' ancient culture, land ownership, and basic means of self-support, and ultimately even the survival of their own language. However, the invaders' land hunger did make one contribution in the form of the first wholesale, carefully written secular records in Ireland. These emerged in County Monaghan and across Ireland around 1663 when the English imposed their fixed system of administration over every townland, parish, and barony that they wished to be measured. This obsession with calibrating property values was in fact based on Roman ideas about maximizing taxation for the sake of the empire's exchequer. Needless to say it stood in stark opposition to the old Gaelic ways of sharing cattle-grazing land and even child rearing in common with an extended but deeply interwoven and communal sense of family identity.

The first powerful tool for solidifying English colonial rule was the introduction of the **Hearth Money Rolls of 1663-1665**, which sought to inventory wealth across the entire island of Ireland by counting chimneys (even though half of the Irish huts had none). These documents reveal the names of numerous property owners in very specific areas at that time and are thus of great genealogical importance.

All told, the Hearth Rolls reference eight males named O'Monaghan living in County Monaghan between 1663-65. Each was residing to the county's north, under the shadow so to speak of the counties Fermanagh and Tyrone and very near the border therefore with the present political entity of "Northern Ireland." Two of these references are for an Art and Pierce O'Monaghan in **Donagh** parish to the north of Monaghan town, whose descendants will be later met again on Prince Edward Island in Canada. Another four – Edmond, Donagh, Patrick and a Hugh Roe (red) – were O'Monaghans living in the parish of Monaghan which encompassed Monaghan town and lay within the larger barony (as opposed to county) of Monaghan. Their address was thus technically Monaghans at Monaghan, Monaghan, Co. Monaghan. Note that a "townland" is the smallest territorial division within Ireland, often about a half-mile square and variably holding one to several dozen families. In County Monaghan, there are 91 distinct townlands – with 51,000 in all of Ireland - grouped into 24 civic (as opposed to church) parishes of around 20-square-miles each.

The 1663-1665 Hearth Rolls also indicate that the last remaining significant chieftain bearing the family surname in County Monaghan was one "Owen Boy O'Monaghan" of the northern parish of **Tydavnet** near the border with County Fermanagh. In reality his name was *Eoghan bui Monachain* "Owen the Blond" since bui meant yellow. It is noteworthy that that this figure is listed six times on the Hearth Money Roll across different townlands in Tydavnet. These many references suggest a sizeable cluster of family gathered around a common grazing valley over which he was forced by the larger English landlord to collect their individual tithes. Owen O'Monaghan undoubtedly was a still reigning chieftain of some stature in 1663, drawing rents off lesser family members because the English authorities by that time forced people in his position to do so. The Hearth Rolls also reference a nearby Cormac O'Monaghan, another likely kinsman.

To the Owenachta

Curiously, references to this Owen O'Monaghan almost vanish afterwards, along with allusions to the O'Monaghan presence in Tydavnet (as do references to the once mighty MacMahon chieftains). The reason is likely not sloppy record-keeping, but rather a deliberate and sustained stripping away of the lands of former Irish chieftains including those of my ancestors. In his history **The Monaghan Story**, Peader Livingston noted that within the four decades since the start of the 1600s, Irish versus invader ownership of the land in their own County Monaghan had plummeted from 78 percent to just 6 percent. One of the ways this occurred was through the deliberate flooding of Ulster with thousands of Scots. They were pushed by English enticements into County Monaghan throughout the 1600s in largely private initiatives off of the larger, systematic so-called **Plantation of Ulster,** as first started by King James II in County Antrim. This was a systematic strategy unleashed by the English aristocracy in order to lock down their dominance and enhance their rent collections.

In 1624, Lord Edward Blaney, his family eventually to be my Monaghan family's landlords, wrote back to London from his seat at the settlement of Castleblaney in the south of County Monaghan, "To speak truly, the MacMahons [the once powerful local chiefs] are neither willing or able to pay anything and that is the case of the whole county, for all is waste, and now I am laboring to get Scotts."

After the Battle of the Boyne decades later in 1690, the Scottish king **William of Orange** ramped up the process by offering his most able lieutenants especially large tracts in the most rebellious reaches of Ulster. Then, 50,000 or more Scots were hurried in and offered a vast smorgasbord of still further newly seized lands. It is almost inevitable that our O'Monaghan ancestors were profoundly dispossessed in the process.

This ousting is the most likely explanation for the strange shift of these O'Monaghans roughly twenty miles south into a hilly, scruffier area of far less-desirable land, at least for the cattle grazing that had sustained the sept for ages, to the civil parish now known as **Aughnamullen**. This name may have derived from *Áth na Muillên* – "the river ford by the mill."

Though the primary Monaghan family chief at this juncture was indeed named Owen, it is entirely coincidental that this Aughnamullen area had long been called the *Eoghanachta* or the "Land of Owens," what with so many ancient figures hereabouts having been named "Eoghan." That tradition likely started in tribute to the fourth-century high king of the Province of Munster, Eógan Mór ("the Son of the Nine Hostages"). Back in ancient Monaghan, the little river that knits together the surrounding loughs of the Eoghanachta was long called (in a hybrid of English and Irish) the "Owenagh." On a summit overlooking nearby Lough Egish ("lake of the learned man") stands a megalithic burial cairn wherein was found an exquisite ancient silver urn that once held the ashes of a very high chieftain, he too likely being an Owen.

The district is dotted with many small lakes and lies within the **Barony of Cremorne**, just above the aforementioned Barony of Farney. Aughnamullen traverses the upper levels of a single sprawling hill that is called **Bunnanimma**, which is actually the highest peak in County Monaghan at 886 feet in elevation. But even at that modest height, in the Province of Ulster mists can settle in for days. In his wonderful **A Topographical Dictionary of Ireland,** Samuel Lewis first explained in 1837 that the waters from Bunnanimma flow either southeast to Dundalk and the Celtic Sea or west-north-west to Ballyshannon on the River Erne in County Donegal

One of the most reliable early Monaghan family records linking to Aughnamullen comes via a weaver named John Monaghan, who is mentioned in the genealogically hugely important survey called the **Flax Growers Census of 1796**. He must be considered an important ancestor, and possibly was my great-great-great-grandfather. There are hundreds of flax weavers in Aughnamullen listed in this census. But John is the only one named Monaghan to be found there at the time, and we know this was a family vocation.

Today the surname of Monaghan – with its many variants – is fairly widespread in the English-speaking world. One 2014 analysis asserted that there were 9,971 people with the name in the U.S, and in England 6,910, with 3,701 in Ireland itself. But in the late 1600s there were only eight known O'Monaghan families who had at least one chimney in the miniature county that shares their name, suggesting a strong possibility that they were all inter-related

In any case, as late as the early 1800s there were still only about 80 families named Monaghan living within the entire county, with a small concentration of these living in the parish of Aughnamullen south of the county's center and larger numbers concentrated around Clones (pronounced "clone-ez") on the border of Fermanagh (again, "Fir [men] of the Monach"). There were others clustered around Monaghan town in the Barony of Monaghan, about twelve miles north of Aughnamullen.

The precise family connection to Aughnamullen is made clear by the oaths of naturalization sworn in Massachusetts by my great-great-great uncle Owen (probably Edward Owen), a weaver and "wool scourer," who indicated in

1842 (when about 35) that he was born in the Aughnamullen townland of **Lurgachamloch** (to the English, "Lurgahamloe"), and by the 1853 declaration of his younger brother Andrew. The later-arriving Andrew Monaghan (likely more officially named at baptism Charles Andrew) was my great-great grandfather and he was born on August 1, 1822. His oath of allegiance to America in 1853, with obligatory rejection of the authority of the British crown, said that he was born in the townland of "Laty Crum," which is to say a half-a-square-mile quilt-work of cottages and fields, whose proper spelling is **Lattacrom**. The two townlands of Lurgachamloch and Lattacrom in fact abut and the family farm likely straddled the invisible "border."

This was the same Aughnamullen parish where the aforementioned John Monaghan was awarded by the English in 1796 a free loom to expedite the family's increased capabilities for spinning flax into linen, one of the crucial land management initiatives of that time. It now seems likely that Owen and Andrew's mother was an Elizabeth or Mary Elizabeth **Henry** – and possibly in some earlier strain a Protestant. The second son, Owen, was possibly named with a nod to the Owen O'Monaghan chieftain(s) of yore – and to the Owenachta region of his birth. The namesake of my own second son, this Owen would rove far and serve as a beacon for various family members in the decades ahead.

The family's holdings in Aughnamullen clearly lay in the western end of the parish and close to the once-bustling linen and livestock market in the small, Scots-Protestant-dominated town of **Ballybay** (which was the center of a larger civic parish of the same name). According to the **Tithe Applotment Books** of the late 1820s, at least seven independent households within this 30,710-square acre parish of Aughnamullen were then headed by people named Monaghan. An Edward Monaghan – a vital family forename for generations – held at least three acres in Lurgachamloch around 1829. Between the births of Owen and Andrew, there may have been as many as ten other Monaghan children, according to tradition and one line of family lore, as well as per many newly recovered records. In all, there may have been 16 or even 17 children in the family, with several preceding even Owen.

One family historian, a Daniel T. Monaghan, a professor of biology at the University of Nebraska and who is DNA linked to this family, believes that John Monaghan of Tievaleny had a succession of three wives (presumably due to two deaths during childbirth). This might explain the considerable age spread apparent between both the definite as well as strongly inferred siblings of my great-grandfather Andrew Monaghan. The biologist Daniel in personal correspondence traces his own lineage to a son **Patrick** (b. about 1800) whose first stop from County Monaghan was in the Canadian Maritimes, as was common in the early Irish crossings from Ulster, before ultimately making it to the American Midwest. His research points toward a brother **James**, a name ubiquitous in this family, being born around 1804, and Francis around 1812. The aforementioned Edward was either an esteemed brother of John of Tievaleny (and thus a great-great-great-great uncle) or the true progenitor of the family line concentrated upon in this book. My guess remains that he was the former. But there may well have been a previous Owen and Patrick among the 1770s-1790s siblings as well.

In any event, the Aughnamullen Monaghan children of the late 1700s and early 1800s may have enjoyed a fairly bucolic upbringing. The area then was still realizing a thriving linen cash-crop trade that put ample food on the table and created work for nearly all. But this situation was not to last. By the time of Andrew's birth in 1822, this cottage linen-making economy's best days were receding and indeed the whole gently sustainable way of living in Monaghan was already under deep threat from over-population as well. Thousands of young Monaghan people lost all prospect of self-support and great numbers of them set off to Scotland for paying work in the fields and also the textile mills around Glasgow and Greenock. Another incentive for evacuating Aughnamullen was that by the 1820s tensions between the natives and the planters from Scotland had grown so ugly there were hints of possible civil war in the making, especially in the tinderbox of nearby Ballybay.

Personal Encounters in Monaghan

My interest in the family's history was partly seeded by the early genealogical research conducted by my uncle Walter Edward Monagan, with the aid of his cousin John S. Monagan. It was further prompted by my studying at Trinity College in Dublin when young and moving permanently back to Ireland with my family in the year 2000. Close family guidance from my cousin Michael Monagan and his cousin Andrew Pierce ultimately directed me in 2009 to Aughnamullen, and the doorstep of a particular long-held ancestral home.

The destination was a townland a mile west of Lattacrom called **Tievaleny** "the hillside of the meadow" – which lies close to a crossroads called Shantonagh. Tievaleny is just one of 1,852 townlands in County Monaghan. But a definite plus for this place was that it bordered a small reedy lake whose surrounding lowlands would have been excellent for growing flax. From flax was made linen, the all-important cash crop in this area for generations – and the key to my family's past.

Naturally, I felt some trepidation back then about barging up the drive to the particular farm that Michael Monagan had identified, the one with generations of my family's past apparently woven into its every inch. But I was warmly greeted by a most hospitable, if by now distant cousin named Sean Monaghan. His house stood atop the knoll and commanded panoramic views over a rolling, intensely green landscape. Sean soon showed me around his surrounding farmlands, which had been worked by our common ancestors for many generations. One heard cows lowing, chickens cackling, and a tractor grumbling in the near distance – all very transporting. The farm had a number of old outbuildings, some sagging with the weight of time. But the centerpiece was a large new metal dairy barn, glistening in the late afternoon sun. Sean, around 50 years old, praised its efficient milking facilities, especially important after he was left to work alone following the death of his brother **Edward**.

Down the back slope of the farm and beside the winding Lurgachamloch Road, the small Tievaleny Lough was dotted with birds. The panorama on all sides was as serene as a Zen painting and one could imagine the many rough dwellings that would have once lined this small valley. My ancestors would have been proud to live in Sean's house at the top of the knoll, which had only four rooms in its early years, because they then would have been among the lucky ones. In the early 1800s a good 40 percent of the natives' huts in Ireland were still only one-or two-room hovels with a mud floor, sod walls, and a roof of dried reeds.

After our walk, Sean invited me in to meet his wife and daughters. We looked over photographs and discussed the olden times. I tried to imagine my great-great grandfather Andrew's presence here as a boy in the 1820s, and his excitement at the periodic returning home of his big brother Owen from his evident stints at Scottish woolen mills. We spoke of many family puzzles, including the matter of religion. This pertained to a mysterious old farmer named James Monaghan, who was burrowed away in the back time just a mile or so to the northwest in the aforementioned Lattacrom townland and yet was scarcely seen. James, Sean warned, was a rather virulent Protestant who denied his family ever had a genetic thing to do with any Monaghans of the Catholic sort hereabouts.

What a gulf of understanding lay ahead. I spent the night in the nearby small town of Castleblaney, near the border of County Armagh, which remarkably exists in the separate country that is Northern Ireland.

Gleaning no particular knowledge in the cafes and pubs, I visited the historic grounds of Lord Edward Blaney, the former chief landlord for Aughnamullen – and made governor of all of County Monaghan in 1607. He received extensive lands in return for promising to build a fortress to establish a secure halting-place for Royal forces daring to venture out of Dublin en route to a barracks at Monaghan town 11 miles to the north, or Londonderry another 60 miles further on. Blaney's descendants collected his Aughnamullen rents through middlemen. The man extracting the rents of my ancestors in the early 1800s was named Andrew McMath, and his family had a substantial house here. Blaney's own former estate hugged the shores of Loch Muckno, which looks across to woodland beyond where the Republic of Ireland suddenly turns into the United Kingdom. This was interesting to me since a nearby pig farmer named "Slab" Murphy who was thick in the Irish Republican Army was often in the news for handling the attempted serving of Northern Ireland arrest warrants at his front door by walking out the back door and into the Republic to tend to his swine.

Muckno and Blaney's lands were in the dead middle of the route that Walter Devereux, Queen's Elizabeth's "Earl Marshall of Ireland," first took north from Dublin, laying waste to most everything in his path with an advance team of specialists in burning and smashing Irish cottages, which made the area safe for lesser gentry like Lord Blaney. But now, in 2009, the original old great house had gone to seed and a few years later, teenage vandals burned the place into obliteration.

The next day I drove back to the townland of Lattacrom, the same place that my great-great grandfather Andrew Monaghan swore that he had been born in 1822. The object was the farm of the cantankerous James Monaghan about whom I had been forewarned. This proved to lay at the end of a long tree-lined and hidden lane protected by a corroded, metal gate with a wildly painted "Keep Out" sign at its start. Up past small woods the lane crossed open fields sporting a few grazing horses. It then turned to a very trim, low whitewashed farmhouse and surrounding barns. Within resided the ancient but fit looking bachelor, James Monaghan, who, despite my long journey, declined to invite me in. As noted, his family had "gone Protestant" many years ago – a very controversial thing to do in this border region beside modern Northern Ireland.

James indeed got a little worked up by his assumption that I was, in contrast to him, "a Papist." But the man was living half-magically, or half-madly if you wish, in some other age. He fiercely rejected the idea that we could possibly be relations, even that Sean so close by shared any ancestry with him either. "Aye, we are not from the same tribe!" insisted Jim. Despite his advanced age, he still pedaled his bicycle three or so hilly miles each way to the nearest shops or his doctor in Ballybay, often smoking his pipe as he rolled up the boreens like some bizarre figure out of the novels of Flann O'Brien. But Jim had to be wrong. Both Monaghan-owned farms almost certainly shared ancient connections since we are talking here about an extremely small slice of Ireland. And Lattacrom in its former heyday was so small that it would have held only about a dozen families living side-by-side.

Problems with Records

There are a lot of reasons why people in County Monaghan, like Jim, could lose a firm grip on their lineage. One had to do with the loss of countless national census and inheritance records from the last seven hundred years due to the burning of the Four Courts in Dublin during the Irish Civil War of 1922. What happened to the Catholic baptismal and wedding records of Monaghan until about 1840, prolific in so many other counties, seems to be a mystery unto itself. Another problem, historically, has to do with the fact that many families struggled to stay put for long in any particular dwelling after their ancient lands were reassigned to waves of military adventurers and Scottish planters. Only a small minority of Irish families had much chance of keeping to a single hallowed plot for generations through time.

The central issue was that the native Irish were simply not allowed to own any land in their own country for generations. Nearly the entire populace, even proud chieftains, had by the late 17th century been reduced to peasants subsisting on English estates. To make matters worse, their leases typically expired at 21 years (although they were often renewed). Evictions could occur without notice all along the way and for any number of reasons, beginning with the failure to pay the rent due to the landlord, or his middlemen. Failing to pay "tithes" to the Church of England, whose houses of worship natives would never set foot in, could also get your humble hut leveled. Given these conditions, tenant farms changed hands frequently in the 1700s and early

1800s. Many dispossessed families also kept vying for better land throughout this period as their next generation expanded in numbers dramatically.

There are only a few surviving indices for ascertaining basic facts about the distant history of Irish families, so it is fortunate that several of these help clarify the early O'Monaghan presence in Aughnamullen. The next substantial nationwide survey after the Hearth Rolls of 1643-45 was the **Flax Growers Census of 1796,** by which the English awarded spinning looms for making linen to the most industrious flax growers in each district. As noted, a John Monaghan of Aughnamullen (specific site unmentioned) was one of these. The next important annals were the **Tithe Applotment Books of 1829**, and the somewhat sketchy **Griffith's Valuation**, printed in 1861. These later two inventories underline the expanding presence of the Monaghan clan in Aughnamullen in these years, with a number of them surely being descendants of the 1796 flax grower John.

In 1829, when my great-great grandfather Andrew was still a boy in Aughnamullen, there was both a new generation John Monaghan and possibly six other heads of household named Monaghan scattered throughout the civil parish. But some of these individuals appear to have worked more than one holding, or to have subdivided their lands. Back then the peasantry in Monaghan were also required to pay a separate rent on whatever piece of boggy wasteland in which they were allotted to dig peat to heat their homes, leading to some duplication.

The Tithe Applotment Books of 1829 identify no Monaghan with a residence then in Lattacrom. But they do name an Edward Monaghan working three acres as a farmer in adjoining Lurgachamloch, the townland that my great-great-great uncle Owen identified as being the true place of the family's origin.

It is interesting that Edward was liable for roughly twice the tithe payments of neighboring farms two and three times larger, suggesting his land was either of better quality or better managed than his neighbors. This Edward had to have been a direct ancestor. It is possible that he was Owen's oldest brother or else his father, meaning my great-great-great grandfather, though my guess is that he was an uncle. The name Edward has certainly been repeated through at least four generations of my family to follow. In any case, the Monaghan family did not stay put on the farm straddling Lurgachamloch/Lattacrom, but rather seems to have taken control of the larger farm in Tievaleny a half-mile south – in short, the one worked to this day by Sean Monaghan. Perhaps this change happened when the family's numbers had become too large to subsist on the three acres in Lurgachamloch/Lattacrom. At the end of the day, the three townlands pinpointed in this narrative – Tievaleny, Lattacrom, and Lurgachamloch – must just be considered as one central nexus of a large ancestral family. Every ancestor would have grown up in and worked this territory in close proximity.

Scattered around other townlands in the vicinity in 1829 also were other Monaghan-surnamed property holders named Patrick, Peter, James, Michael, Anna, and indeed a John Monaghan – he very probably of a next generation from the Flax Census. Some 30 years later, **Griffith's Valuation of Ireland** (principally printed in 1861) – gives valuable insights on the succeeding generation. It lists the 1850s Monaghan householders in Aughnamullen as including an Anne, Mary, Margaret, and Honora, as well as John, Hugh, Peter, Patrick, Owen, and Bernard (who seems to have also retained a shop in Ballybay). Every one of these is likely a genetic relative. Some of these associations will be discussed in more detail later, but to understand this family history and how it led to a great diaspora to Scotland and North America, it is time to step back and more closely examine the lives these denizens of County Monaghan surely once lived.

II.

STRIFE IN OLD MONAGHAN

The Penal Laws

Following the defeat at the Battle of the Boyne in 1690 of the last major Gaelic uprising for generations to come, the English unleashed a mighty vengeance upon the whole rebellious Province of Ulster. To eradicate the last vestiges of power from the likes of "Owen Boy O'Monaghan," vast swaths of land were reassigned to various captains-for-hire and thousands of lowland Scots, with promises of nearly free land if they would just help hold the line against any further uprisings. The process was more systematic in several counties to the north, but it was the bane of County Monaghan as well. The natives were summarily stripped of the right to bear arms, or to hold onto much of anything beyond the most marginal acreage for renting. Any Protestant admiring a Catholic-owned horse could demand that the rider dismount on the spot and turn his steed over for an amount never to exceed 5 pounds sterling. Thanks to the in-flooding of the Scots across County Monaghan and the numerous mercenaries from Wales who had served with Cromwell, a handful of small towns – such as Clones, Monaghan, and Carrickmacross – arose as places for the newcomers to cluster together with muskets loaded after dark.

To consolidate their power further, the English introduced in the early 1700s other "Penal Laws" that were aimed at effectively destroying the natives' last vestiges of independence. Each civil parish was now allowed a maximum of one priest, where there might have been dozens before. Any newly disenfranchised priest who still attempted to say Mass or visit the dying had a 20-pound-sterling bounty placed on his head. The education of children was forbidden. A separate reward of 10 pounds was offered for informing on "hedgerow teachers" who attempted to keep giving forbidden lessons to Irish children out of sight of the English authorities. Thus, actual Irish people in their own land took to offering secret signs on the road as to when the next Mass or even school lesson might occur. Any commercial pursuits judged to be in competition with the English back home were simply prohibited, spelling the end to the woolen trade in Ulster.

Inevitably, the native Irish boiled with resentment. A new class of avengers called "Reparees" came to life in County Monaghan, some lurking in the woods quite close to Lattacrom. They regularly pounced upon and robbed English wayfarers with daggers drawn. As the raiders' numbers grew and the destitution in the region became clear to all, the more progressive English landlords began to insist that the powers in London tone down these ghastly Penal Laws. A general amelioration did in fact begin to unfold in the second half of the eighteenth century.

Linen and the Good Times

As the late 1700s ticked along a modicum of prosperity ebbed back into County Monaghan, in large part due to a burgeoning cottage industry in growing flax and rendering it into linen for export to England and Europe.

The flax-to-linen trade provided a vital means for the peasantry to earn desperately needed cash to supplement their marginal farms. The whole process absorbed countless hours through great stretches of the year and became a fundamental part of the local culture. That the rising prosperity from the linen trade also contributed to an amelioration of relations with the more progressive English landlords is illustrated by an article in the *Dublin Journal* in September 1790 pertaining to a remarkable celebration at a big house in County Cavan – at most six miles south from Aughnamullen:

"On 1 September at Cootehill, Co. Cavan, about 500 of the linen weavers of that place, together with the linen drapers, walked in procession with a machine carried [on certain backs], on which a boy was weaving and a girl spinning, dressed in linen and white gloves ornamented with orange and blue ribbons, after which Mr. Coote gave a grand dinner at his house." Much drink was served, and apparently some of the natives even raised toasts to the English king George III.

Considering the proximity, and the great number of linen tradesmen involved, John Monaghan of Aughnamullen was likely in on the party. This linen making was a social pursuit at various times, although it was a bit segregated with the men generally handling the more arduous and more remunerative weaving side of things, and the women the spinning. Being Irish, they could sometimes make a great party of it. According to Denis Carolan Rushe's, **History of Monaghan for Two Hundred Years: 1660-1860,** the women of a townland might join together on certain summer nights in a farm house's central living area to do their spinning from flax to linen while exchanging stories and taking turns at rendering songs. The men typically pursued various sports outside while perhaps passing a jug of poitin, the wild potato whiskey of the land. The woman usually talked in Irish, but the men liked to show off their prowess in English with taunts, boasts, and oaths. Here is one song, which sadly exists now only in English, which the women sang:

> The neighbor has come in
> With the wheel on the shoulder, playfully
> To sing, to chat, and to spin,
> And when at gloaming the lads would come
> And shyly open the door.
> The wheels would birl with a louder hum
> Than ever they did before.

And here is one the children sang:

I see the moon, the moon sees me,
God bless the moon, and God bless me.
There's a grace in the cottage,
And grace in the hall,
And the grace of God be about us all.

The late 1700s saw many good harvests and a reasonable equanimity prevailing among the population. Paintings from that time suggest that for some reason the people of Monaghan were obsessed with the color blue. Oddly, the young ones often sported light blue in their leggings, but the grown-ups invariably went for darker, more indigo blue in their garments. Through much of the year, the ladies were wrapped in heavy cloaks, with a hood that could be lifted over their heads when the rain lashed down. The grown men sported tall, stove-pipe-shaped woolen hats, whereas the boys went about in tight-fitting round caps. Most in fact did have shoes, and the meals were not all porridge, potatoes, and broth then. In these years beef or mutton were common Sunday fare, and goose was served at special occasions and especially Christmas.

In this period, the natives of Monaghan enjoyed frequent diversions with parades and other celebrations, typically paired with a major sporting event. There was always a passion for hurling, that wildly roving ball game played with long bladed sticks that first began with rival tribes belting around skulls rather than sliotars. On alternate Sundays Gaelic football games were carried out with cow bladders sheathed in rawhide and kicked up and down the drumlins. Horse races provided the occasions for especially memorable celebrations, sometimes embellished by side acts like cock-fights, and contests of discus-like stone throwing. The children had games like "Scotch hop" and marbles (of baked clay), and puppetry with raggedy dolls. Fiddlers, pipers, and ballad singers (some in English, more in Irish) descended in numbers, and a wandering harpist was a rare treat. The fiery poitin and terrific ale from

Castleblaney flowed. On certain nights the people of Aughnamullen would join in step dancing until dawn, with the more boisterous affairs occurring at a big crossroads like Shantonagh, just down the road from Lattacrom.

Even more colorful were the county-wide celebrations in Monaghan town where great throngs joined to celebrate St. Patrick's Day and also the mid-August feast of the Assumption of the Virgin Mary. For the ensuing parades, the people of every parish – children and adults alike – were dressed in their finest and sporting green sashes and marched behind their own raucous fiddle and pipe bands mounted on horse-drawn carts. These were times when young and old met with their cousins from around the county to talk and court. There was drinking and dancing aplenty, too.

The marvelous **History of Monaghan for Two Hundred Years** nicely describes how a year's farming in County Monaghan might play out in a good season at the end of the eighteenth century. The average family farm then

was 10 acres (some even 30) with a core 1 and ½ acres in potatoes, 4 aces in oats (sometimes mixed with wheat), ½ an acre in flax, ¼ acre in vegetables, ¾ acre in meadow, 2 acres in grazing. Typically there were 2 milch cows on the land, 1 horse, 1 or 2 pigs, and an ass. When it came time for spring plowing the neighbors locked their horses together within a heavy wooden yoke and worked as a commonweal through each other's fields. For fertilizer, the animal dung and the ash of turf fires were spread with marl far and wide. So at least in the more benevolent years, life did have its glad moments.

As my 2009 host Sean Monaghan recalled, his ancestral Tievaleny house was originally comprised of four rooms and ringed by various outbuildings, and this was larger than many other local family dwellings back then. The house's dimensions and the little lake below, ringed as it is by a substantial area of low clayey ground, speak back to the old flax economy. We know that this crop's cultivation was important to the family by at least 1796 when the Flax Grower's Census cited John Monaghan as qualifying for a free spinning-wheel, as per the Crown's dispensing one of those for each "rood" of flax grown (about a quarter of an acre). This John Monaghan, farmer, may have been a person of some esteem locally and more heavily involved with the flax-to-linen trade than meets the eye now, since on March 23, 1774, John (or his same-named father) is cited several times as the key witness to a property transfer to an Isaiah Breakey of Creve townland near Ballybay, whose French Huguenot family essentially started and dominated for decades the entire region's linen trade. John's vouchsafe must then have been good as gold, suggesting that at this time the family was not down at the heels. (See, with thanks to Andrew Pierce: thesilverbowl.com/documents/1774)

Following the Flax Grower's Census, 384 spinning wheels were distributed throughout Aughnamullen parish in that year's sudden bonanza of British husbandry. Any enterprising family blessed with sufficient numbers of hands for the work was getting busy at turning flax into linen by then. But this was a laborious job, requiring up to twelve boilings of the raw material and as many bleaches of it with a mixture of cow urine and dung, buttermilk, pota- toes and salt, and much else. Then the material had to be hammered into pliant obedience upon a flat stone with a wooden mallet and dried in the sun. Only after many weeks was the flax ready for spinning into yarn – that task mostly assigned to the women – and then weaving by the men into linen. The process typically took six months to complete from April to September. One nineteenth-century observer said, "It required continuous attention and was, from beginning to end, primitive and disgusting to the utmost degree."

It helped that West Aughnamullen (the parish had two districts at first) was crisscrossed by small streams between the little region's many lakes, since these provided a ready means of power for more ambitious flax-production schemes. In fact, according to **A Topographical Dictionary of Ireland,** a single stream running through the nearby townland of **Carickatee** (where a Patrick Monaghan lived for years) held in that small space 14 flax bleaching mills "on its short course northward to Ballibay [sic] water, the tail race of one serving as the head of the next below it; the lake [beside Ballybay] is under the care of an engineer, or waterman, so that a deficiency is seldom experienced..."

In his 1801 **Statistical Survey of Monaghan,** the aforementioned Charles Coote noted, "Scarcely a cabin is to be seen without a loom or two, and many of the occupiers rent the cabin and the loom from the master weaver, who may be said to be above want. The women spin all the yarn and are extremely industrious. Many of them will earn 6d. [per day]. The children are also employed and will earn from 2d. to 4d. per day, so the more numerous the family is, the better they can afford to live."

In short, it is likely that flax growing and rendering consumed many days of the year through several genera-tions on the Monaghan family's farms in and around Tievaleny. Every child of a certain age would have participated in the laborious harvesting and curing of the reedy plants and steady refinement of the harvest into a woven cloth fit for sale in the local markets. And every child would have thrilled to attend the Saturday sales in Ballybay (until they became plagued by vicious sectarian rancor).

But apart from the side-lines of flax harvesting and linen trading, these were hard lands to farm, with marginal soil quality and protracted rainy seasons. A family might have a total of five or even ten acres to work, but in many cases this might be divided among several grown sons and other relatives in need. Each might be living in their own hut but paying some minimal rent to the main lease-holder before he had to ante up the whole kitty to the likes of Andrew McMath and his armed escorts from Castleblaney. To generate more cash, many farmers distilled the fiery, mind-altering poitin, which the landlords despised for being a bulwark of a secret and thus untaxed economy. But flax was the main ticket. My extended ancestral family undoubtedly trudged off many the Saturday with their laden donkey carts to the great flax and linen marts in the nearest small town called Ballybay ("approach to the ford of the birch trees"). Ballybay was then a predominantly Scots-Irish settlement of some 1200 residents and an appreciation of its tumultuous past is vital to the understanding of the Monaghan family's history. Many relatives with names like Henry and Duffy likely came from the townlands around Ballybay. [The author's Scots-Irish maternal Hawthorn ancestors most certainly came from Ballybay, though they left for South Carolina in 1759.]

For years, Ballybay's streets were lined with linen buyers every Saturday, as even the modest-sized parish of Aughnamullen had up to 1,500 occasional weavers working on making linen in the early nineteenth century. An additional 8,000 to 12,000 "stones" (14 pounds) of raw flax were sold in Ballybay as well. Horses, cattle, pigs, and chickens were all traded too – always for silver coins, or outright barter, since paper money was loathed. The town had 24 public houses for celebrating the closing of the day's deals. One can imagine the rising chatter and boisterous singing in the Irish tongue that would have gone on within a few of those shebeens in the olden days (while forbidden most everywhere else).

Constant Subjugation

Even when the flax economy was thriving, life was never easy for the natives of County Monaghan. Most were not only poor but also bitterly resentful when moments of particular oppression arose. Their greatest antipathy was reserved for the rent-collecting agents of the landlords and for the proxies of the Church of England who would thunder in with a posse on horseback at their sides to demand payment on the spot. The "tithes" to be paid to the English churches were especially despised because no Catholic would ever even set foot into one of those. Additionally infuriating were the demands for additional rents to be paid just to cut turf from boggy wastelands. To keep the population paying up, the larger landlords employed a considerable web of enforcers and spies. These included process servers; "grippers" to impound livestock until all arrears were settled; and what was called the "crow bar brigade" who would burn and demolish houses at bayonet point and leave the suddenly homeless families to seek shelter in the wilds. A fourth element were called the "watchers" and these included destitute natives paid to betray their neighbors at the slightest sign of possible secret assets, such as a poitin stills hidden in a back field.

The resultant inspections could be brutal, especially in the late 1790s when militia units were dispatched to scour the south of County Monaghan for poitin making. As the heavily armed dragoons rode up to some peasant's front door, the children would hurry about the neighboring lanes banging pots and blowing horns in order to foment instant angry crowds. The result was often a mob screaming insults and throwing stones at the dragoons, who were all too willing to begin bashing and slashing away with their swords.

A particular horror occurred on April 12, 1797, at the crossroads and lakeside village of Ballytrain at the western end of Aughnamullen. Today, a Mary Monaghan McConnell, a cousin of mine and sister of the aforementioned Sean Monaghan of Tievaleny, owns with her husband a sizeable pub there. It's a quiet, lightly inhabited locale with a pretty lake below. But once the British dragoons set to their ransacking in 1797, an angry crowd of hundreds of natives materialized, shouting, waving pitch forks, and grabbing at the horses' reins. The troopers reared up and unleashed several broadsides into the throng, killing at least 15, and wounding many more. Three of the militia men were pulled from their horses and beaten to death by the mob, and several others maimed. This of course sparked such ugly retribution by the English that Aughnamullen essentially fell into a churning darkness that malingered for years.

The Anglo-Irish gentry had been on extreme edge for a long while anyway. They were terrified for years by the sweeping reach across Europe of the revolutionary ideals and bloody ways of the French Revolution (1789- 1799) and were convinced that shadowy French agents were circulating across Ireland and preaching wild anarchy. In truth, the French had attempted one botched invasion of Ireland's northwest in 1796, and the important **United Irishmen** movement was gaining considerable force across the island by then. By 1798, even disaffected Scots-Irish were taking up arms in a furiously growing nationwide insurgency against the English. A crisis point was reached when the French in August 1798 brought an invasion armada into Bantry Bay in West Cork, although this was scattered by a ferocious gale. Still, the United Irishmen Rebellion pressed on. Yet they achieved little beyond the death of 10,000-30,000 rebels by the end of 1798.

For my ancestors, the results were not good. The British responded to the rebellion of 1798 by stripping away almost every right the Catholics had been ceded with the phasing out of the Penal Laws. Their new "Acts of Union" were copper-fastened for the next 30 years and they were fierce. A core decree involved denying the Irish the right to hold title to any office whatsoever in their own country – while packing off to London from Dublin every last vestige of independent administrative control.

The Irish of Aughnamullen plodded on stoically for a while, but eventually Catholic resentment began to seethe with a renewed fervor. By the 1820s, a fresh uproar spread across the island, which was called the **Catholic Emancipation Movement**, and led most notably by the brilliant solicitor Daniel O'Connell, called "the Liberator" and an Irish hero to this day. The tension grew especially explosive around Ballybay. A ruffian element there took often to taunting and beating Catholics at the end of the linen and cattle fairs. In July and August they reveled in their drum-thumping, and invective-spewing "Orange" parades celebrating the subjugation of the natives across Ulster since 1690. One Ballybay demonstration in the early 1820s drew a tumultuous crowd of possibly several thousand Protestants, many armed, to remind Catholic agitators just who held the real power on the streets.

Sam Gray and Near Civil War

A good deal of the strife around Ballybay was fomented by an infamous figure named Samuel Gray. Gray was one of the most bigoted and heavy-handed "tithe collectors" in the land and it is no exaggeration to say that he did his best to drive Ireland to the brink of civil war. By day, Gray ran an ale house called the York Hotel, which catered to the most virulently anti-Catholic denizens of the region, be they transplanted Scots, the descendants of Welsh soldiers, or farmers from northern England just looking for a new lease on life. The York Hotel doubled as the headquarters of a notoriously belligerent "Orange Lodge" or local chapter of an arch-Protestant frater-nity, of which he was the local "Worshipful Master," that started spreading across Ireland in 1795. Its members – called "Orangemen" now – sported orange sashes and orange ribbons (never green) and staged wildly militaristic summer parades across Ulster in particular with booming, orange-rimmed drums and the brandishing of orange-sheathed swords. These came to a crescendo on each July 12, when the fanatics swore eternal fealty to Prince William of Orange for having on that date in 1690 (in the old calendar) routed the Catholics at the Battle of the Boyne. Amazingly, in Northern Ireland these rites are fervidly reenacted each and every summer to this day as a celebration of "the Glorious Twelfth."

Sam Gray's infamous York Hotel.

Vengeance was Gray's game. In its pursuit he was appointed for at least 17 years as the "Tithe Proctor" in nearby Aughnamullen. In that capacity he constantly worked at intimidating the Catholic peasantry to fork over their tithes for the Church of England and the wealth of its local vicars and bishops – or else face his unholy wrath. In the event of a failure to pay, Gray typically arrived at the door of recalcitrant peasant families at dawn with a dozen heavily-armed and liquored-up ruffians on horseback whooping around the property to scare the living daylights out of those inside. To those who pleaded they had nothing to give, Gray's next move was often to toss a flaming torch into the thatched roof. If rock-throwing mobs materialized, he knew how to put them down. For nearly 20 years, Gray was accused of bludgeoning and murdering a remarkable string of Catholics who dared to resist him in any way. Though a psychopath, his friends on the stacked juries in arch-Protestant Ballybay acquitted him time after time. As early as 1824, the May 22 edition of the distant *Waterford Mirror* reported that Gray was implicated in the murder of a rural Monaghan Catholic named Bernard McMahon who was kicked to death in a sectarian brawl at the Ballybay linen market, but that the local constabulary refused to arrest him. Reports of his atrocities regularly made their way into the London newspapers.

Eviction was never happy.

Even there, more progressive voices began warning that the man had gone berserk and become the epitome of the worst aspects of the English tyranny in Ireland. But Gray's star somehow kept rising back in central Monaghan. This partly owed to the fact that the Catholic Emancipation movement of Daniell O'Connell was then unnerving a lot of Protestants. As Catholics began staging mass protest rallies and even occasionally raiding Protestant country houses in search of firearms, the Scots-Irish of Ballybay responded by making Samuel Gray their High Constable.

On the night of September 20, 1826, a mob of drunken Orangemen in Ballybay offered their response to the Catholic Emancipation movement by pelting the local rectory with whiskey bottles and unloading their pistols into its windows. Chanting "No Popery!" they threatened death to the priests inside. Constable Gray arrested no one. Instead, he founded a county-wide vigilante group which he dubbed the "Domination Party."

On the other side, a Dublin rabble-rouser who called himself "Honest Jack Lawless" took to staging mass rallies throughout 1828 to stir up Catholic rage. The supremely eloquent Daniel O'Connell called him "Mad Lawless." Nonetheless, Lawless's protest rallies attracted thousands and he constantly cited Samuel Gray of Ballybay as the avatar of the Protestant tyranny fouling the entire land.

In response, Gray on July 12, 1828, staged a huge Orange Order parade through Ballybay. Lawless went tit-for-tat by staging further mass rallies in and around the south of County Monaghan. He preposterously claimed that he would soon lead a protest march of 250,000 Catholics into the very maw of little Ballybay. To the area's Protestants, this sounded like a declaration of impending Civil War. At the appointed date, thousands of them poured into Ballybay, most heavily armed. They were joined by an infantry brigade from the town of Clones, lancers from Cavan, and droves of police. All told, nearly 5,000 armed men were arrayed close to the Aughnamullen border, just waiting for the Catholics to come close.

On the morning of September 23, 1828, Jack Lawless did set off from Carrickmacross (less than ten miles southeast) toward Ballybay with a vanguard of priests and other true believers, followed by a three-mile-long stream of roughly 10,000 Catholic peasants – by no means a quarter of a million – reciting the Rosary and chanting out their slogans and songs. Some of the advance guard carried pikes, but very few had firearms, these being forbidden to Catholics. The Aughnamullen Monaghans had to have witnessed this approaching spectacle, or even participated in it.

At the last minute, however, emissaries from Ballybay persuaded Lawless to disperse his marchers and avert a blood bath. A letter from Gray to Lawless read, "Hearing you intend to disturb the peace and quiet of this Protestant village by your driving into this town with a Popish mob, with green banners and devices emblematic of rebellion." Gray warned that he would soon execute Lawless and his son. He signed off, "No Surrender 1690, Samuel Gray." Halfway through Aughnamullen, Lawless made off on a fast horse, ultimately for the good of all.

In the next days several peasants and priests were ambushed and beaten around the outskirts of Ballybay, with a couple left dead. The area's tensions were only marginally calmed with the passage in London of the Catholic Relief Act of 1830, which finally allowed Catholics to again hold lesser seats of government within their own country, rights that had been barred by the "Acts of Union." If they somehow had the funds to do so, they could even buy a piece of their native land now.

In 1831 Sam Gray was made the "Officer Commanding for Aughnamullen Yeomanry." That year a number of citizens of Aughnamullen filed a joint complaint in Dublin about Gray's penchant for breaking down doors and threatening death. In November 1832, Gray was said to be an accomplice in the premeditated murder of an Owen McGurk. On that December 14 while serving notice at the home of a Duffy family – the Monaghan ancestral line from this stage was likely thickly mixed up with Duffys – his posse began stabbing wildly with fixed bayonets at a newly arisen mob. He was never convicted (see the *Belfast Newsletter,* July 26, 1833). Gray, creepily dressed up as a kind of ghoul, next shot to death an Owen Murphy over an inheritance that he thought better belonged with his sons.

41

Over 90 leading citizens and priests in Monaghan petitioned publicly and at risk to themselves in 1838 that Samuel Gray be stripped of all his official duties and privileges. But this was of course pointless. Instead, he was appointed to become "Sub Sheriff "of all of County Monaghan – the top policeman of them all. In that capacity, he declared that no Catholics could enter Ballybay after dark without a special passport issued by him alone. No wonder my great-great grandfather Andrew Monaghan got out of Aughnamullen.

III.

THE EXODUS BEGINS

The Call To Scotland

The other driver of the Monaghan diaspora was the decimation of the linen trade. Although the mass production of woolen and cotton goods had been well underway since the start of the nineteenth century, linen's turn to industrialization came much later. The inherent roughness of the flax fiber that yielded linen simply defied mass processing until around 1825 when an effective spinning jenny for linen was finally devised. Hulking factories in Belfast, northern England, and Scotland inevitably then began to churn out linen goods with such speed and low cost that the demand for craft-linen from the likes of the Monaghans of Aughnamullen quickly collapsed and many of the quaint old markets effectively went belly up. By the early 1830s, rural Monaghan was facing financial ruin. In 1987, brothers Peader and James Murnane addressed this situation in detail in the splendid County Monaghan history journal called the *Clogher Record*:

> "Living standards collapsed and hardship was common throughout the county. In evidence of the Poor Law Commissioners in 1836, Rev. Charles Evatt of Monaghan stated 'that a person cannot form any just estimate of the North of Ireland without considering the linen manufacturing, which but a few years since afforded full and ample employment to both sexes and to all ages; but this has been abruptly and totally abstracted. The consequence is the demand for their services is so limited that the average earnings appear almost indefinable."

With the demise of the linen industry and the continuing sectarian rancor at home, County Monaghan began to experience a mass exodus years before the actual onset of the Great Famine. By 1830, up to 8,000 Monaghan residents would hurry off each year to work in the textile mills in Scotland, Liverpool, or Belfast. Considerable numbers also began heading to **Prince Edward Island** in Canada, which was being billed by some as a sort of County Monaghan reincarnate – a beckoning isle with land for the taking and already thick with McMahons, McKennas, McCabes, Kellys, Duffys, and even certain ancestors of this Monaghan family.

But Scotland with its giant textile mills (primarily handling cotton, wool, and silk gauze) around Glasgow was the chief draw for many who had grown up "carding" – picking off the thick linen dross – scouring, spinning, or weaving linen as a way of life. Scotland was not all that far from County Monaghan and it was in relative terms booming. Ironically, the country was short of labor partly because so many thousands of lowland Scots had moved away to Ireland, or else to America. Even the landed estates were crying for laborers, since so many tenants farmers had vanished. The people of Monaghan were happy to oblige.

Travel back and forth to Scotland had become commonplace from Ulster by now. Certain spots in County Antrim lay only about a dozen or two miles away after all. County Monaghan was a bit more distant, but no humongous trek either. The disenfranchised young men of Monaghan originally led the way, at first on a seasonal basis leading up to harvest time, but others soon stayed much longer to work in the mills around Glasgow. From Aughnamullen, the journey started with maybe three days walking and sleeping by the roadside or in some rough inn in order to reach Belfast, 55 miles to the north. Then you could take a packet ship over to Scotland for as little as one shilling and make it in a day. Within a few years entire families were doing this in large numbers, many never to return.

My great-great grandfather Andrew Monaghan definitely made this journey in the late 1830s when he was about 18 years old. His older brother Owen appears to have found employment in the Scottish textile mills considerably earlier, perhaps by the late 1820s and possibly in tandem with other siblings. That he was a skilled textile worker is established by later records. Demand for that trade was certainly high around Glasgow in the 1820s and early 1830s. In fact, nearly 80,000 people were employed as power-loom weavers alone in this region in those years, including in the nearby towns of **Paisley** and **Greenock** with their many additional great mills. Nearer to home, Owen may have also worked early on in one of the large nearby flax mills in County Monaghan, notably the Cunningham's operation in Creve at the top of Aughnamullen, close to Ballybay (where the region's linen trade was first started by the French Huguenot Breakey family, mentioned earlier). Owen clearly left for America in 1834.

John S. Monagan, the custodian of many of the earliest Monaghan family records, had been an avid listener to the stories of his grandfather John Stephen as a boy. The grandfather held it firmly that Andrew Monaghan also worked in the Glasgow mills before emigrating to America. In a stroke of great fortune, I discovered that the Scottish census of 1841 showed Andrew to be living with what had to be close relatives in the oddly named parish of "Barony" on the Sandyford estate on the north side of Glasgow. This was sprawling farmland then, but not now. Andrew's job at that moment was listed as "ag lab" – agricultural laborer. He was 20 years old and living in the household of a Patrick and Bridget "Marrin," both 30, and their son Joseph, ten. A few years later Andrew and Bridget and her family will all be found side-by-side again in the County Monaghan townland of **Ummerafree**. This was clearly Andrew's final exit point to America. These combined facts create a very strong suggestion that Bridget "Marrin," properly spelled Marron and a name common in County Monaghan, was Andrew's older sister. [Surely pertinent is the fact that modern DNA testing identifies eight descendants of the Marron family as 4th cousins (sharing from 37 CM over 3 segments to 21 CM over 1 segment of DNA of this author), and 178 other Marron descendants in the massive *Ancestry.Com* data base are linked as 5th-8th cousins. Considering the times, Andrew was lucky to have any floor to lie upon in Glasgow. That summer of 1841, a total of 57,651 Irish, most of them forlorn and poverty-stricken young men from Ulster, crossed to work on the Scottish harvests and mills.

There is no reason to doubt that Andrew worked not just in the fields but also in Glasgow's mills, as family lore has long held. The region's textile mills were concentrated both along the River Clyde in the city and a few miles southwest in the town of Paisley. (Others lay further out on the Firth of Clyde in Greenock.) The Paisley specialty was in producing bright silken shawls and scarves of "imitation Kashmir" that were the rage across Europe for a while. Most of the Irish peasants working in these mills lived in meager shanty towns, whether in Paisley or Glasgow or Greenock. They were despised by the Scots for working for too little money in their 12-hour days and praying in the wrong sort of Gaelic. At the end of the exhausting week many huddled together in their own dark shebeens to drink and talk of a better life somewhere, anywhere else.

Nearly every week the trans-Atlantic shipping companies' shills appeared to tell young men like Andrew that they had no chance of a decent life unless they booked passage to America. But where should one actually go? Stories about spectacular opportunities in Massachusetts had to be in the air, especially talk of a frenzy of hiring in the mills around the towns of **Andover** and **Lowell**.

These young Irish exiles in Scotland were a fairly desperate bunch and no wonder. Even this new economy soon started collapsing before their eyes. Europe's appetite for fake Kashmir suddenly evaporated in the early 1840s, and the shock waves hit Scotland hard. Between 1841 and 1843, 67 of the 112 textile mills in Paisley shut down altogether and thousands of semi-skilled workers were left to scrounge for their survival. It was in this context that a likely distraught young Andrew gave up on Scotland, perhaps at his sister's bidding, and decided to give his native County Monaghan one more try – this time in the townland of Ummerafree plumb in the middle of the vast **Shirley Estate**, just a few miles south of Aughnamullen. But the situation there grew desperate all over again, and directly led to his departure for America in 1844.

Escaping Ummerafree

A chance discovery from the records of the Irish American Folk Museum of Northern Ireland has been vital to this new understanding. It makes it clear that Andrew did not linger long in Scotland, but instead moved back to that townland of Ummerafree located several miles south of Tievaleny and within the vast holdings of the wealthy Shirley family from Warwickshire in England. They were absentee landlords who mainly summered on their Irish lands. Andrew was unquestionably drawn to that obscure location by the fact that this was now the base of the aforementioned Bridget Morran – almost certainly an older sister – and her husband Patrick, the couple that had hosted him near Glasgow in 1841. This connection is made clear by the exact ticket voucher for Andrew to make his way to America which is visible in the files of the wonderful Ulster Folk Museum. This is recorded as "Shirley Immigration Ticket No 24. Carrickmacross 26 April 1844." To be at the top of the list, as Andrew was, is curious, since the Shirley Estate, which touched against the underbelly of Aughnamullen, was comprised of 47,734 (English) acres, making it one of the largest in all of Ireland. By 1840 some 20,500 people – among whom Andrew drew his escape ticket No. 24 – were struggling to provide for themselves on these lands, and a great many were failing. The story of this place goes to the heart of a long stretch of Irish history, as will be shown.

The Shirley Estate had been the property of that family since 1646. It came to them through intermarriage with the family of Walter Devereux, the First Earl of Essex as appointed by Queen Elizabeth and discussed earlier. Devereux made his initial mark upon Ireland by landing in Antrim with hundreds of armed consorts in the spring of 1573 and starting a campaign of killing and mass havoc there before slowly murdering his way south. Next, he succeeded in luring the Irish "Lord of the Great Ards" in County Down, Brian McPhelim O'Neill, and his extended family to join him for a three-day feast. Before they settled in, Devereux had 200 of these visitors either shot or hacked to death. Then the guests of honor, Brian and his wife and the brother Ruari (Rory) Oge McPhelim, were brought to Dublin and drawn and quartered for public display, to the hopeful appreciation back in London of Elizabeth, "the Virgin Queen. "

To curry further favor, Walter Devereux launched a scorched-earth campaign across Ulster in 1574. In a letter to the Queen's Privy Council dated March 10, 1575, he described his recent march of terror through "Mageoghagan's country" – meaning along the border of counties Armagh and Monaghan. To properly subdue the Mageoghagan area, his soldiery were accompanied by 600 ruffians employed to burn and demolish everything in their path. He noted that he had used the same tactics in Tyrone at the previous harvest and "they were utterly without bread or horsemeat...And their next harvest shall be by all likelihood twice as unquiet. And therefore it is certain that they must either obey or starve very shortly."

Devereux indicated that he had gone even further in "Mageoghagan's country" and the "Barony of the Fues" (Armagh). Through forested passes he had also felled thousands of trees so that 14 calvary men could ride abreast. "The inhabitants fled with their cattle to Henry MacShane's sons [sons of the still regionally powerful chieftain Shane O'Neill] leaving their corn behind them, which I have wasted and spoiled together with such habitations as they had in that place."

This swath of destruction was concentrated a few miles east of Aughnamullen but must have incited a virulent hatred among our nearby ancestors against the English invaders. Devereux himself would die soon, but not before he (and his heirs) were awarded the vast lands of what ultimately became the Shirley Estate.

At the time of the Shirley family's ascendancy over the Barony of Farney, its modest settlement of Carrickmacross was evolving into a bustling trading center. However, the hinterlands remained an iffy and unevenly populated world. The Shirley's themselves were generally living on their Monaghan lands for only the summer months. But powerful land agents closely managed the family's affairs and kept detailed records that provide a fascinating lens through time now.

For gentry of the Shirley's stature, summers in Ireland were meant to be a romantic idyl, a time for jaunting between "big houses" for glorious long stays, when not angling and shooting and dabbling in drawing and writing by dreamy lakes, after the morning business meetings were done. Yet for all their wealth, the Shirley family never quite managed access to the more rarified layers of the Anglo-Irish social world. Thus in 1826 when Evelyn John Shirley (1788-1856) gained the County Monaghan seat in the English Parliament, he decided to make the Shirley family presence more impressive by constructing a spectacular mansion on the shores of Lough Fea outside Carrickmacross. The ultimate result was a stunning 27-bedroom great house with elaborate French and Italian gothic styling and multiple wings and a separate chapel and several annexes. Its central hall was 75-feet long and 33-feet high, with enormous windows looking out to exquisite gardens and the pretty lake.

The Shirleys' grand estate.

He relied of course upon his peasants' rents to maintain all this. From 1829 until his death in 1843, the chief overseer for the Shirley Estate was a much despised Samuel "Sandy" Mitchell. By now County Monaghan's linen economy had collapsed, but Mitchell would not relent on his domain for a second. Even as the whole county fell into desperation, he kept raising the rents and evicting the most destitute. He also employed a network of devious spies and garrulous drunks to inform on their neighbors. But history will note that he was far more reviled for his treatment of women. "He never spared any man in his anger or woman in his lust," one observer noted. When women came into Mitchell's Carrickmacross office to remonstrate about rent payments or other problems, his first act was to lock the door. Such was this trustee of English honor. Not surprisingly, at Mitchell's sudden death in March of 1843 bonfires of celebration were lit across the drumlins of south County Monaghan and people drank, danced and sang all night. Mitchell's right-hand man was the sub-agent William George O. Smith, and he was a little better. He was effectively the financial controller and a man who would become instrumental in determining the fate of several of my Monaghan family ancestors. Smith had many sources of power to do his bidding – armed yeomanry, powerful middlemen, the networks of secret watchers, process servers, and all the rest. But at least he helped instigate useful new programs in land drainage, road building, and rudimentary school building for the lucky few.

My great-great grandfather Andrew Monaghan relocated from Glasgow to the Shirley Estate by about 1842, when he was 20 years old. His new dwelling place was in the aforementioned townland of Ummerafree, toward the northern end of these lands. Andrew settled there beside the same Patrick and Bridget Marron with whom he had boarded in Scotland. But he was likely just a subtenant with a crude hut and a small patch for some crops. A James Monaghan, a possible brother and born around 1826, lived next door. A Terence Monaghan had farmed here in 1823. Within Ummerafree also resided the family of Edward Monaghan – possibly an uncle or older brother or even the same figure seen in Lurgachamloch beside Tievaleny in the

Tithe Applotment Books of 1829. All must have been related. Meanwhile, Bridget's extended Marron family controlled nearly every other acre of Ummerafree, as well as many of the farms in the next townlands. It is nearly inevitable that there were other intermarriages between the Monaghans and other Marrons, since modern DNA results indicate such a strong interconnectedness between that family and my own, as mentioned earlier.

The man the Shirley's chose to succeed the overseer Samuel Mitchell in 1843 was named William Steuart Trench. Hundreds of peasants – some claimed thousands – greeted his arrival in Carrickmacross with an all-out riot in demand of rent reductions on the spot. Perhaps adding to the day's volatility was the fact the town had gone heavily into the business of brewing porter and distilling whiskey and poitin, making 200,000 gallons of such hard stuff a year. In any event, the riot peaked in the early afternoon, then petered out.

William Trench only lasted a year and a half at his new job. He wrote a book about his brief time at the helm of the Shirley Estate called **Realities of Irish Life, 1843-45.** Trench had been sagacious enough to appreciate that the terrible struggle for survival playing out on all sides of the Shirley Estate had much to do with its explosive population growth. In 1841, the Barony of Farney, of which the Shirley Estate made up over half, had more than 600 residents per square mile (93 percent of them Catholics), or about ten times the number of people who live there now. The small county of Monaghan had about 200,000 residents then. Twenty years later, after the Famine did its work, the total dropped to some 130,000. In 2016, the populace numbered about 60,000.

Trench's purview was not easy. By early 1843 swarms of starving people were already being driven into the poorhouse at Carrickmacross with their upkeep to be paid for mostly by Evelyn John Shirley, the boss. By the end of the year, Trench began exploring new options for handling the most impoverished (or most agitated) tenants across the Shirley estate and devised an early trial of what has been called "assisted emigration." This meant paying for actual tickets to America, with food and clothing allowances added in many cases, to cull the great estates of a large number of their subjects struggling to survive. By March, Trench and the sub-agent William George Smith had pieced together their initial lists for assisted emigration. Remarkably, none other than the young Andrew Monaghan, my great-great grandfather, was selected as the 24th person among the thousands of other potential candidates from the vast Shirley Estate to be offered free travel across the seas. There had to be countless others more infirm or desperate than this not quite 22 year-old with no wife or children in need of support. Perhaps he was perceived as some kind of trouble- maker – or maybe he or Bridget Monaghan Morran had certain connections.

In any case, Smith followed through on Trench's plan and reached an under-standing with the young Andrew. His next step was to notify a Thomas Eliott in Liverpool – a factotum there who happened to be married to one of Smith's cousins – of the imminent arrival of my great-great grandfather.

The note read:

To be presented within ten days. Particulars:

No.	Name	Age
22	Andrew Monagh	22

{signed]
W.G. Smith
To: Mr. Thomas Elliott, 11 Waterloo Road, Liverpool

> Sir,
> You will please give to parties mentioned on the book here on
> Credit in regards Passage to America to the amount of two
> Pounds/s/- Sterling and charge the same to the account of [to be
> filled in]
> Your obedt servt
> W. G. Smith

Some firebrands in academia have gone so far as to call the assisted emigra-tion program "a conspiracy to exterminate the Irish race." But Trench and others argued that the goals at first were quite humanitarian. A letter dated April 22, 1844, from Elliot in Liverpool back to W.G. Smith in reference to the departure of the earliest batch of assisted emigrants from the Shirley Estate certainly does not sound very dastardly:

> "The last paid of your people got off yesterday all in excellent humor and I must say most grateful they all appeared for the trifling friendship and attention I tried to show them. They one and all desired I should write to you to let you know how they prayed for your success as they termed it. The ready cash they all get clearly does much for them and tends to make them very cheerful." Elliott added that it seemed that 70 pounds of bread was required for each passenger's crossing.

These were early days before the full horrors of the Famine struck, but the issue of over-population was becoming increasingly concerning to the big landlords in County Monaghan. The new idea was that a steerage class ticket to America, combined with a small stipend for food and clothing, might end up costing the landlords half the tariff of a year in the poor house while free-ing up land for older, more reliable replacement farmers who might provide steady rents for years to come. In the selection of Andrew Monaghan for free passage to America – with an evident brother James to follow before long – there could have even been personal factors involved. Perhaps these related to the good offices of Andrew's apparent sister Bridget Morran, who in Griffith's Valuation of Ireland of 1861 is found as a widow looking after the caretaker's house and that portion of the lands in Ummerafree belonging directly to Evelyn Philip Sydney. Bridget herself lived on until January 24, 1877.

Andrew Monaghan's 1844 travel voucher was for him alone. But that same year the Shirley estate agents also vouchsafed payment for departure from the next townland beside Ummerafree of **Rafferagh** for one Edward Monaghan,

44, and his wife Mary, and their children Anne, Catherine, Elizabeth, Patrick, James, and Mary. Their destination might have been Australia, since from the same townland in 1849 a "Frank" or more likely Francis Monaghan, 21, received his traveling money from the head office to venture off with his wife Mary, 17, with a reasonable clothing pension included – for him, five shirts, two pairs of shoes, one jacket, a vest, a pair of trousers, and a suit. Mary got vouchers for stockings, a gown and petticoat, and five shifts.

In his departure from Liverpool in 1844, Andrew would have encountered moments of strange pandemonium. That city had become the paramount embarkation point for all of northern Europe in the surging eagerness to get to America or Canada as cheaply as possible. The docks there were a scene of constant cacophony as people piled in from not only Ireland and Scotland, but the Netherlands, Germany, Belgium and France, few knowing which way to turn. Many the pickpocket or shill would be sizing up each arriving lot as they stood gawking at ever-larger emigrant ships keen to pile up to 600 destitute souls into their fetid holds. At least in their upheaval in leaving

Departing Liverpool was tumultuous.

County Monaghan forever, the poor from the Shirley Estate were lucky enough to fall under the genial ministrations of Thomas Elliott.

In 1846, the Shirley Estate decided to clear out of Ummerafree two further Monaghan family households from that townland. One of these was the aforementioned James Monaghan, possibly a younger brother of Andrew. Also in 1846 the sizeable family of Peter Monaghan, aged about 40, was sent off from Ummerafree, possibly to Pennsylvania. Cross searching within the DNA banks of Ancestry. Com suggests links to several living descendants of this Peter J. Monaghan in the area of Luzern County, Pennsylvania, through his son Patrick J. Monaghan (1839-1907) married to Mary Cassidy. Other offspring of Peter included Peter, Jr. (1837-), Edward (1846-) and Bridget (1835-). It is noteworthy that a cluster of several Monaghans living in Brooklyn, New York by the 1840s and 1850s have descendants DNA-linked to this researcher.

Of course, by 1846 the Famine was in full rage, and hundreds of thousands of Irish people were clawing to get away as fast as they could. As the "Great Hunger" wore on, terrible scenes erupted around the country. But certain newspapers kept highlighting in particular "The Shirley Tragedy" (notably the virulently anti-English *Freeman's Journal* of Dublin of September 28, 1849) regarding the forced evictions of half-naked, fever-wracked souls utterly unable to pay their rents. One report homes in on the death from "fever" following eviction of a widower Brian McQuillan of Ummerafree. His two children were said to have soon died thereafter.

But the decidedly pro-English *Belfast News* of October 4, 1850, had a very different take, reporting on "Brutal Outrages in the Barony of Farney, County Monaghan" regarding the near beatings to death of two different rent collectors on the Shirley Estate. Either way, it was no happy place.

IV.

LANDING IN AMERICA

Owen's Crossing

Preceding Andrew Monaghan to America by a decade was his much older
brother Owen, who had arrived in Boston on August 14, 1834 (as noted
on his 1842 naturalization oath). Within a couple of years, Owen settled in
North Andover, Massachusetts about 25 miles northwest of Boston. He may
not have been the first of the Aughnamullen Monaghans to set off across the
Atlantic, but his long-term immigration story is essentially one of the earliest
that can be tracked with confidence.

That he declared that he arrived specifically in Boston is intriguing, since
the ports of New York, Philadelphia, Baltimore were all far more often
the points of call for trans-Atlantic immigrants crossing from the likes of
Liverpool and Glasgow in the 1830s. In contrast, the vessels delivering people
directly from Irish ports still tended to favor Canada over America as their
destination then. A great many of Boston's Irish arrivals in this period thus
first landed in the Canadian Maritimes, then found their way down the coast
to Massachusetts in smaller vessels. This seems to have been Owen's route,
since he fits so closely with the profile of the Owen Monaghan, 26 and thus
born about 1808, who landed at St. John's, New Brunswick on June 16,
1834, on the ship *Betsey Heron* out of Belfast.

This was a 250-tonne brigantine launched in Newcastle in England in 1832
and commanded by the master James Storey, with nine other crew.
He set off from Belfast on May 6, 1834, with 220 paying passengers whose
names read like a roll call from County Monaghan – McKenna, McCabe,
McKeon, Kelly, Trainor, and Duffy strong among them. *(See **Passengers to
New Brunswick: The Custom House Records:** 1833, 34, 37 & 38.* Saint

John, N.B.: **The New Brunswick Genealogical Society,** 1987.) This was a classic result of the "escape to North America" marketing schemes that were then targeting various parts of Ulster as international shipping syndicates sought to sign up an endless stream of passengers for their Atlantic crossings. Owen's interest may have even been sparked by some tout slapping out flyers at a Saturday fair in Ballybay. It always seemed unlikely that he set off alone, and indeed the Betsey Heron's newly available manifest lists a couple of fellow passengers who may have shared in the planning for the great crossing: namely one **James Edward Henry**, 36, and called a "laborer" (like every adult male on the manifest), and his wife Margaret, and a baby delivered on board and not yet Christened. (Alexander would be the name). James was possibly an uncle of Owen, or else a first cousin. He likely hailed from the Aughnamullen townland of **Corkeeran** *(Corr Chaorthainn)* beside a lovely lough at the beginning of the road to Cootehill that pointed south from Ballybay. It is noteworthy that in the 1850s Owen would name his final son James Henry as if in a continuing homage to this fellow traveller. A number of other intriguing new discoveries have further illuminated the connections between the Monaghan and Henry families of Aughnamullen as they eventually regrouped in Massachusetts. Whether some of these Henry passengers were at first heading toward the rapidly growing "Monaghan Settlement" on Prince Edward Island is not clear.

It does appear that Owen's travel-mate James Henry, born around 1797, ultimately settled down to a long life of farming in New Brunswick's southeastern Charlotte County, in a place called St. Andrews that was close to the border with Maine. The 1851 census there shows his children to have been Alexander, Jane, Hugh, Racheal, and James.

In contrast, my great-great-great uncle Owen Monaghan pushed on to Boston that August. Likely he was seeking to make a beeline to the region's booming textile industry. Owen's later naturalization oath of fealty to the United States asserts that he landed in Boston on August 14, 1834. No ship arrival from across the Atlantic on or around that date is apparent, and not many did ply that route. But coming down from Charlotte County in New Brunswick – only 325 miles to the northeast – even a coast-hugging fishing smack could have done the job of getting one into the United States for a farthing. Nobody was recording every last person to skip ashore from such vessels then.

Owen's initial whereabouts in late 1834 and 1835 remain a puzzle. He could have just stayed in Boston itself for a while – where an older Owen Monaghan, another potential uncle, was well established. Alternatively, he could have been adventurous enough to even travel to upstate New York where there seems to have been a pull of long-term family allegiance starting early on.

But where Owen was really headed for within a year or two at least was the not quite famous small town of **North Andover**, Massachusetts, and specifically its "West District." There were under fifty adult males living in this section in the early 1830s and the town's meticulous tax records show that very few others were Irish and none were named anything close to Monaghan. But the May 1,1833 tax rolls show that a **John C. Henry**

(1810-1873) was already at work in a local mill and generating an annual tax bill of 75 cents. He may have been the same as the John Henry who moved to the neighboring town of Salem and married an Elizabeth Hayes there on August 30, 1835.

Somebody put the right word in Owen's ear, since as it happened, my great-great-great uncle was finding his way to what would become the epicenter of the American Industrial Revolution. Owen clearly spent most of 1836 in North Andover, likely in the Ballardvale section, since he shows up on the tax ledgers in North Andover on May 1,1837 as having a payment due of 90 cents for his work in the previous year. That town and neighboring **Lowell** were by then experiencing a huge growth in textile manufacturing, thanks to the harnessing of waterpower from the fast-flowing Merrimac River and its tributary of the Shawsheen River in North Andover.

The Monaghan and Henry connections will be returned to shortly, but the point is that it is foolish to think of the family's migration as having been the work of one core pioneer setting out alone, as some have speculated. It did not work that way very often for the Irish. In fact one possibility is that Owen might have been initially attracted by stories of other ancestors who immigrated not to Massachusetts but to extreme upstate New York. He does seem to have been quite an adventurer, no matter how you cut it.

New York's North Country

Owen and Andrew Monaghan certainly followed through on a long-planned relocation to Franklin, New York in their later years, but it is anybody's guess when the idea first took root. We can be sure the notion was not random. In fact, it is possible that the earliest close relative to arrive in the United States proper was an enterprising Thomas "Monahan" (the dominant spelling in English, instead of "Monaghan," in the early 1800s). He appears to have made the journey when aged around 30 on board the ship *Atlantic* from Belfast arriving in New York on May 28, 1827. Thomas and his wife Mary headed for **Fort Covington**, New York, a growing village just below Canada's mighty Saint Lawrence River, and at the northern edge of the Adirondack wilderness. For hundreds of years this area of bitter winters, lofty mountains, and wild rivers belonged to the Iroquois Confederation of the "Five Nations" – the Mohawks foremost, and to the west the Onondaga, Oneida, Cayuga, and Seneca. In consort with their British allies and sly manipulators, the Mohawks ferociously raided the American frontier outposts and homesteaders' farms in their region during the Revolutionary War.

In retaliation, the fledgling U.S. government in the 1790s seized control of *five-million acres* from the Mohawks for a pittance. This was then put up for sale to a first wave of speculators who bought immense tracts for next to nothing and began subdividing and reselling these to whatever takers they could scare up. Out of this hubbub there emerged some unique settlements, including a cluster of Irish enclaves in the middle of the primeval wilderness, which just happened to attract some very naïve people from County Monaghan.

That specific phenomenon was brought about by a second-wave speculator named Michael Hogan. Hogan was an Irish sea captain and ship owner who never let moral scruples stand between him and the possibility of making obscene profits. Over a long and rapacious career, he grew wealthy on the East India trade, as well as on piracy, transporting convicts to Australia, and selling opium and slaves. Much of the latter business was conducted from a manor in South Africa. Hogan eventually moved to a 100-acre residence in New York City with a wife he had romanced in India's Bombay. In 1816 he purchased three thousand acres in Franklin County for the sum of $1. While Americans were still reluctant to move to the remote North Country, Hogan wagered that his fellow Irishmen wouldn't have a clue about the forbidding climate or black flies by the millions there, and he staged a promotional tour across his homeland to sell off every possible patch of his purchase he could unload.

Ultimately, Thomas Monahan made his way to the area in 1827. He certainly did not go to Fort Covington by chance, since it was 370 miles due north from the port of New York. Thomas arrived with his wife Mary Healy and likely a brother, possibly of hers. The U. S. census of 1830 for Fort Covington listed Thomas's household as including two "white males aged 20-29" and a female who was almost certainly Mary.

Fort Covington was created as a redoubt against a feared invasion from Canada during the War of 1812. A British invasion force in fact did plunder and burn nearby **Malone**, the Franklin County seat, in late 1813. The Little Salmon River, descending from the Adirondack peaks, made its final surge to the St. Lawrence through Fort Covington, providing limitless waterpower. As settlers eventually trickled in, grist and lumber mills sprang up and by 1821 the community also had its first cotton carding mill and by 1828 its first woolen mill. Perhaps it was while working in a Scottish textile center around Glasgow that Thomas Monahan heard about these developments, possibly from the master Scottish weaver Robert McPhee who was seeking craftsmen for the mill he was setting up in Fort Covington. In 1833 the western part of Fort Covington was subsumed by the newly created township of Bombay, New York, named after the birthplace of the wife of the land speculator Michael Hogan. In fact, Thomas Monahan's lands were near an outlying crossroads known as **Hogansburg**.

Whether they were married in New York or Ireland is unclear, but Thomas Monahan and Mary Healey had a son named John in Fort Covington in 1831. Around 1834 the couple had a daughter named Mary and a Bridget followed in 1836. The Monaghan connections to the "North Country" deepened. A Bridget Monahan joined Thomas in Fort Covington or Bombay by at least 1835 and married a Richard Moore in early 1836 in the St. Patrick's Church there. The couple's children included a Martin and Mary. Bridget seems to have lost her husband Richard Moore early on and moved to New York City with her children. Around 1839 an **Artemis** (with many spellings) Monaghan arrived in Malone, and he may have been closely tied to our family line.

There are no records to prove that Owen Monaghan made any trip to Franklin County, New York in these early days. But he surely did begin exploring the region a decade and a half later and with his brother Andrew ultimately spent the later years of his life within two or three miles of Thomas Monahan's family in Hogansburg. He would have had had many occasions to meet both Artemis and a subsequent **Arthur** Monaghan who arrived in the area in the 1850s after first landing in Canada's Prince Edward Island, and next living in likely close contact with Owen and Andrew in Massachusetts.

Owen in Andover

As noted, Owen settled in the town of North Andover, Massachusetts, about 25 miles northwest of Boston. The idea may have come from other relatives in the Henry family or possibly a **William Stephen Monaghan**. Someone clearly spread the word about the tremendous opportunities for textile workers arising there. Even by 1836 the place boasted several four-story red-brick mills beside the Shawsheen River. The Osgood and Sutton flannel mills were among the forerunners, but Owen more likely took up early employment at the Marland family's brand new worsted woolen mill, the first in the U.S. Owen prospered in Andover for years to come.

North Andover's early textile mills.

Returning to the yearly tax records for the "West District" of North Andover, one finds a faint and scrawled companion name in the registry of May 1, 1838 (amidst entries for only 60-plus neighbors) – still almost none of the others yet Irish. Though automated computer scans have failed to discern this, just two lines above Owen "Monagan's" entry for his meagre tax debt for the year of 1837 of $1.12 is a notation specifying that a **William S. Monhan** owed the relatively whopping sum for those times of $17.36. In other words, William's tax bill is about 16 times greater than Owen's, which obviously suggests that he was making a lot more money, and thus undoubtedly residing longer on the scene or holding a particular highly-valued skill. He may in fact have been a skilled tailor. Though William S. Monhan vanishes from the local records after that, he must be considered as a candidate to be Owen's close relation, even a brother (or uncle), and another personal guiding star, since in 1843 Owen named his first son **William Stephen** Monaghan.

My great-great grandfather (Charles) Andrew named his second son **John Stephen**, and his apparent third "son" **Thomas William** (a controversy to be addressed later). Many names in succeeding generations expand on the "Stephen" link – including my great-grandfather and my father; my oldest brother and his son and then his son after that; and the late U.S. Congressman from Connecticut, John Stephen Monagan. But note that the middle (or first) name Stephen was not common among the Irish in the early 1800s, and nobody knows its origins within this family. The William S. Monhan of Andover in 1837 may have restarted the name on American shores.

Alas, Andover's William S. Monhan remains invisible to the later records in Massachusetts – although he is conceivably the same person as William "Mangin" who lost a three-year-old daughter Anna to measles in Lawrence on May 18, 1849, and his wife Mary soon after. The best guess is that William S. was a tailor "born in Ireland," who arrived in New York on the bark *Tay* by way of Halifax, Nova Scotia on October 8, 1833, at the age of 25. This would again point to the remarkable County Monaghan link to the Canadian

Maritimes. William the tailor remarried a ten-years-younger English woman named Elizabeth and in the 1840s they had a number of children, including a Mary and William James. In 1846 there followed the twins **John S.** (Stephen?) Monaghan and Thomas Patrick, and next a **Jane Elizabeth**. He may in fact be the same William Monaghan who moved on to New York, where there was at least one other newly arriving DNA-linked Monaghan in Brooklyn, and then began working in the other great American textile center then emerging in Patterson, New Jersey. This whole family moved across the Hudson by the census of 1850 to Patterson.

That a number of other relatives were present in Massachusetts's Merrimac Valley well before the Famine becomes evident when one focuses on the boom town of Lowell – by the mid-1830s this indeed embodied the heart of the industrial revolution in America. Lowell's mills by then already employed thousands, with the numbers of Irish just starting to jump up rapidly. Among the Lowell citizens of the 1830s were a variety of Monaghans with first names like Patrick, Hugh, Edward, and Margaret. They were all likely in frequent close communication and related somehow or other in those early years. It is only after 1850 that tracking the surname of Monaghan (or its variants) in this region becomes a lost cause, following the flooding of the state with people escaping Ireland during the Famine.

But the United States census of 1840 indicates that there were only a few dozen immigrants in the entire state of Massachusetts then named Monaghan or its variations. A lot of these were gathered around Fall River or Holyoke. Thus the earliest clustering of people with the name Monaghan within Andover and Lowell was unlikely to have arisen by chance. Rather, it seems clear that this was a particular family group steeped in the linen-making traditions in Ulster who gravitated together in some kind of medley toward the very center of the textile industry in America. Along the Merrimac and Shawsheen rivers, wool was now king. If one had any skill with it, employment was guaranteed. The need for strong laborers of all kinds soon became constant as well, and the word of all this incredible opportunity in Massachusetts ricocheted back to the most destitute precincts of County Monaghan.

While North Andover was thriving, Lowell was bursting at the seams. With its direct rail link to Boston, thundering energy source in the Merrimac's Pawtucket Falls, and an interconnected canal system, new mill construction took hold with a vengeance there. Its 1825 population of 2,500 jumped to 18,000 by 1835, and 30,000 by 1850, the final growth owing in large part to masses of Irish pouring in during the Famine years. Most piled into freezing and clamorous boarding houses that typically held dozens of immigrants crammed up and down the stairs. In Lowell, the Irish first lived in a part of town variously called "Paddy Camp Lands" or earlier "The Acre," because of its huge squatters' camp for the Irishmen digging the town's canals.

Apparently on the mill floor in North Andover, Owen early on met his bride Catherine McNamara, who was born in Charlestown, Massachusetts around 1818. They declared their intention to marry in North Andover on July 20, 1839. The actual wedding occurred on August 4 in the area's only Catholic church then, St. Patrick's in Lowell. Owen's last name then was spelled "Monahan," the most common rendering in the early 19th century. The witnesses were an Arthur Killen of Andover and Elizabeth Short. Back in Ireland, there were five Short families living around Ballybay in this time and another one residing in Aughnamullen. As we shall see, some of these Shorts had moved to Lowell by at least 1832, and they too, though possibly

Protestants, were likely relatives – or perhaps Elizabeth was a Monaghan who married a Short. (In fact, DNA analysis within the Ancestry.Com database identifies seven current descendants of the Short family as being 4th cousins to this author, and 87 as being more distant 5th to 8th cousins.)

At marriage, Catherine McNamara was a decade younger than my then 31 year-old great-great-great uncle Owen. A spartan construction initially, St. Patrick's was the region's first Catholic church to cater to the early Irish immigrants. Its wonderfully preserved and deeply indexed records provide many vital keys to the history of the Monaghan family. Near it lay the local court house where Owen applied to become a U.S. citizen on July 30, 1842 (an action which was not sanctioned until the applicant had been in the country for at least five years). On his oath of naturalization Owen declared that he was born December 11, 1813, though every other time in his life he answered census takers – both federal and state and both in Massachusetts and New York – that his birth date was in late 1807 or early 1808. However, immigrants had many cloudy and possibly strangely apprehensive reasons for lying about the dates of their birth on their oaths of naturalization, fearing that these could be important documents regarding future employment or military service.

In any case, Owen's oath of allegiance to the United States as recorded in Lowell on July 30, 1842, is a wonderfully detailed, if half-blotchy document. He swears that he is now 29 years-old and has already been in America for just shy of eight years. He explains that he was born in **Lurgachamlough** (now spelled Lurgahamlough) in County Monaghan. As noted, this little slice of land nestles tight between both Lattacrom and Tievaleny. That the younger Andrew referenced the former townland's name instead may have merely indicated that the family threw together a new cottage on the same farm in the intervening years between his older brother's Owen's birth and his own.

Other aspects of this declaration add further intrigue. Foremost is that Owen in this formal setting declared that his last name was not Monaghan nor

Monahan but **Monagan**. The origins of that spelling, ultimately only agreed to by my particular family in Connecticut in the early 1890s, have mystified all of my relations for ages – as well as 99 percent of the Irish who have never seen that spelling or heard that pronunciation before in their native country. But there in Lowell in 1842 occurs something like the first raising of a banner. This cannot have been haphazard since Owen somehow dictates the correct spelling of the impossible Lurgachamlough before affixing his signature as Owen Monagan. But through many later records over many years, it looks as if he backed off this act of defiance and let people call him "Monaghan" again as life wore on.

Owen was an interesting figure. Though a mill worker toiling for endless hours when young, he was definitely literate in English – which was not true of the majority of the Gaelic-speaking Irish of Aughnamullen of his vintage. In the 1840s he is repeatedly identified as a fee-paying subscriber to the *Boston Pilot*, a broadsheet which for decades served as the primary source of news and political discussion about the homeland for Irish immigrants throughout America and Canada, but especially around Boston. The masthead was wrought with images of a benevolent damsel representing America extending a hand of resurrection to a despairing beggar representing Ireland.

One reason for Owen's fascination must have had to do with the publication's running dozens of articles about Ballybay and its environs, pinpointing its citizens and highlighting that little town as a flashpoint for so many tensions and changes occurring within Ireland. The thuggery committed by Sam Gray and other "Orangemen" in Ballybay was a continuing focus of the *Boston Pilot*.

But the doings around Ballybay were not the only thorns in Owen's side. On August 26, 1843, he is seen in the Pilot as a signer of a nationwide petition by the "Repeal Association of America" demanding immediate annulment of the Acts of Union of 1800 whereby the Irish Parliament was dissolved to make way for total control of Ireland from London. In the late 1700s the native Irish had been gaining a modicum of genuine political power in the country's Protestant-dominated parliament in Dublin, which made many English aghast (partly due to fear of collusion with the zealously revolutionary French). The Acts of Union overturned all that and even forbade any Catholic to stand for election to represent his own people. These laws were despised in Ireland from the start, but it was not until the rise of the Catholic Emancipation League under Daniel O'Connell that the uproar became general, leading to that march on Ballybay that almost sparked a nationwide civil war in 1828. As a teenager in the 1820s, Owen may well have participated in some of the mass protest rallies against these so-called Acts of Union, and he undoubtedly knew all too well of the brutality Sam Gray rained upon the peasantry of Aughnamullen.

Owen of course had other facets. An item in the *Boston Pilot* on October 4, 1862, shows him to be among a group participating in a fund drive by the Augustinian Fathers of Lawrence, Massachusetts for its "Poor of Ireland" charity. He gave $2 – this was the equivalent of $50 today and not bad for a "scourer" of wool.

Owen was also not the first Monaghan to be married in St. Patrick's in Lowell. Six years before his own wedding to Catherine McNamara, a Michael "Mongan" married Harriet Jameson there on October 15, 1833. On June 14, 1835, a Bridget "Moneghan" married a Michael Boyle there – a possible brother of the James Boyle who married a Sarah Monaghan from Tievaleny. On today's world-leading genealogy and DNA-hosting website Ancestry.com, 57 people with Boyle lineage are listed as 4th cousins of this author, while over 1,100 descendants of the Boyles share 5th-8th cousin lineage. (However, the author descends matrilineally in part from several Scots-Irish families who also may be interlinked with this Boyle name.)

To round out this picture of a myriad collection of Monaghan ancestors arriving in Lowell and its environs early on, it should be remarked that on July 11, 1835 a Patrick Monaghan married an Anna Powers at St Patrick's.

Note that a Patrick Monaghan definitely had been farming in Aughnamullen as per the Irish Tithe Applotment Books of 1829.

Owen's Family Grows

Owen and Catherine Monaghan had seven children in all. The first was an **Elizabeth Ann Monaghan** who was born in Andover on December 16, 1840. They next had a son **William Stephen** on April 9,1843. The baptismal sponsors for William Stephen were a Catherine Cassidy and the **Arthur Killen** who was also a sponsor at Owen and Katherine's wedding. Perhaps he was related to the bride.

It is interesting to watch Owen's annual local tax bills rise. By May 1, 1846, he owed $4.25, almost five times more than he did in 1837. By contrast, the recently arrived brother Andrew (while evidently living in the same household), owed $1.15 for his first full year in the district in 1845. In May 1850, Owen owed $5.01 – nearly four times more than most of the others on his taxation page – and was apparently living in his own house on Abbott Street in what was called Marland Village. This was a cluster of modest (now expensive) houses that the mill owner John Marland and his partners had built for his skilled workers to purchase. This means Owen lived within sight or sound of the Marland Manufacturing Company complex, for which he likely worked then or earlier. He must have been productive, as shown by his tax bill for 1851 jumping another 10 percent to $5.55. In truth, this pattern of variability more fundamentally suggests he may have been a sub-contractor.

In 1847, Owen and Catherine had a second daughter they called **Vezina Jane** (with many spelling variants to follow). Research on this enigmatic name has led nowhere, save the realization that the second part of Jane was employed by our forebears time and again. The U.S. census for 1850 calls Owen a "wool scourer." This would have been a fairly nasty job since it entailed numerous treatments of fresh "greasy wool" with boiling alkalis and the like. But he had come a long way since his first boarding house years in North Andover. Living with Owen and Catherine in 1850 were not only their children, but two boarders, **Terence Henry** and John McCallan, both listed as (wool) "spinners." A variously "Callan" or "McAllan" family can be found living next door to Edward Monaghan in Lurgachamloch townland in Ireland's Tithe Applotment Books of 1829, so both were probably family.

Owen and Catherine's later four children were Alice, **Edward**, Richard, and the last, born in 1860, was a son also called **James Henry** Monaghan. Note that Henry is also a very strong surname from the middle of County Monaghan, with nine families answering to it in Aughnamullen and Ballybay as of the Tithe Applotment Books of 1829. In 1845, Owen had a **John A. Henry** – that name again – living with him and his growing family. The A. might have been for either Albert or Alexander. This John Henry was a shoemaker, and married a Hannah Trow, the daughter of a shoemaker, and they had at least six children together. It is all quite a curious subplot, since there are a total of 70 individuals bearing the last name of Henry today (or descended from someone with the name) with whom this author shares a significant DNA signature. Again, it seems that my great-great-great grandmother might have been an Elizabeth Henry.

Further linking to this Henry name was the almost certain relative named **Arthur Monaghan**, who married a Julia Lynch in St. Patrick's Church in Lowell in 1849. Arthur had first arrived in May 1841 on Prince Edward Island, at the great bay at the mouth of the St. Lawrence River in Canada and by that time in places a virtual colony of County Monaghan. But he left there for Massachusetts by at least 1847 and did not even stay long in Lowell. In the mid-1850s, Arthur moved on to the far upstate of New York. He may have soon served as a key figure there in urging Andrew and Owen to follow – which they later did. Arthur (who went by Monaghan, not Monahan like his own brother) died in 1908 in Malone, New York. His obituary stated that he had an aged brother Hugh Monahan still living on Prince Edward Island, and that they had arrived there together in 1841. Hugh prospered greatly as a general trader with his own swift sailing merchant boats plying the Canadian Maritimes. Importantly, Hugh's second son, born in 1858, was named **James**

Henry Monahan. Henry was not a commonly used forename by the Irish, making the overlap noteworthy, and triggering much subsequent research by this author on both the Henry and Prince Edward Island connections.

The Henrys, From Aughnamullen to Andover

Terence Henry, Owen's 23 year-old boarder in 1850, by now must be considered a definite close relative and likely even a nephew, through his father James Francis Henry. Terence's application for naturalization on December 15, 1852 (granted in 1856) avows that he too was from Aughnamullen and was born there on November 22, 1829. Terence states that he arrived in New York on November 30, 1847, i.e. at the height of the Famine. He was then barely eighteen. His parents were James Francis Henry and his wife Catherine, and they followed Terrence later, arriving in Boston with five younger children on March 22, 1851, on board the ship *Harvard* out of Liverpool. The younger children included a Susanna, James, Francis, Catherine, and Ellen. The father Francis's 1857 oath of naturalization swears that he was then living in Andover and was born in "Aughmacon" in County Monagan in 1796. The witnesses were his son Terence Henry and a Robert Sweeney (likely another relative).

Terrence Henry, resident with Owen Monaghan from around 1848, thus served as a family front-runner, likely helping to secure a residence for his parents and younger kin. The father, mostly called Francis though he was legally James Francis, was already listed on the tax roll in Andover of May 6, 1851, suggesting his work may have even been pre-arranged.

That this family were close kin is made further manifest by Owen and Catherine Monaghans selection of Terrence's father Francis Henry as the godfather of their second son **Edward C.** (Charles?) at his baptism on August 27, 1853, at the new St. Mary's Church in nearby Lawrence. The godmother was **Susan Henry**, likely Francis's wife Catherine's middle name. Other than when being very formal, the Irish in these years in great numbers eschewed use of their first names (typically bestowed as honorifics at birth) and switched to a lifetime of being called by their middle names. It is with the middle names, rather than the first ones, that you generally get down to genealogical reality with the Irish.

Francis Henry appears to have arrived in America with a drive to succeed. The 1855 Massachusetts state census suggests that he was working as a "factory operative" and was renting a respectable flat or even his own house in Andover. Back in Ireland, the *Tithe Applotment Books* of 1829 suggest that his Henry family in Monaghan had included an Alexander and Hugh Henry in the townland of Corkeeran at the northwest edge of Aughnamullen, just on the southern outskirts of Ballybay. This volume also cites a James Henry as living in Ballybay itself. He may have been Owen Monaghan's traveling partner to New Brunswick in 1834. In any case, the Massachusetts state census of 1855 shows that Francis Terry was living in Andover with his eight-years-younger wife Catherine and six of their children – Susan, 18; James, 16; Catherine, 14; Francis, 12; and Ellen, 10 – plus one "Clarence," 26, obviously a mis-rendering of Terence. In 1862, Francis and Catherine's son Francis Jr. was crushed to death in a terrible mill fire in Lawrence.

But Terence was building a respected reputation for himself as a skilled cabinet maker and purveyor of fine furniture. He had married an Elizabeth McGovern from Scotland in 1856 and moved to an apartment on 41 Oak Street in Lawrence (the same street to which his parents relocated). While pursuing his carpentry, he developed a successful trade as a furniture dealer and auctioneer and by 1860 had a shop at the prominent Lawrence intersection of Newbury and Common streets. Possibly because of even better business prospects in the making, he moved to Lowell within a couple of years. When his father Francis died on March 29, 1864, aged 70 – his death certificate cites his parents as being Michael and Ellen Henry – everything changed again. The next day Terrence and Elizabeth's infant son was born. Soon after that the couple took in his widowed mother Catherine, now 59, and the seamstress daughter of the same name, now 21.

Terrence and Elizabeth Henry's middle son John Albert Henry died when very young. The couple's other offspring were named Catherine, Mary Alice, James Terence, and Benjamin. Their progeny remained widespread around Lowell and Lawrence, Massachusetts at the end of the 1800s. Evidently, Terence Henry traded very successfully as a furniture dealer. But his own work became much sought after and he hopscotched back to Andover. On January 1, 1872, Terrence purchased for the then princely sum of $3,000 a substantial two-story house on Main Street in Andover overlooking the town's central Elm Square. This "very roomy" dwelling, according to the *Andover Advertiser,* came with an adjoining brick-fronted display shop and a neighboring field facing Elm Square. This was a superb address, and quite a turn-around from his arrival 25 years earlier. But alas, Terence soon suffered from bowel cancer and died *in testate* at the age of 44. Extensive probate court proceedings ensued, since his wife Elizabeth was forced to hurriedly sell off their lovely property – valued at nearly $3,500 and worth a lot of money then – in order to make ends meet. She perhaps moved back to Lowell since her various children married within that city in the late 1800s.

As can be seen, the connections to this extended Henry family were deep, even if forgotten by later generations. Indeed, a current Connecticut resident named Francis Henry has been identified as a clear 4th cousin (DNA match of 32 cms across 3 segments with yours truly). Within the Ancestry.Com data base, 69 other individuals with the surname Henry share genetic links with this author. In sum, the evidence suggests that my great-great-great grandmother was born a Henry. Considering that both Owen and Andrew Monaghan named their first daughters Elizabeth Ann, her maiden name may well have been Elizabeth Ann Henry.

As mentioned, in 1850 the other boarder with Owen and Catherine Monaghan was a **John McCallan**, a wool "spinner" aged 30 and a different puzzle. He was likely the same as the John "Callan" who arrived with his brother Angus in Boston on November 2, 1848, from Sydney, Nova Scotia (a stepping stone from Prince Edward Island).

While the Henry family's drama played out around them, Owen and Catherine Monaghan produced their own seven children in all. By early 1851 they had a daughter named Alice. In 1853 there was a son Edward, then a Richard in 1856, and finally James Henry Monaghan in 1860, when Owen himself was about 52 (his wife Catherine was a decade younger). Through the 1850s, Owen kept working as a "wool scourer." That meant working with reeking vats of bleach and other horrid potions whose toxins may have contributed to his somewhat untimely death from "lung fever" in 1874. It is noteworthy that people laboring inside the ever vaster textile mills of Massachusetts were typically listed as "operatives," no matter what their role. So the reference in the 1850 U.S. census to Owen holding this separate specialty of "wool scourer" – rather than being a mere "operative" – may indicate that he had found a niche in preparing wool before it crossed through the factory gates, whether in a business of his own or someone else's. By now, he was likely on very personal terms with the Marland family of Andover. Somehow, he was making enough money to put aside sufficient funds to eventually buy a fairly substantial farm in upstate New York.

Andrew Monaghan, Assisted Emigrant

My great-great grandfather Andrew Monaghan was but 12 when Owen left for America. So one can only guess as to how close the brothers were back in County Monaghan. But these two obviously established a bond along the way, as Andrew's destination from his "assisted emigration" from the Shirley Estate was straight to Owen's home in North Andover, Massachusetts.

Andrew declared at his 1853 naturalization application in nearby Amesbury, Massachusetts that he had arrived in New York on July 15, 1844. Currently accessible records do not reveal any immigrant ship landing that day. However, the Irish were already being forced to undergo extended quarantines before disembarkation, and a ship called the *Nile* from Liverpool that offloaded its passengers on August 2, 1844, may have actually arrived earlier. The blurry manifest lists a Mary "Monagan," 23, and an Edward, 32; and though barely legible, what appears to be a "Chs. And" – which would mean **Charles**

Andrew and aged either 21 or 31. It is my strong belief that the full name of my great-great grandfather was indeed Charles Andrew Monagan.

Andrew's citizenship application.

Andrew seems to have enjoyed a fine start in America. Possibly while working side-by-side in North Andover, Andrew quickly met his fiancé Catherine Castle. By the 1840s, the Massachusetts textile mills already employed young women by the thousands. On October 26, 1844, after little more than two months in North Andover, Andrew married Catherine (with some blurry transcripts rendering the name as "Castles") in the Cathedral of the Holy Cross in Boston. Catherine was a County Cavan girl of about 21, and their accents would have been nearly interchangeable. In fact, Andrew's last residence in Ummerafree almost touched the border of Cavan and it is possible that the couple were first introduced there.

In any case, Andrew and Catherine may have even shared rooms at the beginning of their marriage with the older brother Owen on North

Andover's Abbot Street. Note that both Andrew and Catherine Castle left for America before the full onslaught of endemic starvation and disease that was the Great Famine. The terrible statistics of these years have been told in many ways, suffice it to say. Between 1845-1851 nearly one million people fled Ireland to North America. But often overlooked is the fact that thousands more were moving to England and Scotland in this same period.

Even before the Famine's official onset, crop failures were already stirring terrible want across great swaths of Ireland. In fact, half a million Irish moved to England in the three decades before the Famine even started. So the newly booming city of Liverpool, to which many County Monaghan people also fled for employment in its mills, must have exercised a strong attraction to our ancestors early on. It was Liverpool that dominated the diaspora to North America as the prime disembarkation for all of Europe after the 1830s, mainly because the fares there were the cheapest.

Catherine Castle's year of departure from Liverpool was 1840 and her hardships at sea were formidable. She appears to have voyaged on the brig *Cotton Planter* which arrived in New York on April 10, 1840. An entry on its manifest by the ship's master Cornelius Duane cites a Catherine "Costle" or "Costles" – it is a bit blurry – as being from Ireland and 18 years old, which is age-exact. No alternative immigration citations for a person similarly named are apparent anywhere else.

The Cotton Planter was built around 1801 in Stonington, Connecticut and was not commodious, being only 92 feet in length and weighing about 140 tons. The brig appears to have served as a slave runner from Africa in her earliest years, and eventually evolved to collecting cotton in the Carolinas and New Orleans for transport back to Liverpool and then returning with her 20-foot-wide hold packed with as many impoverished Irish and English immigrants as could be squeezed in. Usually she was stuffed with around 150 destitute souls at a time. Their sustenance would likely be two daily helpings of corn meal and maggot-infested bread. The earlier African slaves were treated far, far more unspeakably, yet by the year 1840 the ship as it neared its fifth decade at sea must have leaked and smelled worse than even the slaves ever endured. Such was the morality of the prosperous Yankees out of Essex, Connecticut who commissioned the Cotton Planter and her fellow ships in the Mobile Packet Line.

Andrew and Catherine Monaghan.

It is unclear whether they arrived on the same ship, but Catherine Castle ended up living with or near a number of relatives in Andover, Massachusetts. These included her sisters Rosa, born in 1825 and who died of "congested lungs" in 1867, and Ann who married a Richard Kilby [or Kirby?] there on September 8, 1848. She also had a brother Patrick who in 1850 had 50 cents tax due for his last stint of employment in a North Andover foundry. Another likely brother, born in 1819, was a James "Cassell," son of parents James and Catherine. An Elizabeth "Castles," a weaver and as per her death certificate a daughter of John and Jane, died in the Salisbury area called "the Mills" from poisoning – undoubtedly from the wool treatment vats – on July 12, 1848. Andrew and Catherine Castle Monaghan were living in the same place at that time of Salisbury's "Mills."

V.

THE INDUSTRIAL REVOLUTION IN MASSACHUSETTS

The Lawrence Miracle

Andrew and Catherine were fortunate to have my great-great-great uncle Owen on hand. For most newly arriving Irish, the first stop was typically some tenement house stuffed with up to 200 mill "operatives" and general laborers. Bitter cold in the winter, stifling heat in the summer, and squalor and bad sanitation in every season – that is what your dollar in the booming new factories would buy you at the exhausted end of a thirteen-hour work day.

As the industrial revolution churned forward in the Merrimac Valley, great throngs of men, women and children as young as ten hurried in the darkness to the factory gates to start work at 5:30 a.m. They toiled on until at least 7 p.m., while working an average of 73 hours a week. The noise of these factories was infernal, and the air within them was choking with particles of wool and the stench of smoke and toxic chemicals. Female emancipation? In 1840, some 8,000 women toiled in the woolen mills of Lowell alone. In all, roughly 70,000 people worked in the region's textile mills by the decade's end. In Lowell, there were 40 different mills thundering away beside the once tranquil Merrimack River, with their 320,000 spindles producing 50,000 miles of cloth each year. If all this were not enough, Andrew Monaghan and Catherine Castle happened to be living within shouting distance of one of the most remarkable economic developments in American history – the almost overnight birth of Lawrence, Massachusetts.

Until the late 1840s, Andover maintained a somewhat lower profile than Lowell. The northern half of the township still held many sizeable farms in the fertile plains along the Merrimack River, giving the whole place a kind of balance between heavy industry and gentle rusticity. But that would not last.

The clock, indeed, had been set ticking from the moment a small group of rich Boston Brahmins examined the situation with dollar signs in their eyes. In 1843 they formed a syndicate, soon called the **Essex Company,** whose purpose was to leapfrog booming Lowell by buying up great swaths of Andover's riverside land (along with parts of Methuen across the Merrimac) and create out of farm fields an overnight "miracle mile" of a town to be called **Lawrence.** Their hugely ambitious goal was to first create on the Merrimac the largest dam the world had ever seen, in order to generate such thundering water power that their new town could be stacked from end to end with more prodigious mills than even Lowell could muster. To top the scheme off, they proposed to divert major canals right and left from below the dam so that even more mills could be lined up alongside these.

Andover's staunch old Yankees were horrified, but they were no match for the brute wealth and political savvy of the Essex Company. In Boston in November 1845 the Massachusetts State Legislature obliged the latter by decreeing that Andover should be split in two with the top half handed over to the Essex Company. The transformation that followed was astounding. In 1840 the riverside strip of Andover that had been called **Merrimack** held about 200 residents, consisting of maybe 20 or 30 farm families. But once the thumbs up was given to the onset of essentially a new corporate age, Boston's unemployed surged to the site and along with them the Irish poured in too. By 1848, the newly created town of Lawrence had nearly 6,000 residents – 30 times more than lived in so-called Merrimac eight years before. Of these, 3,750 were native sons, but 2,139 were newly materialized Irish. There was also 1 German, 1 Italian, 3 French, 2 Welsh, and 9 Scots.

The scene was feverish from the start. From late 1845, thousands of men were hired the moment they showed up to help create the so-called **Great Stone Dam,** nearly a third-of-a-mile long and thus the largest ever made. This colossus had to be fed with vast supplies of raw materials. Granite blocks by the thousands were delivered from the quarries of New Hampshire, prodigious loads of lumber were hauled down from Maine, and up to 200,000 bricks a day were hefted onto the building sites springing up on all sides. After the earliest mills began production, up to a million pounds of wool and cotton was being carted through the infernal fug of mud and dust that was Lawrence. The scene resembled the building of the pyramids, but actually on a much larger scale. All of this material had to be hauled in by ox-wagon from the nearest railhead in North Andover. Access roads to the work sites had to be laid and constantly expanded as did the new city's rudimentary first streets, sewers, water pipes, and the beginnings of a new railway line. Workers were sleeping in the fields and in the streets and many got soused at night on cheap whiskey to steel them for another work day to begin before dawn.

The Great Stone Dam.

Lawrence was built out of nothing.

The Lawrence mills, largest in the world.

Child laborers in Lawrence.

For an eager Irish laborer with a stout back like our Andrew Monaghan – who was almost certainly involved one way or another with the building of this American colossus – the sense of almost limitless new horizons for work had to have been thrilling. At first though, the area's offerings to a laborer, which is what he always said he was (rather than say a weaver), ranged between 84 cents and a $1.25 a day. However, those numbers did rapidly rise, since the need for new building became insatiable. In 1847 Lawrence had not a single paved street, sidewalk, sewer pipe, or a church or real school – it was akin to America's "Wild East." The state of housing was deplorable, with tenements sometimes thrown together in three weeks in anticipation of the quick profits to be made by stuffing in the destitute Irish dam builders and canal diggers cheek by jowl. Tuberculosis, cholera, and dysentery ran rampant.

But the first textile factories indeed flew into being and spurned a growth in manufacturing capacity at a pace the world had never before seen. One of Lawrence's first plants was the vast Bay State Mills which opened in 1847. This was followed by the Atlantic Mills, and in 1852 the Pacific Mills with 5,360 employees splayed over 41 acres of floor space. By then, even the smaller-scale Everett Mills, with 750 employees, was producing eight million yards of fabric each year.

A neighboring company had 135,000 spindles turning its cotton, and 25,000 spindles working at worsted wool. Nearly 5,300 employees in this manufactory worked through 65,000 pounds of wool and 116,000 pounds of cotton each week. That company was burning 1.26 million tons of coal each year to help churn nearly ninety 3,000-horsepower steam boilers and engines around the clock. In Lawrence, the scene was of textile manufacturing gone berserk, and it was all complemented by the construction of nine huge paper mills.

Until at least the 1860s, a typical day's work for men, women and children alike in Lawrence would start well before dawn and in winter lasted until well after dark. True, there was abundant work for all – including children as young as ten. But the reality was harsh. Owen Monaghan's children all became child laborers and so too did Andrew's sons Edward and my great-grandfather, John Stephen Monaghan, born in 1846. Starvation was no longer an issue, but killing diseases remained rife. Another problem was bitter resentment of the Irish among a number of nativist young toughs, which led to a full-scale riot in Lawrence in 1853. And inside the sprawling mills lurked the constant danger of industrial accident along with appalling levels of chronic respiratory problems.

Some of the mills were built with great haste. The worst consequence of this was the disaster that occurred on January 10, 1853 at Lawrence's booming, five-story Pemberton Mills. The overall design of the place was reasonably thoughtful, with the spooling and warping at the top floor, then spinning below, and carding beneath that, and the weaving and finishing at street level. The 700 workers there filed in at 5:30 a.m. and toiled away as usual on that January day. Suddenly, just before 5 p.m. and as darkness was falling, the structure's low-grade iron supports began to tremble. Then the top floors with all their enormous weight in brick, timber and iron groaned and then cracked with a deafening roar, with each floor exploding into the one below. The sound of buried people screaming for their lives could next be heard throughout Lawrence.

Swarms of locals began tearing at the rubble to free the trapped and haul away the wounded – members of our family had to have been among them. At least 120 people were killed instantly. As the terrible work continued in the darkness, someone stumbled and dropped his blazing oil lantern. In an instant the wrecked wooden flooring and masses of half-finished textiles erupted into a raging inferno. Everyone in the vicinity would have witnessed the horror as dozens more trapped workers burned alive. Among these witnesses must have been Owen Monaghan and his sister the widowed Mary Burns.

Tracking the Merrimac Monaghans

In tracking the substantial Monaghan family presence in the Merrimac Valley, several facts should be borne in mind. The bewildering variations in the spelling of the family name, sometimes with multiple variations for the same person depending on the transcriber, are one problem. Another is that these towns were deeply interwoven, especially after the 1.5-mile expansion of the rail line from North Andover into Lawrence and the opening in 1848 of a new 9-mile line between Lawrence and Lowell. Even in its first year of operation that line carried 8,000 passengers a day. As J. F. C. Hayes remarked in his **History of the City of Lawrence** (1868), "It seemed as if the entire population of Lawrence was travelling to Lowell, and the population of Lowell traveling to Lawrence." In other words, this triad of mill towns was so interconnected that newly arriving cousins or even siblings could easily live in any one of them one year, then move back and forth to a different one the next.

One way or another, all the earliest Irish Catholics in the area had to venture to Lowell's St. Patrick's Church for baptism or marriage throughout the 1830s and 1840s. A Catholic church was not finally built in Andover until 1852, and in Lawrence about the same time. All the early church records from Lowell must thus be considered as pertinent to the Monaghan family story. One notes that a Thomas "Mongan" buried his two-year-old son John at St. Patrick's church yard in Lowell on May 18, 1840, after the boy's succumbing to croup.

A possible sister to Owen and Andrew was a Sarah "Monan" who married a Patrick Connelly at St. Patrick's in Lowell on April 28, 1848. Back in Tievaleny, three different Connelly families, headed by a John, Terrence, and Felix in the 1850s, lived next door to my Monaghan ancestors. Another possible sibling was a Bernard Monaghan born in County Monaghan on October 15, 1809 and naturalized in Lowell on October 25, 1852 – suggesting as per the five-year rule that he arrived by at least 1847. His wife was another Catherine.

Also of interest is a Margaret Monaghan, a possible first cousin to Owen and Andrew, born around 1823 "in Ireland," who married a baker named William Dalton. Their family lived in Lawrence's 4th Ward. Alas, Margaret, who had a number of previous children, died while giving birth at the age of 47 on May 29, 1870. The death certificate identifies her parents back in Ireland as a Thomas and Margaret Monaghan.

In 1848, a 35-year-old married laborer named James Monaghan, born around 1813, died of consumption in Lowell, possibly contracted on his trans-Atlantic crossing. Was he that other "assisted emigration" brethren from Ummerafree? In June 1849 a newly landed Mary "Monohan," 17, was buried in Lowell after dying from "ship fever." A Lawrence stonecutter named Patrick Monaghan, born in Ireland in 1821, is also of interest, and may be linked to the Prince Edward Island offshoots of the family. On September 20, 1853, he married a Susan McGovern and cited his parents as being a Cornelius and Ann Monaghan.

Also present in Lowell in 1855 were possible aunts to Owen and Andrew named Bridget and Ann Monaghan, born around 1795 and 1785, respectively. An Edward Mongan lived in Lowell for many years until his death in 1887 at the age of 67. By the end of the Famine years, the number of people with some semblance of the name Monaghan in Massachusetts grew with a vengeance – essentially becoming too many to track. In fact, the Massachusetts state census of 1855 listed 478 people named Monaghan or one of its derivatives.

The Sad Story of Mary Burns

One definite relative was Owen and Andrews's widowed sister **Mary Monaghan Burns**, who arrived in early 1846. Mary was born as early as 1801 or as late as 1811. She married an apparent John Burns, possibly associated with the prolific neighboring family of that surname in Tievaleny. They had a run of children including two older daughters plus sons named John, Edward, Patrick, and Peter. But then the Famine hit, her husband died in 1845, and the bottom fell out.

Poor Mary next landed in Massachusetts, likely destitute but with four still young children in her care, including a mortally sick infant. All of these she at first crammed into a boarding house in Andover near Owen. She must have heard from him that here her older sons would find work quickly, and that the black cycle of disease, despair and early death back home could be broken under his watchful eye. Mary also knew that here she would find not only her brothers Owen and Andrew, but also her deceased husband's apparent cousins John and Richard Burns, who were living in nearby Lowell.

But life's vicissitudes kept stalking Mary. Soon after her arrival in Andover, her baby Richard W. Burns, aged six months, succumbed on April 8, 1846, to "brain atrophy." Undoubtedly this was due to tuberculosis, and possibly caught on board ship. She had to have been newly widowed as it was Mary – rather than a husband not mentioned – who alone placed a notice in the *Boston Pilot* of April 1848 beseeching that any news about her missing son John be sent to his "uncle Owen in Andover." This notice (discovered by Andrew Pierce) says that John, "a tailor from Aughnimullen [sic]" was supposed to have set sail for

America from Liverpool in October 1847 but never arrived. In fact, *Griffith's Valuation of Ireland* shows both a James and a Charles Burns – likely brothers of Mary's husband – to have been still living in Tievaleny.

Mary Burns's doomed infant was named Richard, and several years later my great-great-great uncle Owen would name his third son Richard as well, possibly after this lost nephew. Massachusetts census records from 1855 show that Mary (Monaghan) Burns was still living in North Andover, but now joined by her older daughters Catherine 28, and the twins Mary and Sarah, 24. The older girls seem to have waited back in Ireland until the mother gained a foothold in Andover. It was not until 1857 that the daughter Mary married a Michael Connelly, possibly also an emigrant from Tievaleny where the aforementioned family of that name had a strong presence. The mother may have been the same Mary Burns who died in Andover on May 18, 1866.

Arthur Monaghan, Canada to Lowell to New York

Another relative living nearby in the late 1840s and early 1850s was Arthur Monahan (later Monaghan), by his sworn affidavits born in County Monaghan in November 1825. He is an important link in connecting the family narrative both forward from Massachusetts to northern New York and also backward to other ancestors on Canada's Prince Edward Island. That narrow 120 mile-long island in the Gulf of the St. Lawrence attracted over 2,000 immigrants from rural Monaghan in the 1830s and early 1840s and is said to hold the highest concentration of descendants from Monaghan in the world outside the home county.

The most intriguing clues about Arthur's history only came to light in the U.S. census for Malone, New York in 1900 and in a local newspaper article at the time of his death in 1908. The latter noted that he was survived by a brother Hugh on Prince Edward Island in the Canadian Maritimes. Further research made clear that Arthur and Hugh first landed on Prince Edward Island in May 1841 with several other bedraggled siblings disembarking beside their widowed mother. A Canadian newspaper record decades later says she was accompanied by "five or six children" all likely first cousins to Owen and Andrew. But Arthur and perhaps three other siblings moved on to America fairly rapidly, as many did from Prince Edward Island in those days. Remaining behind to face the long Canadian winters was the young but almost instantly prospering brother Hugh Monahan.

Arthur's contingent instead soon headed south toward Massachusetts's booming textile industry. Thus in 1849, when aged 23, Arthur married in Lowell a 20-year-old mill "operative," named Julia Lynch. The couple took an apartment in a nearby boarding house, together with two Lynch sisters named Catherine and Ellen, the latter then 15. On the marriage license Arthur listed his deceased parents as being Hugh and Mary "Monahan." Also marrying in Lowell's Catholic church the next year – to an Arthur Malarky – was Arthur Monahan's older sister Ann, 32, born in 1818.

A John Monahan in Lowell appears to have been Arthur's older brother. He may have led the way there via the small sailing ship *Flora* from St. John's, Newfoundland which arrived in Boston on January 17, 1842 – seven months after the family's landing on Prince Edward Island. At that time John was 22, and he seems to have been the same John Monahan who married a Mary Higgins in Lowell in 1847. John, Ann, and Arthur appear to have brought a Henry Monahan along, too. In fact, Arthur Monaghans sister-in-law Ellen Lynch, who had been living with him and his wife Julia Lynch, on January 28, 1855, married a Henry Monahan.

Andrew Monaghan, Great-Great Grandfather

This narrative's primary interest in these Massachusetts years of course concerns the doings of the great-great grandfather Andrew Monaghan. He seems to have thrived on the rich supply of new work opportunities available after his arriving in America in the summer of 1844, and clearly began to save some money on the side. However, some of his early movements were elusive. Possibly, the administrative mess of carving the brand new metropolis of

Lawrence out of Andover, with an overnight need for a second set of records, may have contributed to some confusion about both the dates of birth and spelling of Andrew and Catherine's first son Edward Monaghan. The Essex County archives ultimately show one Edward "Orne" being born to Andrew and Catherine "Munigan" of North Andover on September 24, 1844. Orne, a department in Normandy, is almost implausible. The name appears to have been a transcription error from an original scrawl, and likely should have read "Owen"or else "Oge" after the Ulster hero massacred by Walter Devereux. The date also had to have been mis-transcribed from 1845 since the former does not add up on several counts. My great-grandfather John Stephen Monaghan was born next on November 4, 1846, in North Andover, where one record keeper this time had the name as "Monhagen." (The formal registration in county records seems to have been delayed until June 4, 1847.)

Then on October 27, 1847, Andrew and Catherine became the parents of a son they named **Owen**, who seems to have died within a few days of his baptism in Lowell on November 1. The baptismal sponsors were the Lowell solicitor Charles M. Short and his wife Mary. Considering the prevalence of the name Short around Aughnamullen and Ballybay, and Andrew's brother Owen having had an Elizabeth Short as a witness at his own wedding in Lowell in 1839, not to mention the fact of so many Short descendants today being DNA-linked to this author as 5th to 8th cousins – one strongly suspects that these Shorts of the 1830-1840s were close relatives. This Charles M. Short was living in Andover by 1832, so perhaps he even had something to do with Owen's initial move to the area. Be that as it may, Andrew and Catherine's infant Owen must have died soon after birth since all subsequent records for him vanished summarily.

Perhaps in order to escape the growing din around North Andover, Andrew Monaghan soon moved his young family to the then expansive neighboring Essex County township of Salisbury. The place had several new textile mills of its own, and yet boasted an unspoiled sea coast to the east. Unfortunately, this relocation came with new trauma. A daughter named **Elizabeth Alice** Monaghan was born there in 1848. Sadly, she died of the whooping cough at age 10 months, 7 days, on April 29, 1849. She was buried in Saint Augustine Cemetery in the Mills district near the town of Amesbury. One of the most touching relics to survive from this time is a 12-inch square tin plate with the infant's name ornately inscribed with her dates of birth and death. Such so-called "coffin plates" become a common memorial in New England by the 1840s and often were placed upon an easel before the casket during the initial wake and later funeral mass. The infant Elizabeth Ann's coffin plate remains in the keeping of my cousin Parthy Monaghan in Virginia, a devoted curator of many of the family's most treasured photographs and memorabilia.

Elizabeth Alice Monaghan's coffin plate.

The 1850 federal census lists Andrew as being a "dyer" in Salisbury, presumably of wool, with Catherine and their sons plus four young women tenants co-resident. The family next moved back upriver to Lawrence where Andrew in the late 1850s can be found listed in the city directories still as a "dyer" (but for one year as a grocer). Contrary to family lore, he seemed to have had no interest in working within the deafening roar of the mills and left all that to Owen. But Andrew is nonetheless found in the census of 1860 as being a resident of Lawrence's heavily Irish Catholic 4th ward, where his sister Mary Monaghan Burns and other family members were already established. Andrew's sons Edward, now 15, and John Stephen, 13, are both already listed as being "mill operatives." Catherine is "keeping house." That my great-grandfather John Stephen later as an adult so roundly impressed people of much higher education seems impressive, considering his humble beginnings. Also remarkable is some very baffling record keeping, which has it that in 1868 the couple – voila! – had a son Thomas William over two decades after the birth of Edward and John Stephen, and long after settling into their later farming life outside Malone, New York. But we shall see.

SOME OF THE ANCESTRY IN ANDOVER AND SURROUNDS – 1832-1868:

Owen Monaghan m. Catherine McNamara

Their children:

    Elizabeth Ann (1840-1920)

    William Stephen (1843-1897)

    Vizena Jane (1847-1916)

    Alice (1850-1899)

    Edward (1853-1904)

    Richard (1856-1900)

    James Henry (1860-1885)

    Catherine McNamara Monaghan's several siblings.

Andrew Monaghan m. Catherine Castle(s)

Their children:

    Edward (1845-1900)

    John Stephen (1846-1929)

Castle siblings, partial list:

    James (1819-)

    Elizabeth (1848)

    Rose (1825-1867)

Mary Monaghan Burns, widow

    Her children: Catherine, Sarah, Ellen, John, Edward, Patrick, Peter.

Patrick Monahan m. Anna Powers, Lowell (July 19, 1835).

Arthur Monaghan (1826-1908) m. Julia Lynch (later Caldwell).

Terence Henry, his several children – Owen, Andrew, Mary, William.

Francis Henry, Terence's father and his several other children.

Various Short relatives, Elizabeth and Attorney Charles, at their American start.

Various Killen relatives.

Mystery relative seen in 1839, William Stephen Monhan

Bernard Monaghan (b. 1809, naturalized Lowell 1852)

Edward Monaghan (29 when marries Bridget Kane in Lowell in 1849)

Hugh Monaghan m. Catherine Didiat, both of Lowell, July 13, 1834

Patrick Monaghan (b.1821-1893) m. Susan McGovern 1853

Bernard Monaghan (b. County. Monaghan 1809, naturalized Lowell 1852)

Michael Monaghan m. Harriet Jameson, 1833

Bridget Monaghan m. Michael Boyle, 1835

Patrick Monaghan m. Anna Powers, 1835

Sarah Monan m. Patrick Connelly 1848

VI.

THE CANADA CONNECTION

Prince Edward's "Monaghan Settlement"

There are many forgotten chapters and mysteries still lurking within the ancestral Monaghan saga. One concerns the role of Canada's Prince Edward Island as an important stepping stone in the family's immigration to the New World, which also serves as an odd but indelible link to the extreme north of New York State.

Prince Edward Island is of interest to this story for multiple reasons. For starters, numerous families known to the Aughnamullen Monaghans would have had ties to this place, since so many people from County Monaghan migrated to that verdant but wintry isle in the 1830s and early 1840s that a central part of it was dubbed the "Monaghan Settlement." The winding dirt road from the docks of the port of **Charlottetown** was even called the "Monaghan Road."

Until the late 1820s, the 120-mile-long Prince Edward Island had remained a virtually uninterrupted wilderness with only a few towns and settlements hugging the coast. But around this time certain large landholders began to actively recruit immigrants from Scotland and Ireland to transform their wilderness holdings into rent-paying farms. To help the cause, an Irish Catholic priest named Father John MacDonald sent an agent named James Trainor around Belfast and County Monaghan to petition for settlers. Another, though later, key priest on the island was a Rev. **James Duffy** from Aughnamullen.

The usual procedure for the island's big landowners was to offer 100 acres of forest rent-free for the first two years to any family who agreed to clear all that

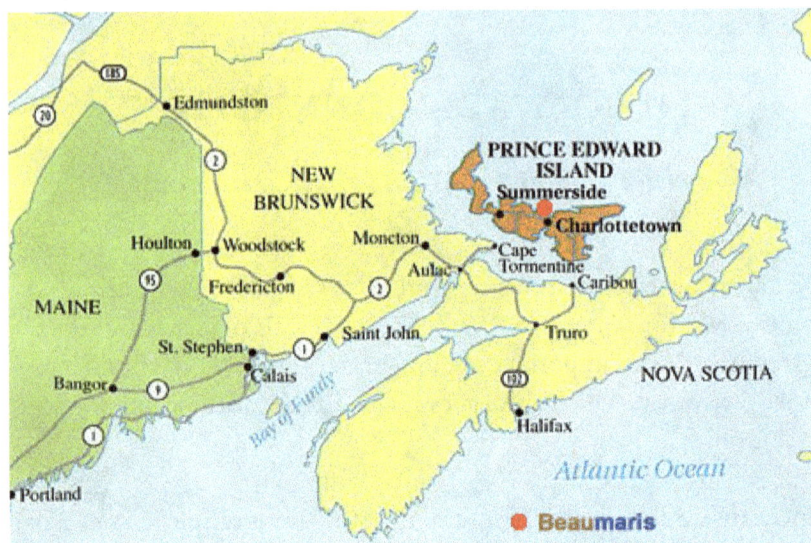

into meadow and farmland. Once a working farm was in place, six pence an acre would be owed to the landlord for the next 20 years. To destitute tenant farmers from County Monaghan, this sounded like manna from heaven, and they signed on in large numbers.

The December 20, 1908, obituary for Arthur Monaghan in *The Malone Farmer* describes his arriving in Prince Edward Island with his brother Hugh, their mother and several other siblings in 1841. Hugh's own obituary in 1913 makes it clear that the family arrived on May 17, 1841, on the *Margaret Pollock*, a behemoth of a transport ship that was a forerunner of the infamous class of "coffin ships" only beginning to ply the Atlantic then.

The typical arrivals from the often harrowing voyages to P.E.I., as it is called, staggered off the boat at Charlottetown in a kind of a daze. As the excellent island historian Brendan O'Grady wryly notes, the locals even had a name for the groups who wore this confounded look and talked in nearly indecipherable English and shuffled along in homespun wool trousers and overcoats that nearly flowed to their toes – "the Monaghans." A good portion of them, including definite relatives of the eventual Connecticut Monagans, stumbled along the Monaghan Road toward a place called **Kelly's Cross**. The Kelly's Cross district of Prince Edward Island began as a small sheep-rearing hamlet near the center of the long island. Here wool was carded and loomed in at least one nearby mill early on. Where two dirt tracks met, there accumulated a collection of Kellys from County Monaghan. Around them grew up a perimeter of Monahans (the favored spelling there). The outer ring also included Duffys, Trainors, and Johnstons – all from County Monaghan. Also for a brief time resided the young Arthur Monaghan who showed up before long in Lowell and later in Malone, New York.

The denizens of Kellys Cross included a "Big Pat" or Patrick Monahan married to a Catherine Johnston, and a "Black Johnny" Monahan (his brother and married to a Margaret Johnston 1802-1884) and his sons called "White Johnny" and "Peter the Great." Of the descendants of this bunch DNA-tested by 2020, this writer appears to be most closely related to Black Johnny Monahan. Peter the Great Monahan's own children were called "Thomas the Great," "James the Great," and "Mags the Great." But Black Johnny, who was born in Monaghan in 1786, had another son on Prince Edward Island in 1833 who he also named Peter. One of this second Peter's descendants is a "Shawn" Monahan, living now in Boston but with many links back to Kelly's Cross. Recent DNA testing reveals Shawn to be a 4th to 6th cousin. His great-grandfather Peter's children included a Thomas, James, Ellen, John, Peter, Mark and a **Stephen**.

A descendant of Big Pat above, or more properly Patrick Anthony Monaghan (1789-1884), also proves out as a 5th to 8th cousin of mine (9 cms overlap) via the Ancestry.Com database. The extensive family tree of this "A.C." indicates that Patrick's parents were a John Monahan and Mary Gill (or McGill) of Monaghan. Patrick's first child born in Ireland was named **Owen**. He was followed by an Ann, Patrick, Mary, John, Michael, James, Ann, and in 1840 a son **Charles** born on Prince Edward Island.

So thickly interwoven were these Monahans of Kellys Cross that a ballad, likely dating to the 1850s, was composed about them. It is quite amusing to realize that this is actually about a particular cluster of our family's ancestors. One stanza went:

> *There was White Johnny,*
> *Black Johnny, Peter and Pat*
> *And twice as many more –*
> *Now how many's that?*

Some of these Monaghans of Kellys Cross are said to have come from Donagh parish in the north of County Monaghan, where potential ancestral links have been previously discussed. That area was only about 15 miles north of Ballybay and Aughnamullen.

The earliest Monaghan on Prince Edward Island was possibly the aforementioned John, arriving by at least 1831 and married to a Margaret Johnston. He is found in the 1841 census as the head of a family of 10 persons. John and Margaret Monahan's daughter Sarah was born on Prince Edward Island in 1831 and in 1856 she married a James Duffy.

Hugh Monahan, Prodigy of P.E.I.

As noted, the Arthur Monaghan connection to Prince Edward Island (and ultimately to Owen and Andrew and upstate New York) was only recently unearthed via an obituary reference to his brother Hugh. Hugh seems to have become a young star soon after his arrival at Kelly's Cross. DNA evidence makes plain that these must have been first cousins to Andrew Monaghan.

Hugh Monaghan was certainly a man of great energy and spirit. His obituary on April 30, 1913, in the Prince Edward Island *Daily Examiner* explains his humble origins. He arrived on May 17, 1841, at the port of Charlottetown with his widowed mother Mary and "five or six" siblings after a difficult journey from Belfast on the 917-ton transport ship the *Margaret Pollack*.

The unheard of number of more than 700 passengers, most of them from County Monaghan, were stuffed into this ship's hold as it set sail on April 9. Alas, a measles contagion spread with terrible consequences for the young. Before the Gulf of St. Lawrence hove into sight, 24 children under the age of five had died on board. When the Margaret Pollack slipped into Charlottetown on Mary 17, 1841, two newly dead infants lay side-by-side on deck.

The Margaret Pollock's sister ship, the *Thomas Gelston,* with 139 passengers on board, was just dropping anchor as well. Its passengers mustered brave cheers to the Margaret Pollack and even pranced some jigs and a reel back and forth. But then both ships were put into a stultifying quarantine that prevented all from disembarking until early June. Only then could the widow Mary Monahan with her children Arthur, Hugh, Ann and possibly John and another unknown (the earlier mentioned Henry?) start their trudge toward Kellys Cross.

As far as can be told, Hugh was the only son who stayed behind on Prince Edward Island. He began making his mark around Charlottetown as early in 1845 as the builder (or buyer among a syndicate) of a new schooner called *Swallow.* Hugh was then about 20 years-old, so this is curious. Hugh was obviously a dynamo and his first sons later also became seafarers in his mold. He soon began trading in all manner of goods via all manner of boats. In October 1856 Hugh married an island-born Anna Jane McMurrow. Their known children were Francis (a "seaman" born around 1860); Patrick (a "sailing master"), Michael, **James Henry,** and finally a girl named Mary Ann. The son Francis died at the age of 30 as did his wife a few months later, leaving Hugh (then about 66) and Anna to raise their grandchildren in their old age.

With his early years spent as a deckhand and then ship's master importing goods from the mainland to the ever-needy island market, Hugh soon became known as one of the biggest general traders in the port of Charlottetown. Rum and whiskey, coal, cotton, salt, and flour – wherever he saw a profit, he bought, and most often brought to the island on his own sailing vessels. By 1864, Hugh was building up his own fleet of brigantines to run down the Saint Lawrence to Quebec and Montreal, and trade with other ports in Canada's Maritimes. Some of his ships included the brigs *Primrose of Ireland*, commissioned in 1865; the *Aereon* in 1866; and then the *Priscilla and Silver Light*. The *Hibernia* followed in 1873 and the Erin in 1880. According to the *Charlottetown Guardian* of February 11, 1909, it was Hugh Monaghan who in 1868 was selected to send the first message from that community to London via a historic new transatlantic telegraph cable. He announced that he was looking for better insurance terms for his ships.

In 1879 Hugh constructed a substantial trading emporium and warehouse on Charlottetown's main street. He acquired several other properties around town and was active in the local Catholic church. But his considerably younger wife Anna Jane died in 1912 and the bereft Hugh then passed away a year later. His cash holdings were so large by the standards of the day – namy millions in present terms – that his wealth was talked about even in the distant *Saskatoon Daily Star*. He signed his will on April 25, 1913, only about two days before he died. Looking to smooth his way to the Great Beyond he asked that $2,0000 (about $50,000 today) be directed to having high masses sung for the repose of his soul and his deceased wife's, and another $5,000 be given to St. Dunstan's Basilica straight out.

Hugh's brother Arthur, who next showed up from Prince Edward Island in Lowell, Massachusetts and married Julia Lynch there in 1847, must have been some kind of adventurer. As early as September 1850, Arthur was already visiting New York's North Country in Franklin County, hard by the Canadian border and where farmland remained cheap. While exploring the region's opportunities he undoubtedly visited Artemis Monaghan there. Important new railroad links were just being forged to the East Coast, so the place must have been in the news. From Andover, Owen Monaghan was poking about the area himself by March of 1850, according to the waiting letters column in the Malone *Frontier Palladium*. He could have met with Artemis right then as well. As he was related to Arthur and Arthur clearly was to Artemis, thus all three were kin.

If it weren't for pre-existing family connections, why else would an enterprising 24-year-old like Arthur, recently arrived in Massachusetts from distant Prince Edward Island, develop a craving for this strange little corner of upstate New York? Why, too, one might ask, did Owen become so interested in this same area around the same time, unless there was an interwoven familial thread? The name of that missing thread perhaps should be filed under "Artemis."

One Artemis Monaghan of Malone

As discussed, a Thomas "Monahan" of Bombay had been a fairly early settler in Franklin County by dint of his arriving in the late 1820s. But possibly more intrinsically related to this story was an Artemis Monaghan who arrived in 1839 and quickly set to farming and siring many children. Artemis, with his unusual and variously spelled first name, appears to have been an uncle of the 24-year-old Arthur who had bounced all the way from County Monaghan to Prince Edward Island, and then on to Lowell, Massachusetts beside Owen and Andrew. In some oddly purposeful mission for such a young man, he pushed on to one of the most obscure places left in the eastern United States of that time – Malone, New York. But there he took up residence nonetheless and close to Artemis.

Artemis, mostly recorded as another "Arthur" and undoubtedly called that in everyday living, is listed with his wife Catherine Bannon as a resident in Malone, N.Y. in the census of 1840, when that township had 3,229 residents (almost five times more than in 1810). Possibly, he himself was urged there by Thomas Monahan. In any case, Artemis and Catherine Bannon had their first son named James in Malone in 1840, and he was followed by Mary in 1841, and John on April 16, 1844. Then came Ann, Peter, and Artemis, Jr., with Francis following in 1855. By 1860, "Artimas Monacan" (in 1850 "Monchan") was farming a bigger spread in Belmont, just southeast of Malone. Artemis was a prosperous farmer until his death in 1877 at the age of 66.

By 1850 the remote, half-Canadian world of Franklin County, New York was opening up to destinations south and east. The important Northern Railroad (later the "Ogdensburg and Champlain") was just completed with a depot in Malone and affording direct connection all the way through to Boston, Massachusetts. A waiting letter for "Owen Monahan" is noted in the *Malone Frontier Palladium* of April 11, 1850, as having been at the Post Office since March 31. Owen surely wasn't traveling to extreme upstate New York in late March, scene of some of the coldest winter temperatures in the U.S., on some site-seeing tour. Possibly Owen, laboring endlessly over the highly toxic bleaching vats for "greasy" wool, sensed that his future health demanded that he remake his life. He may have quickly grasped that the opening of Malone's new rail line would create direct access for the area's dairy farmers to the big markets of the Northeast. In fact, through links with what became the Vermont Central Railroad, new creameries in Franklin County rapidly began dispensing bulk shipments of butter to Boston. For a moment, it was "let the good times roll" for an extraordinarily isolated part of upstate New York.

VII.

UPSTATE NEW YORK

They were a hardy lot, these Monaghan immigrants. By the 1850s they had all weathered tremendous hardships and perilous journeys to lands unknown, while leaving behind a homeland they would never see again. Arriving in America – or Canada at first – from the hinterlands of rural Ireland and essentially another age and foreign way of speaking, they would have been constantly misunderstood. But they sired and raised children well in settings of great want, even if they had to watch some of these perish when heartbreakingly young.

Through his early years in America, my great-great grandfather Andrew Monaghan clearly labored intrepidly and saved as best he could. What he was eventually striving for was a third act of his life, by re-immersing himself in an agrarian world in an American style of what he had known as a youth in County Monaghan. The last records relevant to his tenure in Massachusetts come from the 1860 census showing him to be a resident in the 4th Ward of Lawrence with his wife Catherine and sons Edward and John Stephen, with the two boys already working in the mills.

In this same census of 1860, Andrew's older brother Owen is listed as a "wool scourer" – and thus dealing with horrendously toxic early bleaches for up to 13 hours a day. Meanwhile, Owen's wife Catherine was busy raising her brood of seven children. The oldest girl, Elizabeth Ann – the same name Andrew had tried with his little daughter who died in 1849 – was then 19 and working as a weaver in the mills. The oldest son, William Stephen was 17 and working as a wool "carder." Vezina Jane – a gnomic name if ever there was one and spelled at least half a dozen ways by various record keepers – is another child laborer working as a weaver at age 12. Alice, Edward, Richard, and James are aged four to nine.

Somehow, our family tradition managed to forget that it was neither Andrew nor Owen who was the first to abandon the heavy industry of Massachusetts for the quieter rural Franklin County, New York. The real pioneer there has to have been the close cousin Arthur who made the move in the early 1850s. Arthur and his wife Julia Lynch had a daughter Bridget around 1852, following the death of the infant Mary Ann. In 1855 they had a girl named Frances. Their first son, born in 1856, was named Hugh.

Julia Lynch Monaghan died, and six years passed before another child was born to Arthur. But with his second wife Alice Caldwell there arrived a son George in 1862. This son George later had a son **James Henry** who in turn had a son Edward James (1918-1974); the latter had a daughter named Loryn Elizabeth Monaghan (1944-2015) who married a Charles MacDonald and their offspring, including a Michael MacDonald, show up as 5th to 8th cousins of this author according to Ancestry.Com DNA records. This strongly corroborates the idea that Arthur was a first cousin connecting to Owen and Andrew.

Back in June of 1863, Arthur registered for the American Civil War draft in Malone, but he may have paid some surrogate to fight in his stead, as there are no records of his service easily found. He and Alice next had a daughter named Mary Ann in 1864. Arthur's third son, born in Malone around 1866, was formally named **Artemis** with clear reference to the unusually named Artemis Monaghan who had arrived in the area in 1839. The older Artemis appears to have been an uncle. Arthur's next son was a William, born in 1867. In 1868, a daughter Julia arrived. An Elizabeth was followed by a John and an Alice in 1873. Finally, the couple had a Lawrence Francis and in 1878, when the mother was 51, an Edwin.

Meanwhile, the family of the early Franklin County farmer Thomas Monahan continued to expand in the nearby Hogansburg district of Bombay. His son John on March 1, 1862, married an Elizabeth Daly, and they quickly had sons named John and Thomas. Then followed Thomas,

William, Mary, Catherine, Anna, Daniel, and Edward. The father Thomas and his wife Mary passed away in the early 1870s.

Andrew Monaghan, Farmer Again in 1863

In 1863 my great-great grandfather (Charles) Andrew followed in Arthur's Monaghan's footsteps and moved to upstate New York with Catherine and their two sons, Edward and John Stephen. Andrew purchased a 55-acre farm about five miles west of Malone in a place called **North Bangor**, which was just south of Fort Covington and not far from the Canadian border. In doing so they were moving to within two miles of Thomas Monahan's family in Hogansburg.

For my great-great grandfather, the fresh air and profound quiet must have felt like heaven at first compared to the noise and toxicity of the ever-more clamorous Merrimac Valley in Massachusetts. To the west now lay the Adirondack wilderness with its countless lakes and rivers and teeming wildlife. But in winter this area was as cold as any place on the contiguous American continent. The snows were heavy, the freezes unforgiving, the soil rocky and the growing season short. The summers also brought insatiable black flies and mosquitoes by the millions. Other than the saw and grist mills, and a few iron mines, industry here was scarce. Farming and lumberjacking were the main trades, although smallish textile mills had been cropping up around Malone. Perhaps Andrew considered that to be a fallback.

But a big plus was that the Vermont Central Railroad now stopped in route to Rutland, Vermont at a Bangor crossroads depot only a mile or so away called **Brushton**. There beside the Little Salmon River you could get a bite to eat and trade news at the Railroad Hotel or even buy an ice cream after Sunday Mass. That depot would have made access to cities like Boston and Lowell, Massachusetts available nearly every day.

Edward, John, and the Civil War

The transition to upstate New York had to have entailed both excitement and much trepidation. For this was also a time when America was still convulsed with its ghastly Civil War. Young and even middle-aged males from every town and village were being sucked into the fight – 6.3 million in all would serve on both sides. One of these soldiers for the Union was Edward Monaghan, my great-great uncle. On March 7, 1864, and when aged about 20, he joined the 96th New York Volunteer Infantry Regiment, which was originally mustered out of nearby Plattsburg in 1862 and included an entire company formed from volunteers in Franklin County. This unit soon saw nearly continuous action in Virginia, including Williamsburg, Savage Station, and the bloody Seven Days Campaign. Then it suffered further terrible attrition throughout Virginia and North Carolina in the year 1863. When Edward enlisted in this regiment, he claimed he was 22, but was lying. Age lies were commonplace in hopes of adding to one's chances of gaining a higher rank or pay scale.

The regiment was then desperate to refill its depleted ranks in advance of a major assault that was meant to break the Confederacy's back. The target was the railroad hub of Petersburg, Virginia, lying along the James River some 25 miles southeast of the Rebel capital of Richmond. Here Edward was pressed into action on May 9th, notably as part of a force of 14,000 Union infantry and cavalry seeking to destroy a key Confederate railway line by a place called the Arrowfield Church. On that day a force of 4,200 Confederates mounted a wild counter-attack and the young Edward Monaghan, enlisted two months previously, was badly shot up. According to the U.S. War Department records, he was carted off to a field hospital the next day.

The Confederates rapidly created a fierce line of fortifications stretching for nine miles before their capital of Richmond. Swelling to some 70,000 soldiers, the Union forces under Ulysses S. Grant gathered for a long siege. Into this stalemate, Edward Monaghan was shoveled back to endure the terror of constant bombardments, screaming Rebel assaults and sniper fire from dawn until dusk. Field notes by Edward's fellow 96th New York infantryman Kenneth Lang (posted generations later in the *Wisconsin Post Crescent* of June 9, 1977) described the horrors in detail. He dwelt on the terrifying exchanges of shelling commencing on June 26, followed by a Confederate frontal assault commencing on June 29. That day Edward Monaghan was shot up again. On June 30, 1864, Edward was hurried to a nearby field hospital.

Perhaps Edward's wounds went gangrenous, or maybe he had gone shell-shocked and incapable of returning to duty. In any case, Edward was transferred on August 31 to the major long-term Union army hospital that had been created at the Episcopal Fairfax Seminary in Alexandria, Virginia, just across the Potomac from Washington. The place had a campus-like setting with two large red-brick dormitories constructed in 1821 for a few dozen priests in training then. But the world changed and 1,700 gravely wounded Union soldiers were treated there during the Civil War, with 500 buried on the grounds. Iconic photographs show clusters of bandaged and half-uniformed soldiers gathering on crutches between the stately elms – young men in their prime reduced to amputees. One of these could have been my great-great uncle, since it was two months later that a "special order"

Recovering Union soldiers at the Fairfax Seminary.

of the War Department, No. 356, signed by the Assistant Adjutant General, B.D. Townsend, decreed that, owing to the gravity of his injuries, Edward should be (honorably) "discharged from the service of the United States." This document is viewable on *Ancestry.Com*. The timing of all this fits with our family's history in upstate New York in multiple ways. Also, there is no trace of anyone else with the same name in this region in 1864.

To have their 20-year-old son Edward return home so brutally battered by the war must have been agonizing for my great-great grandparents and also for my great-grandfather, Edward's younger brother John. It may have been this that even enraged him enough to join the fight. John Stephen Monaghan himself did not reach the enlistment age of 18 until November 1864. But for whatever reasons it was only on March 24, 1865, that John too enlisted in the Union Army, as an 18-year-old substitute for some other draftee. For this he would have received $300, even though it was becoming apparent in the North that the war was won. From today's vantage point, John's enlistment's does not seem especially heroic, but he remained very proud of it for the rest of his life.

In his tenure as a private in Company G, the 193rd Regiment of the New York Infantry, John Stephen Monaghan had a drastically different experience than his older brother Edward. He would have had little danger lying in wait since the Confederate commander Robert E. Lee surrendered two weeks later at Appomattox Courthouse in Virginia on April 9th. Whether Andrew witnessed the Battle of Sailor's Creek, Virginia, three days before that, is doubtful.

In any case, John served for about ten months in the "army of occupation" intent on seeing that the South would not rise again. He was mustered out of service still hale and hearty at Harper's Ferry, Virginia on January 18, 1866. John S. Monagan (JSM), the United States Congressman, later noted: "His discharge described him as a 'farmer,' five feet, three inches tall with a 'fair' complexion and 'gray' eyes... Now 19 years-old, he returned to 'York State' as he called it and resumed farming with his father."

JSM absorbed many stories about these times as a young teenager at his grandfather's side, and especially on one memorable trip with his grandfather and his father Dr. Charles Monagan back to Lawrence, Massachusetts and then Bangor, New York. While serving much later for seven terms in the United States House of Representatives in Washington, D.C., JSM did invaluable research about our family history. In his own 2002 memoir *A Pleasant Institution: Key C-Major* John observed of his grandfather:

> "Andrew appears to have done pretty well, since he owned land and had a house at "Snipe Island" which I saw in the late twenties [1920s] He farmed 'wheat and barley–20 acres each.' [An underestimate.] He made a will in 1876 under which he left his property to his widow Catherine for life and to his son Edward as remainderman. In the same neighborhood lived Patrick Nolan, born in County Cavan, Ireland, in 1824 [actually 1826] and his wife, nee Mary Clark, also from Cavan.... They married and their daughter Ann, born in 1853, was my grandmother."

> "Malone and Bangor lie in the St. Lawrence River plain where the land is flat and formidable. It is also cold in the winter when the winds sweep down from Canada. I remember hearing my grandfather tell how the rivers froze over and the boys could skate for miles on the frozen surfaces." The Snipe Island above must have been the site of some kind of summer cottage, possibly with additional grazing for the cattle or a team of horse, since it lies in the middle of the huge Saint Lawrence River.

Owen Follows to New York

Meanwhile, Owen Monaghan, the pathfinder brother in earlier days, had lingered in Massachusetts for several years after the younger Andrew's departure to upstate New York. The 1865 census showed him to be still resident in Andover with Catherine, now 48, and their children Elizabeth Ann, 25; William Stephen, 22; the curiously named "Vezina" Jane, 17; Alice, 15; Edward, 12; Richard, 10; and James Henry, 8. Only the younger three sons would be brought along to New York.

Owen finally purchased a 117-acre farm near his brother Andrew in Bangor around 1868 and judging by the size of it – census records indicate it was initially twice as large as Andrew's – he had accumulated considerable savings. A great aid in tracing these farms is the exquisitely detailed *D.G. Beer's* 1876 maps of Franklin County. The one for North Bangor also boasts an advert for **A. Monaghan, Farmer and Dairyman**. The North Bangor map shows his farm to be at parcel No. 57, with his neighbors being a W. Morehead and a Mrs. Tracy. Just north of the Vermont Central railway line lies the farm of Owen listed as parcel No. 34. A mile or so to the northeast of Andrew's primary lands lay a second parcel he acquired as No. 77, which may have consisted of fields or orchards without a house.

Just across the town line from North Bangor can be seen the lands of John (son of Thomas) Monahan in Hogansburg close to the St. Regis River. In the D.G. Beers maps, Artemis and Arthur are each listed as "A. Monigan," a spelling of some novelty. Artemis was buried at the age of 66 on November 24, 1877, in St. Joseph's Catholic Cemetery in Malone. His wife Catherine lived until 1885.

John Stephen Marries Ann Nolan

After returning to upstate New York after the end of the Civil War, my great-grandfather John Stephen Monaghan apparently enjoyed a heady social whirl that ended up with the courtship of my still quite young great-grandmother-to-be, Ann Nolan. The young Union army veteran seems to have returned in high spirits as he initially joined his father Andrew in tending the family's dairy herd, orchards, and fields of wheat, barley and corn. He may possibly have in time also found work at one of the small nearby mills, since he clearly did not take to farming and spent all of his post-Bangor life in industrial work.

The young John Stephen Monaghan.

Congressman JSM passed on these observations: "Apparently John was a bit of a hell-raiser and 'the life of the party.' He was not always invited to the more decorous gatherings, but according to my grandmother [Ann Nolan Monagan] the girls would send a boy to tell "John S." about a party (perhaps a "sugaring party" celebrating the maple syrup harvest) to which he had not been invited. He would then appear and stir the gathering into excitement – a role not appreciated by the hostess."

The point is that after returning to North Bangor in 1866, young John Stephen Monaghan had many chances to consort with that close neighbor named Ann Nolan as she blossomed into a young woman and he finally asked for her hand in marriage. Judging by early photographs, John was a strapping if lanky young man, and bursting with self-confidence and oddly bearing a decided resemblance to my own older brother Stephen John Monagan, a fighter pilot when young. The original post-Civil War John Stephen Monaghan wore a moustache to beat the band. Judging by old photographs, Ann Nolan had a theatrical flair and often wore a very mirthful, half-winking look. The two seemed to have enjoyed a great chemistry from Day One.

The Brushton Hotel.

The couple were married on November 18, 1869, in a double-wedding ceremony in North Bangor with John McGowan and Margaret Riley (a first cousin of Anna; but the McGowan's also had been intermarried with Henrys in County Monaghan). Anna was just 17 then. The couple quickly established a separate residence in the vicinity and stayed there for about four years, with Anna working as a school teacher at first. They obviously enjoyed a warm relationship with the McGowans since they remained lifelong friends, with John and Margaret making trips all the way to Connecticut years afterwards.

Anna's grandparents were a **Matthew** and **Anna Clark** (born in Ireland around 1787 and 1795 respectively) and who immigrated to Cohoes, New York in 1829. Their second daughter **Mary Ann Clark**, born around 1825, was another great-great grandmother of this author. She is thought to have worked in a hotel in Cohoes when very young. Perhaps once again in pursuit of cheap farming land, the Clark family headed north to Franklin County, although the draw may have also had to do with a number of relatives having already settled there.

Records from St. Joseph's Cemetery in Malone indicate that the father Matthew Clark was buried there in 1842, when he was about 53 years-old. But the Clarks stuck around Franklin County for years. The 1850 census indicated that Anna Clark was widowed and aged 55 and left alone with the farm and its large household in Malone. Her children included Flora (Clark) McIntosh, 33, apparently also widowed and with a little girl, and the younger sister Mary Ann – my great-great grandmother – aged 25. The others were Charles, 23; Hugh, 20; and Catherine, 13. Charles Clark later ran a hops farm in the village of Constable.

Importantly, also resident in this same house in 1850 was one Patrick Nolan, 27, the hands-on farm manager. The records suggest that he may have been fairly recently arrived from Ireland and thus another product of the Famine's diaspora. In any event Patrick Nolan and the daughter Mary Ann Clark soon wed. They then began farming a bit east in North Bangor and had their first child James there in 1851. Anna Nolan, my great-grandmother, was born the following year. Meanwhile this now very basic last name got hit with all kinds of permutations. Thus, at the time of the 1860 federal census my great-great grandmother Mary was called "Nowlan." In their crowded household now were seven young children: James (1851-1933); my great-grandmother Anna; then Thomas, Hugh, Margaret, Mary, and Ellen. But the family had four more children to follow: a Catherine in 1862, Elizabeth, William, and Agnes, the youngest. The farm to feed them all totaled 56.5 acres.

A variety of records indicate that there may have been an extended Nolan presence in upstate New York beginning much earlier, perhaps another fall-out of the early wheeling and dealing of the Irish land speculator Michael Hogan, whose "Hogansburg" village was more or less just over the hill from the Patrick Nolan farm.

Mary Clark Nolan, years later.

The first child of John Stephen and Anna Nolan Monaghan was a daughter named **Mary Agnes**, born on September 15, 1870 and soon and rather permanently called "Minnie." Mary was the name of Anna's mother and Agnes was the name of her youngest sister, showing that women were gaining a hand in the once rigidly male Irish naming protocols. On June 1, 1872, John and Anna next had a son named **Charles Andrew Monaghan**. The middle name certainly references John's father, and so likely does the first. My great-great grandfather was almost surely a Charles Andrew who dropped his everyday use of his first birth name altogether, as was so common among the Irish. In 1873, John and Anna Nolan Monaghan departed the North Country forever via the Vermont Central Railroad for the brighter lights of Connecticut, with their two little children at their sides. This move had to have been carefully planned and aided by prior reconnaissance. The net result was to leave John's oldest brother Edward alone to help with the parents' farm.

The Fishy Thomas Monaghan

But not long before John Stephen and Anna vacated the area, the family was supposedly being repopulated by the arrival of a half-miraculous child named **Thomas William Monaghan**. According to some kind of long-retailed story, the baby from out of the blue was born to my great-great grandparents in 1868. At this point Catherine was about 45 years-old and had not given birth to any other known human being for almost 20 years.

This may have been a remarkable biological occurrence. But the truth would seem to be that this particular child had a very confusing lineage and most likely was adopted. He is listed as Andrew and Catherine's 12-year-old son in the U.S. census of 1880 and living with them in Franklin County (as was a farm hand named George Gibbs, even though Edward was clearly in the same house and should have been in his farming prime). The problem is that this William Monaghan was not even mentioned in the 1870 federal census ten years earlier, which showed Andrew and Catherine "Munigan" as living solely with their older son Edward, aged 26. (The newly married John Stephen and Anna Nolan had already moved out.) Curiously, there is no toddler resident with them by any name, definitely no Thomas. So where was this Tom in 1870 – hidden in a back room? There certainly is no birth record of anyone with his name in Franklin County in these years.

The 1875 New York state census has the aging Andrew and Catherine also residing with Edward, then 31, in their same house, with nobody else at the breakfast table. Thus there persists the very deep conundrum that there is again no mention whatsoever of young Thomas, the supposed third son – who should be a seven-year-old and about four feet in height and quite rambunctiously visible by now. Unless of course he is somewhere else altogether with his real parents.

Family lore had it that Edward never married and there are no New York State records to suggest otherwise. We do know that neither of the two farm holdings of his father Andrew were ever put under the administration of Edward even though his oldest son worked by his father's side for nearly 30 years. In fact, there is no indication of anything that Edward achieved in upstate New York and one cannot help but wonder again about the severity of his injuries or their psychological aftermath that caused his early discharge from the carnage of the American Civil War. Or perhaps the problem became alcoholism. Edward lived a relatively short life, dying at age 55 in Bangor in February 1900. He was unmarried then, and with no cause of death documented. Also curious is the fact that Edward later was simply not much talked about by the increasingly upwardly mobile family of my great-grandfather John Stephen Monaghan, Edward's only sibling on earth. The penchant for constantly tidying up one's family memories may be universal, but the Irish have certainly been masters at it for ages. Something must have been "off" with Edward. But my ancestors seem to long ago have decided to close the door on the subject forevermore.

In light of all this what seems likely is that Thomas William Monaghan was the child of some other forgotten relative in New York City who had died or dissipated. Thomas was a real person, about that there can be no doubt. From about 1887 to 1889, when he reached the age of 20, he mostly lived in Bristol, Connecticut with my great-grandfather John Stephen Monaghan. He worked nearby as a machinist in the "lamp burner shop" of the Bristol Brass and Clock company – a job John very likely landed for him. But he soon quit Bristol for the Lowell/Lawrence, Massachusetts area to enjoy the company of the many cousins living nearby. He obviously had had no desire to linger on in Bangor with Edward, the only immediate family member left behind there and thus all the more likely who was not his father in any shape or form.

Later, when taking out a marriage license in Lowell in 1898, Thomas avowed that his parents were Andrew and Catherine Monaghan, all right, and that he was born 30 years before then, true to the chronology of the 1880 census. But he attested that he was born in New York, New York, and thus almost 400 miles from remote Bangor. This further suggests that he was adopted. But why would this come about? It is hard to imagine that my great-great grandparents suddenly looked at each other one cold night in Bangor when approaching 60 years-old and set off to New York City on a whim to adopt anyone, unless there was some profound connection speaking to their hearts.

In any event, Thomas William's life is fairly traceable from 1880 onwards. In Lowell, he married a Mary Dunn, a "mill operative," on April 21, 1898. Their first children were an Edna born in 1902 and on June 11, 1904; then followed the twins Irene and **William Thomas**. It seems noteworthy that neither the first daughters nor three more to follow were named Catherine after Thomas's supposed mother, my great-great-grandmother. Nor was the name Andrew ever used in honor of Thomas's purported father.

As iffy as it may seem, my best guess is that Thomas's father might have even been the **William** "Monhan" vaguely glimpsed in Andover and Lowell in 1838 and 1842 before evidently moving to New York. The grandchildren living now of this enigmatic Thomas, born in 1868 and raised by Andrew and Catherine Monaghan, still posit on Ancestry.com that he was born in New York City – not Lawrence or Lowell or North Bangor, New York. It happens that a William Monaghan was buried in the Greenwood Cemetery in Brooklyn, New York on May 20, 1875. This is rather in keeping with the idea of Thomas's being adopted in New York by our great-great grandparents sometime after the state census of 1875. Perhaps some future scribe can better clarify all this.

It bears repeating that the pathfinder Owen Monaghan back in 1843 in North Andover named his first son William Stephen. And my great-grandfather John Stephen Monaghan named his second son, born in 1876, **William Henry** Monaghan. This was less than a year after the death of the William Monaghan in Brooklyn, which might be pertinent. As a grown man in Connecticut, my great uncle William Henry referred to himself as William Monagan II (as shown in city directories in Waterbury in 1914 and New Haven of 1937- 1941). So there clearly lived somewhere a William Monaghan of importance and great linking power to the previous generations.

To return to the life of the baffling Thomas William Monaghan, he and his wife Mary Dunn Monaghan had a tragically short-lived daughter Nellie in 1905, a Bridget in 1906, and an Agnes on Oct. 3, 1907. Next came a Harold Edward on September 4, 1909. So there is no indication that he was much enamored with his memories of Bangor, New York or even Bristol, Connecticut. Thomas died in Lowell on June 7, 1917, at age 49 of chronic nephritis and was buried in St. Joseph's Cemetery there.

VIII.

THE FADING OF THE UPSTATE MONAGHANS

Owen and the Massachusetts Roots

By the early 1870s, a generational change was unfolding among the Monaghans in the North Country. Over in Bombay, New York, Thomas Monahan of Hogansburg, born in 1797 and an early settler, died in 1872. In that year also, my great-great-great uncle Owen made out his last will and testament, the date not very long after his arrival in North Bangor. He was likely already struggling with debilitating emphysema or lung cancer, thanks to working so long as a "wool scourer" (if not also smoking too much tobacco). Poignantly, the 1875 state census (obviously conducted in the previous early autumn) lists Owen as living at that moment in the younger brother Andrew's house, when the two siblings plainly owned separate farms. The reason had to have been that Owen was desperately needing additional care of some kind that could be better provided there. His death occurred on October 23, 1874, with the cause listed as "lung fever."

More than a year after Owen's death there appeared the following notice in the December 16, 1875 edition of the *Malone Palladium*: "In pursuance of an order of the Hon Albert Hobbs Surrogate of the County of Franklin, notice is hereby given to all persons having claim against Owen Monaghan, late of the town of Bangor, deceased, that they are required to exhibit the same, with the vouchers thereof to the subscriber and executor of the will of the deceased at his store in the town of Bangor, on or before the 14th day of February 1876. Solon Reynolds Executor."

The next to die was **Artemis Monagan**, on November 24, 1877, at age 66. His last will and testament, entered in the Malone courthouse with immaculate penmanship, clearly demonstrates that he now preferred that his last name be spelled and pronounced "Monagan." Our family lore long held that this peculiar spelling – a great curiosity in Ireland itself – was initiated by my great-grandfather John Stephen around 1898. But the exquisitely legible last will of "Artimus" (often Artemis) makes clear that this was not so.

My great-great grandfather Charles Andrew must have been wrestling with his own health concerns, since he initially made out his will in 1876, when still only 54. Meanwhile, his brother Owen's widow Catherine kept struggling to manage her nearby farm with her three growing and evidently restless sons – Edward, Richard, and James. Their enthusiasm for the area had clearly waned. Catherine can next be found in the 1880 census living now with only the youngest son James Henry, aged 20, and a "hired farm boy" named Jerry Donahue, aged 12 – likely some other family orphan. The *Malone Palladium* of April 28, 1881, gave further notice on the demise of this Monaghan family's history in upstate New York

"Farm for Sale

The subscriber offers for sale her farm of 117 acres near North Bangor and all the stock and implements and farming on it. It is situated within half a mile of Depot [North Bangor's rail stop at Brushton], contains two good orchards, is well watered, and is all under cultivation. There are good buildings on it, and the property is in every way desirable. Ten years' time will be given if desired. For further particulars apply to Catherine Monaghan, North Bangor, N.Y."

Catherine's sons had lost all interest in continuing with the family farm and even in remaining nearby. Her Edward, 27 at the time of the 1880 census, had already moved back to Lawrence, Massachusetts – from which area his four older siblings had never strayed. Richard, 24, had by then moved out of the farmhouse too, and was working on the nearby Bangor farm of a Patrick

Garvin. Richard was soon to marry and return to Lawrence as well. Once the farm was disposed of – possibly by lease to a tenant farmer – the son James Henry fled for Massachusetts as rapidly as he could too, essentially drawing to a close one major family connection to this unique corner of the world.

The descendants of Owen Monaghan were likely among the most numerous constituents of Lawrence and Lowell in the late 1900s to bear the Monaghan family name. Following the sale of the family farm in North Bangor in 1881, Catherine took up residence at 85 South Broadway in Lawrence, where she was surrounded by all of her seven children and their spouses, various cousins, and many grandchildren. There were certainly many other relations in the area, including the latest generations of the Henry, Short, and Killen families. There had to have been connections among the Duffys and possibly also the Sweeneys around. There also must have been many of Catherine's McNamara relatives in the vicinity as well. Nearby at 2 Railroad Street lived the family of the stone-cutter Patrick Monaghan (1830-1901), including his wife and daughter Susan and sons Thomas, 22, and Matthew, 18. Lawrence was still an extraordinarily Irish-American dominated city in which there were likely more Monaghan kin existent than will ever be known.

The first of the Monaghans of Bangor, New York, to move back to Massachusetts was Owen's second son Edward. By 1880 he was already living in Lawrence with his 25 year-old wife Margaret **Allen** in the house of her brother Thomas Allen (who was married to none other than Owen's daughter Elizabeth Ann Monaghan, born in Andover in 1843.) Margaret must have died while giving birth since in the following year of 1881 both Edward and his next youngest brother James Henry, 21, were sharing an apartment as bachelors on 19 Pacific Avenue in Lawrence. Both were working as teamsters, or horse-drawn cart drivers of bulk materials rumbling in and out of the mills. On August 2, 1890, Edward remarried to a "Kate" Finn, who unfortunately also died young. He continued to work as a teamster through most of the following decade, but eventually took a job in a Lawrence paper mill. Edward died at age 50 on July 28, 1904.

The oldest of Owen's children, Elizabeth Ann, had married the above Thomas Allen in Lowell on December 16, 1860, and never left. Vezina Jane, born in late 1847, had married a Timothy Hayes in 1870 and stayed in Lawrence until her death on September 4, 1916. Alice, the youngest of Owen and Catherine's daughters, and born in 1851, had married John Moran in the mill town of Somersworth, New Hampshire in June 1870. Both daughters had numerous children. Alice appears to have had a second husband with the surname of Mullen.

Owen's oldest son William Stephen Monaghan, born in Andover in 1843, had also never left the area. By 1860 he was already working as a 17-year-old "carder" in one of the Lawrence woolen mills. (That year his sister Elizabeth, 19, was a weaver in the mills, and so was the 12 year-old Vezina Jane.) On April 14, 1866, William Stephen married a Margaret or "Maggie" Mullen, whose father was working in a mill across the nearby New Hampshire border. William and Margaret's children were Gertrude, Vezina Frances, and William **Charles**. The latter may be a reference to his uncle Charles Andrew. A George Monaghan (later a boiler maker in Patterson, New Jersey) was born in 1873, and he was followed by a Mary, called "Della," who also moved to Passaic County, N.J., as an adult – as did the son William.

By 1880 William Stephen and Maggie moved back to Lawrence from New Hampshire and he now became a "watchman in a mill." Further underlining the family's interwoven ancestry, the couple in 1877 had a boy named **Arthur** but he died of meningitis in 1880. In 1881, the Andover city directory shows William to be working now as a "gas-fitter," meaning on one of the early lighting and heating schemes transforming life then.
The return to Lawrence did not do a lot of good for the youngest son James Henry, either. After working with Edward as a teamster, he became a general laborer. Alas, he contracted tuberculosis and died at the age of 25 on December 30, 1885. The story of Richard, the second youngest son, is perplexing. He evidently stayed behind in Bangor for a while and kept working on the Garvin farm there. On January 31, 1887, he married a Garvin

daughter named Mary in Brushton. It was only on June 16, 1888, that the *Adirondack News* noted "Mrs. Richard Monogan [sic] went to Lawrence, Mass., Monday to join her husband who has been a resident of that place for about a year."

Richard and Mary resided in his mother's South Broadway house. He worked in several later capacities, including as a tobacconist, "paper maker," mill operative, and watchman. Richard and Mary had three children – Catherine, and in 1891, James Edward, and in 1895 a daughter blurrily recorded as something like Gladys. Richard died in Lawrence in 1900 at the age of only 44, of "fibrotic myocarditis." Catherine McNamara Monaghan, Owen's wife from their marriage back in 1839, lived on until January 13, 1894, when she finally succumbed to heart disease at age 76. At that point, the family seems to have defaulted on making any further payments regarding what might have been a second mortgage on Owen and Catherine's sizeable North Bangor farm. Apparently in this regard, eight years later lawyers for a Franklin County money lender named George Sabin had tracked down most of the descendants of Owen as named above to hit them all with a lawsuit to be prosecuted in the Malone, New York district court on December 29, 1902. [See the *Malone Palladium* of Nov. 27, 1902, for one of many notices on this.]

As mentioned earlier, around 1889 the likely adopted Thomas Monaghan abandoned Bristol, Connecticut and moved to Lowell, Massachusetts. He had clearly lived with my great-grandfather John Stephen for a while, as seen in several Bristol city directories. *The Malone Palladium* of May 12, 1887, had noted, "Thomas Monaghan is home from Bristol, Connecticut to spend the summer here." In Massachusetts Thomas worked principally as a machinist and married the aforementioned Mary Dunn.

The Passing of Andrew and Catherine

Catherine and Andrew Monaghan must have been saddened as the 1880s wore on to see so many of their loved ones abandon the North Country. This could not have been the outcome they dreamed of nearly 30 years earlier when trying to recast the family's way of living. But the clock was ticking for them too.

Andrew ultimately died on October 27, 1890 and was buried in the St. Augustine Cemetery in North Bangor. His will (first made out on February 2, 1878) bequeathed the core 55-acre family farm to Catherine, with the lands only after her death to be transferred to their son Edward. Andrew's personal possessions were bequeathed to neither of his sons Edward nor Andrew but to his close friend and neighbor Solon Reynolds (the executor of the estate and a prosperous landholder). One gets an impression of family discord.

The figure of Solon Reynolds (1839-1914) bears some consideration. Scores of newspaper references to him, following his 1860 move to North Bangor from Gross Isle in Lake Champlain, make it clear that Solon was one of the most admired men in Franklin County. A Second Lieutenant in the Civil War, he ran the general store in Bangor and most anything else of note locally, as he was justice of the peace and an overall formidable force in town and county politics. He became a large landholder, at one point in the early 1870s selling off 1,025 acres of forest. His lengthy (for those times) obituary of April 15, 1914, in the *Malone Palladium* spoke of "universal sorrow" at his passing and spoke of him as a "a man of keen intelligence and superior judgement" and "a citizen of brains, positive force and integrity" who helped guide the whole region forward. It is interesting that my great-great grandfather Andrew – on the surface a humble laborer and hardscrabble farmer numbered among the closest friends of this learned and discerning figure.

My great-great grandmother Catherine Castle Monaghan died of a cerebral hemorrhage in 1891, the year following the passing of her husband Andrew. The *Malone Palladium* of that December 17 revealed that her son John Stephen made it back from Connecticut for her last days: "John Monaghan is here from the East visiting his mother Mrs. A. Monaghan who is very low – having had a shake of paralysis." Catherine and Andrew's oldest son

Edward labored on alone for another decade at the Bangor farm. He was the last immediate family member keeping the lamp aglow until 1900 when Edward suddenly died at the age of 56, the cause unclear.

Monaghan Relatives in Franklin County, New York – 1870s, Partial

Matthew Clark (1787-1843) m. Anna (b. 1795-)

Charles Clark (1820-) m. Flora McIntosh

Mary Margaret Clark (1825-) m. Patrick Nolan

Hugh Clark (1830-)

Catherine (1837-)

Patrick Nolan (1826-1897)) m. Mary Margaret Clark (1825-1910)

James (1851-1933)

Ann (Oct. 9, 1852 -Dec. 9, 1933–wife of John Stephen Monaghan)

Thomas (1854-1904)

Hugh (1855-)

Margaret ((1856-1946)

Mary (1857-) – marries Arthur Devlin

Catherine (1862-1889) – marries Thomas Miller

Elizabeth (1865-) – later "Sister Ushina"

William Henry (1867-1924)

Agnes (1868-)

Ellen (1872-)

[Francis Nolan, shepherd brother of Patrick]

[Mary Nolan, 1819-1889, mother of Margaret Nolan who married John McGowan)

Owen Monaghan (1807-1874) and Catherine Monaghan (1817-1894)

Edward (1853-)

Richard (1855-)

James Henry (1860-)

Note four children left behind in Lawrence, Massachusetts.

Artemis Monagan (1812-1878) m. Catherine Bannon (1818-1885)

James (1840-)

Mary (1842-)

John (1844-)

Ann (1846-)

Peter (1848-)

Artimus, Jr. (1849-)

Jane (1850)

Francis "Frank" (1855-) (Children all born In New York)

(Children all born In New York)

Andrew Monaghan (1822-1890) m. Catherine Castle (1824-1891)

Edward Owen – or Oge? (1845-1900)

John Stephen (1846-1928) m. Ann Nolan (1852-1933)

Mary Agnes (1871-1938)

Charles Andrew (1872-1931)

Thomas (1868-1915)

Arthur Monaghan (1825-1908) m. Julia Lynch

Bridget (1851 –)

Frances (1855 –)

Hugh (1856 – first child to be born in Malone)

2nd Marriage, 1860 – Alice Caldwell

George (1862-)

Mary Ann (1864-)

Artimus (1866-)

William (1867-)

Julia (1868-)

Elizabeth (1870-)

John (1872-)

Mark (1873?)

Lawrence Francis (1874-Alice (1875-)

Edwin (1878-)

Note: The descendants of Thomas Monahan are not yet proven relatives.

The Monaghan Legacy in Franklin County

Despite the late 1800's clearing out of Owen and Andrew Monaghan's families and the Nolans, a scattering of the more extended Monaghan clan remained in Franklin County for years to come. Some of their stories are fascinating, especially those of the family of Arthur Monaghan, the definitely DNA-linked cousin. As early as November 9, 1871, this elusive ancestor is referenced in the *Malone Palladium* as selling what may be his first farm, a holding of 28 acres located three miles east of Malone – evidently to finance the purchase of a larger one in the nearby village of Belmont. As noted, Arthur's children with his first wife Julia were Bridget, Frances, and Hugh. Following Julia's death he remarried to the younger Alice Caldwell from Fort Covington and their children included George and Mary Ann; Artemis [named after his nearby uncle but called "Arthur" in everyday parlance], William, Julia, Elizabeth, John, Mark, Lawrence Francis or "Frank," Alice, and in 1878, Edwin.

In addition to farming, Arthur Monaghan assumed control in 1879 of the State Dam Hotel in Belmont. The *Malone Palladium* reported on April 1, 1880, that Arthur was now selling off two separate farms, this time a main one of 284 acres, but also a second holding of 124 acres with a "first classwood lot."

Arthur's offspring were embarking on several new enterprises of their own. In March 1882, the Malone newspaper boldly announced: **"Monaghan and Skelly Have Just Opened a Tin and Stove Store."** That business was still thriving on June 23, 1892, when the Malone Palladium noted that "William Monaghan (another son of Arthur) has been licensed to become a purveyor of ale and beer."

Other young men of the family were laboring in the 3,500-foot-deep and mostly open-pit iron mines some miles to the east in Rogersfield. The *Palladium* of May 11, 1883, rendered horrendous news in that regard: "Frank [Francis] Monaghan of this village [the youngest son of Artemis] received a dispatch Wednesday from Lyon Mountain stating that his half-brother Arthur [Artemis Jr.] was killed in the mines the day before."

The *St. Lawrence Herald* of May 19, 1883, offered a far more graphic account: "Franklin County. Last week Tuesday night, Arthur Monaghan, Jr. [technically Artemis Jr.] gave the signal in one of the mines at Rogersfield [an iron mining district just east of Franklin County] for a car loaded with ore to be hauled out of the pit, and then remained standing at the bell cord. The car proceeded nearly to the mouth of the pit, when it in some way became disengaged from the hoisting chain, and went careering down the slope, gathering momentum with every revolution of its wheels. Monaghan was struck by it on the leg and the back of the head. His leg was broken in four or five places and the entire back part of the head torn completely off. Death was, of course, instantaneous. Deceased was 18 years of age and was the son of Arthur Monaghan. residing in the eastern part of Malone, and brother of Frank Monaghan [likely Lawrence Francis] of this village [**Malone**]."

Altogether strange is a report a few days later in the *Gouverneur (N.Y.) Herald* of May 24, noting: "Hugh Monaghan of Malone, an employee of the [Chateauguay) Iron Co. of Rogersfield, was killed by a loaded ore car which had broken from its fastenings and returned at a rate of speed into the pit on Tuesday." Was this really a case of lightning striking the same family twice in a matter of days, that these half-brothers – Hugh and Artemis Monaghan, Jr. (Arthur) – were killed in the very same week?

Sadly, that is exactly what seems to have transpired. Hugh was a son of Arthur and his first wife, so it seems the half-brothers were working side-by-side in the Rogersfield/Chateauguay Iron Ore Company mines just over the eastern boundary of Franklin County. There were as many as 2,500 men at a time working round-the-clock on both the vast open pit and the off-shooting one-and-a-half-mile-long subterranean veins bored every which way from its depths. The scene must have been a hellacious inferno since the mine's many forges required 27,000 bushels of charcoal along with 195,000 cords of firewood to keep running 24-hours a day throughout the year (save Sundays). In December of 1883, the company's huge supply of dynamite blew up in an explosion that shook every hut for the 3,000 workers in the shanty village to the skies.

Life in upstate New York was easy for no one, of course. Arthur's son "Frank" was the subject of the below article in the May 5, 1885, *Ogdensburg Journal* which speaks for itself:

"Great Noise and Little Fire
Malone. May 4, 1885

The chimes made discordant music Sunday morning just before church going time, and the steam whistles joined in the chorus. The noise brought out the fire brigade and everybody else and they all hastened to the residence of Frank Monaghan in the southern suburb of the village where the cause of the disturbance existed. A fire had caught in the attic near the chimney, but the bucket brigade squelched it before more damage could be done. Monaghan and family were attending early mass and when they returned to their home, they found the house stripped of furniture, doors, windows, and everything not spiked down. Loss covered by insurance. **Jake"**

My great-grandfather clearly kept in touch with the local kith and kin for some years after his leaving for Connecticut. That is seen from newspaper references like this one in the *Malone Palladium* of August 17, 1905, noting: "John Monagan of Waterbury, Conn. is spending a few days with some of his old friends and neighbors." He must have visited his failing cousin Arthur, and some of his sons and daughters.

Arthur Monaghan himself was gifted with a long life. The 1900 census showed him at age 74 still enjoying as a house mate his daughter Alice, 25, and a grand-daughter named Luelle Donahue; plus, a brother-in-law named Clarence or Clemence Caldwell, aged 70. He had several children and grandchildren living in separate residences nearby. Arthur finally died in 1908, the last of my great-great grandfather's generation still standing in Franklin County, and apparently in touch until the last with his brother Hugh on Canada's Prince Edward Island.

One gets an unusual update on our extended family's reach in the North Country from notices posted in the region's newspapers around 1915, apparently regarding some conflict over either inheritance or distribution of proceeds from a major lawsuit. The *Malone Farmer* of January 4 of that year referred to this bitter struggle being waged in the Supreme Court of New York by a George and Frank "**Monahan**," plaintiffs in Bombay, against a Sarah, Lawrence, Mabel, Julia, Mary, Alice, John, Mark and Katherine **Monaghan**, a number of whom are scattered to the Midwest. These appear to be the children, with some spouses added, of the deceased Arthur Monaghan.

Profound tragedy eventually befell many of the descendants of this early arrival in Fort Covington in 1827, Thomas Monahan. As mentioned, Thomas married a Mary Healey and by 1832 had his first son John, who was followed by the daughters Mary and Bridget. They were all raised on a farm near the village of Hogansburg in the township of Bombay. This was former Mohawk Indian land beside the St. Lawrence tributary of the Saint Regis River, in earlier days teeming with Atlantic salmon. Thomas's daughter Mary married a Peter Daly in Hogansburg from a family that had lived there for generations.

Thomas Monahan's son John assumed control of the family farm in Hogansburg at his father's death in 1872. John and his wife Elizabeth provided for a large household. The 1880 federal census shows these to include their eldest son Thomas, 17; William 13, who would head to Montana as a young man; Mary; Catherine; Anna; Daniel: and the newborn Edward John. John's wife's mother Mary Daly, 83, was living alongside also.

After John's death in the 1890s, his oldest son Thomas ran the farm for many years. Peculiarly, most of his third-generation siblings never much budged out of the household or married. The group grew increasingly eccentric. Within a few years various local newspapers would run regular bulletins about one or the other of them making it all the way from Hogansburg to Malone – a distance of perhaps six miles.

Chirpy news items about these "Monahans" in Hogansburg continued until the start of 1929 when Franklin County was hit with a terrible influenza epidemic. While nowhere near as globally devastating as the 1918-1919 "Spanish flu" (which may have actually started in Kansas) that eventually killed 40 million people, this contagion hopscotched over the map to cause havoc in select communities. But in Hogansburg the Monahans became as mortally afflicted by it as any family in America. In the depths of winter, five of these ancestors – all grandsons and granddaughters of the early settler Thomas Monahan – succumbed one after another. *The Fort Covington Sun* introduced the story on January 31, 1929, thusly:

"Double Funeral for Two Pneumonia Victims Tuesday

Ed and Dan Monahan of Bombay are dead and buried. The former passed away on Saturday evening and the latter on Sunday morning. The direct cause was pneumonia. Their two sisters, Misses Ann and Kate, are also very sick with the same disease. Another brother Thomas Monahan has been ill but is now able to be out. Another sister, Mrs. Parker died last week. The funeral of the brothers was held in St. Patrick's Church, Hogansburg on Tuesday morning. We understand a brother who resides in the far west is expected home...

****

Later – As we go to press, we are advised that Miss Ann Monahan has passed away and will be taken from the hospital to the family home tonight. Aged 56 years."

IX.

A NEW LIFE IN CONNECTICUT

Arrival in Bristol

In 1873, John and Ann (Nolan) Monagan set off on a steam train to Vermont and then headed south on another until they with their two little children reached Bristol, Connecticut, a small city in the upper reaches of the Naugatuck Valley in the western half of the state. The area's economy, earlier based on wooden clock making but now increasingly involved with brass manufacturing, was booming. Nonetheless, one has to wonder what possible "family factor" informed the couple's choice to wave goodbye to a whole way of life and both of their families in upstate New York for this particular place.

Perhaps the persuasive voice came from earlier forays by Ann Nolan's slightly older brother James who was one of her earliest siblings to join in what became a family migration out of North Bangor. Possibly relevant is that a young John Nolan was mustered into the Connecticut 25th Infantry from Bristol during the dark days of the Civil War and was now living in close-by New Britain. Possibly John Stephen and Ann Nolan Monaghan had made an earlier newly-wed trip to visit some such relative and liked what they saw.

No one knows. The 1869 city directory for Waterbury, Connecticut – the city that would be the family's ultimate destination – alternatively references a John Monahan dwelling at the intersection of Scovill and Cole streets and being an employee at the S.L. Bradley Company. In 1881 this apparently same Monahan, John, was managing the Scovill Billiard Rooms and living at the Scovill House in Waterbury – an inn at the town center, whose next iteration as "the Elton" would host the American president-to-be John Fitzgerald Kennedy for a truly historic night in 1960. This address was tied in with the management of the premier brass producer in the state, the **Scovill Manufacturing Company**, which would transform my great-grandfather's life and the family's history. Maybe this John Monahan of 1869 was actually some kind of cousin?

John and Ann Monaghan's first residence in Connecticut was in Bristol's Forestville section. Lying two miles east of the town center and just beside the Pequabuck River, Forestville had its own rail stop and this boasted service to Waterbury and Hartford or Winsted as many as 13 times a day. The most prominent employer here was the sprawling red brick **Bristol Brass & Clock Company** where John Stephen would work for nearly two decades. The complex also included the so-called Lamp Burner Shop for making brass lamp fittings that became prized by millions of households across America. The idea for the initial brass and clock enterprise arose during a meeting of 16 of the region's prominent industrialists in the local Foster's Tavern on April 3, 1850. The group's leaders were Eliza Welch and an Israel Holmes (1800-1874) of Waterbury, lower down the Naugatuck Valley.

Holmes was an extraordinary figure who had a profound impact on the Monaghan family's history. He started out as a traveling "Yankee peddler" of brass buttons and hats in the American South, an iconic role in that day. After returning to Waterbury, he joined the then modest Scovill family's brass plant of the 1820s as an accounts clerk. He rapidly rose through the ranks and made it his mission to transform the business into an industrial powerhouse. The English completely dominated the world's brass trade to this point, thanks to having the best machinery and unrivaled craftsmen, both of which assets they fervidly endeavored to keep out of foreign hands. Holmes solved that problem in the brash new American style by spending his way through these constraints. In three separate trips to England he acquired critical brass sheet-rolling machinery and the best craftsmen that money could buy. His first poaching mission netted a skilled die maker, a gilder, and a burnisher. In 1831, Holmes fetched an expert caster – or mixer of the alloy of zinc and copper that is brass – as well as a roller, wire drawer, and tube maker, and 14 of their family members. Three of these workers were hidden in wine casks on the Liverpool docks before being smuggled off to Waterbury – or so the story goes.

Holmes's raids on English manufacturing led to a stunning transformation of the production capacity and quality of brass products coming out of the Scovill company and helped raise the skill base of associated industries throughout the valley. Before long, the region's factories began diversifying from brass buttons to fabricating all manner of new and shiny products – brass hooks and eyes, hinges, pins, toys, photographic plates, and fittings of every description. This dizzying array of expanding uses of brass transformed the Naugatuck Valley and attracted droves of workers from afar.

After starting a variety of new businesses to the north of Waterbury, Holmes inevitably turned his attention to Bristol's celebrated but fastidiously slow, hand-made clock-making industry. At its peak, this small city had 280 separate enterprises involved in clock-making, with several hundred thousand clocks made there each year – the community's name being synonymous with fine clocks world-wide. But profit margins grew increasingly thin in this demanding artisanal world, and Welch and Holmes spotted a major opportunity for their magic potion of ever malleable brass. With a small syndicate they set out in 1850 to transform the business of clock-making by replacing the painstakingly hand-fashioned inner workings of old with mass-produced brass fittings. Their new operation included an on-site brass rolling mill to provide endless supplies of raw product.

Meanwhile, a revolution in lighting, for ages dependent on whale oil or lard candles, was in progress across America with the mass manufacture of kerosene lamps. Kerosene was only first successfully distilled from petroleum in 1854, but its potential became abundantly clear with the discovery of vast petroleum "rock oil" deposits in western Pennsylvania in the late 1850s, which could then be refined into a near endless supply of kerosene. This led to a great clamor across the nation to acquire the new wonders of kerosene lamps. But the burning of the wick and the level of illumination had to be fidgeted just right for these new contraptions to be effective. Here again, Israel Holmes and colleagues saw a "glowing opportunity" and set up their own "Lamp Burner Shop," whose initial thrust was to produce reliable internal wick holders by the tens of thousands. These were instantly gobbled up across America. In time, the company also produced beautiful floor, wall, and desk lamps out of brass, designed with all manner of scroll work and filigree. This side business of Bristol Brass & Clock took off like a rocket. It long employed my great-great uncle James Nolan, John's Stephen Monaghan's oldest brother-in-law.

John Stephen first reported for duty at the three-story Bristol Brass and Clock Company in 1873. At that time the company had about 300 employees. Many were of Irish extraction like himself, since by now the word had spread far that Connecticut's "Brass Valley" in general was experiencing something like the second coming of the industrial miracle earlier seen in the Merrimack Valley in Massachusetts.

Invaluable to the understanding of these early years in Bristol have been the writings of the late United States Congressman John S. Monagan

Mary Agnes and Charles Monagan as little children, Bristol circa 1875.

(JSM), who listened closely to his grandfather's recollections while he was growing up. JSM remarked that the family's house in Forestville was a modest wooden affair on Broad Street. It was likely No. 472 and on the corner with Preston Street. This dwelling soon became jammed with people. The 1880 census cites John, now 33, as "working in brass mill" and Anna, 26, as residing with their brood with modernized nicknames, beginning with Mary or "Minnie," age nine; and Charles "Charlie" Monaghan, age eight. Also on hand were Catherine or "Kitty," six – apparently named after John's mother

Catherine Castle Monaghan and a son William Henry, born on December 2, 1875. The third child to be born in Bristol, in 1877, was a Thomas, likely named after Anna's next sibling, but who died around age four. Next came a Helen called "Nellie," born on April 29, 1878. In this Forestville house then were also a Matthew Kane, 38 – who may have been a cousin of some sort – and Anna's slightly older brother James Nolan, 26. James Nolan was the first of a number of Nolans who would work within the Lamp Burner Shop. Then came the enigmatic young Thomas Monaghan, described earlier. In June 1880, Anna Monaghan, named after her mother, was the next child born in Forestville. On January 10, 1882, there followed my grandfather Walter Edward Monaghan. Possibly after subsequent miscarriages, on February 8, 1891, John and Anna had their last child, a daughter named Marguerite Bernice Monaghan.

The Transplantation of the Nolans

John Stephen and Anna inspired quite a number of the Nolans to follow them to Connecticut, and the families remained deeply interconnected for decades. But the Nolans did not abandon their North Bangor crossroad called "Cook's Corners" all at once. The 1875 New York state census shows that the core Nolan household held for the moment not only the parents but their oldest sons James and Thomas; a daughter Margaret; "Katlen" meaning Catherine and born in 1862; "Liza" or Elizabeth, 10, who became a nun called "Sister Ushina"; plus William and Agnes. Missing from the census are Hugh, 19, and for some reason, Ellen, 13 – possibly another nun in the making. Though only 16, Mary had already married an Arthur Devlin from a West Bangor farming family.

By the 1880 census the oldest sons James and Thomas had already relocated to Connecticut and found work in the Lamp Burner Shop of Bristol Brass. Thomas, born in 1854, married an Elizabeth Smith in Bristol by about 1877. The couple had a son James in 1878, then a Mary Elizabeth, George Thomas, Josephine, and Frederick after that.

Playing with fire was always risky but for John Monagan it bore rich fruit.

The town of Bristol was compact in 1878.
Bristol Brass buildings were at its center.

A stock certificate from Bristol Brass. Note emphasis on railway connections.

The lamp burner shop moved into filigrees.

An 1870s Bristol Brass bicycle lamp.

A gilded Bristol bucket.

Forestville's little train station. Next stop for John – Waterbury, Connecticut.

The daughter Mary Nolan and her husband Arthur Devlin made their way to Bristol a little later with their sons John, James, and Raymond, and a daughter Bertha. A Leo George Devlin was born to them in Bristol in 1884. Arthur Devlin's new work as a "pressman" – meaning physically working at a metal printing press – must have been profitable since he next bought a house in nearby New Britain. According to the *Hartford Courant* of February 24, 1898, the couple had just lost "a young child" – with no name given – to "malignant scarlet fever," a periodically rampant and often fatal disease in those times. Another transplant to Bristol's Forestville section was the daughter Catherine Nolan, possibly arriving in the late 1870s.

In the Lamp Burner Shop, Catherine's brothers James and Thomas Nolan were working shoulder-to-shoulder with a number of **Miller** brothers who lived

The young Catherine Nolan.

Her husband Thomas Miller.

close by. This was well and good since Daniel Miller, perhaps the oldest, ran the entire facility. But it was the younger brother Thomas Joseph Miller, a handsome, sandy-haired young man with fine features and rather doleful eyes, who captured Catherine Nolan's heart. They married in 1885. Thomas Miller had arrived in Bristol in 1879 and worked at first as a metal buffer. His other brothers were Frank and William and they all lived next door to John Stephen and Ann Monaghan at the intersection of Broad and Preston streets.

Back in Bangor, New York, the Nolan parents Patrick and Mary sadly watched the progression of their children's departures. Yet still they kept the farm going. Finally a mid-March 1888 item in the *Malone Palladium* revealed that Patrick Nolan was recuperating from some long illness. It was apparently the last straw. Before long Patrick and Mary called it quits on the North Country and made their own move for Connecticut with the youngest son William and their unmarried daughters Margaret and Agnes.

Once arriving in Bristol, these Nolan ancestors took up residence at 30 Henry Street, which was just a little outside of Forestville. The son William got a job in the brass spoon-making department of Bristol Brass and Clock. Their newly married daughter Catherine and her husband Thomas Joseph Miller also moved into this residence with their first child, a daughter born in August 1887 and named **Lorena** or "Rena." The young Catherine, a faded daguerreotype shows, was a tall slender woman with an hour-glass figure and waves of lovely brown hair. In April 1889, Catherine gave birth to a son named **Howard Joseph,** but she died while bringing him to life. In time both Lorena and Howard would become all but adopted by my great-grandparents, and thoroughly interlinked with the Monagan family in Waterbury for nearly three decades.

The Road to Waterbury

John and Anna Monaghan were obviously a very hospitable couple. Within their packed house at Broad and Preston streets there must have been a constant clamor and much pressure to provide, as well as to entertain the comings and goings of the various Millers and Nolans from their nearby bases on Henry Street and elsewhere.

For whatever reasons, John may have grown over-fond of the drink, according to an account related by Congressman Monagan: "At this time, my grandfather was still a free wheeler and liked an occasional nip – conceivably in part due to crowded conditions at home. But it was here, according to family tradition, that he came home one night a bit worse for drink, as they say, and frightened his little son Walter [this author's grandfather], or "Eddie" as he was then known, so that the little fellow burst into tears. Whereupon John S. said, 'If liquor makes me look that way to my own son, I'll never drink again.' And he never did." This must have been in the late 1880s.

Despite the cramped scene, the children managed to thrive in the local schools. In fact, the oldest son Charles Andrew achieved the highest marks in his 1889 graduating class at Bristol High School. But the powers-that-be still

Great-grandmother Ann Nolan Monaghan.   The young Charles Monaghan in bow tie.

scorned the rude Irish enough that certain local authorities tried – ultimately unsuccessfully – to prevent his being honored as the class Valedictorian. Charles next enrolled at the highly regarded Trinity College in Hartford, a place so staunchly Episcopalian that it had only recently begun accepting any sons of Catholic Ireland. For a long while he commuted back and forth by train to save money. He excelled at baseball and swimming at Trinity and graduated near the top of his class, determined to become a medical doctor. However, the family's primary commuter at this time was actually the father John Stephen, by now a maestro at casting that alloy of copper and zinc that is brass. A curious fact is that the Bristol city directories of the late 1880s already listed John as being an employee in Waterbury and not Bristol. It would appear that John had been wooed to make the big switch, evidently for significantly more money, by one Chauncey Porter Goss, then the vice president of Connecticut's premier brass enterprise, the **Scovill Manufacturing Company**. The twosome came from radically different backgrounds. Chauncey Goss was almost akin to a Connecticut aristocrat and gifted with an expensive private education, whereas John Monaghan had little book learning, having effectively been a child laborer in the Massachusetts textile mills. But John had such native wit and poise and by now such a growing self-confidence that the two became fast friends.

In becoming an expert caster of brass, John Monaghan was assuming a pivotal role in the production of that fickle but lucrative alloy that in Connecticut was akin to gold. Blending copper and zinc at the perfect ratios and temperatures and durations required for each particular product was exacting work. One can barely imagine now the cacophonous noise and fumes and black grime that came with that job, but John Stephen Monaghan somehow managed to handle it all with aplomb. Reportedly, he walked into each shift with a kind of effortless insouciance. At Scovill's, he quickly moved from serving as a foreman on the day shift – fueling the process that created millions of dollars in profits every year – to a later overseer of the night shift, which kept the inferno of production running around the clock.

It must have been quite a thing to commute from the small city of Bristol to booming Waterbury in the late 1880s, which had taken to calling itself the "Brass Capitol of the World." Here, new construction was progressing frantically on all sides, with trolleys clanging all day and factory whistles screeching at every shift change in the mad bustle of a once obscure city coming of age. By 1890 Scovill's employed around 1,500 workers with the numbers constantly growing since the brass industry was enjoying a headlong boom. Meanwhile, several smaller players in the brass sheet-rolling business abruptly merged into a single powerful new entity called **American Brass** which was backed by New York financiers. The other big player, Anaconda American Brass, would eventually be listed on the New York Stock Exchange. That company would soon employ 5,000 workers to labor in its sprawling plant beside the Naugatuck River. Raw copper was pouring in from Montana and zinc from New Jersey by the hundreds of thousands of tons, and if you were a Lithuanian, Italian, Irishman or some other new immigrant your chances of finding employment were near 99 percent if you showed up and looked half fit.

Chugging down the Naugatuck Valley each morning around 1889-1890 from Bristol, John Stephen Monagan must have felt like he was gliding into a kind of fantastical realm. The "Brass City" then had about 32,000 residents, more than half of them of Irish descent, and loads of these Irish were making more money in a month than their parents could have dreamed of in a lifetime. But passenger trains back and forth to Waterbury from Bristol took about a half hour either way, and the commute had to grow tiring.

A gala Spencer Avenue dinner around Helen's wedding. Closest to camera Anna, next Rena Miller, "Lizzie," John Stephen, Helen, Ann (striped shirt), Willie, then "Kitty" (across the table).

Ultimately, my great-grandparents packed up their Bristol house in 1890 and moved the whole family 12 miles south to a rental address at 9 High Street in Waterbury. It appears from many indicators that John Stephen was already being very well paid by the Goss family. On June 5, 1895, he bought for $2,700 a three-story house on 15 Spencer Avenue, a modestly affluent address on a hill overlooking the center of Waterbury. The money was not small and the seller was a George L. Lilly, the future Governor of Connecticut. The house had five bedrooms, a living room, formal dining room, and sizeable kitchen and was outfitted before long with an upright piano for the musical daughters Helen and Anna.

Congressman Monagan recalled: "These were the days when brass was still cast by hand with the casters personally determining the composition of the elements and determining the speed in pouring the metal. They were independent contractors and in a sense were like today's atomic scientists since they alone knew the secrets of their trade. Our men were personable and reliable and endeared themselves to the owners so that Willie [John's son William Henry, born in 1876] rose to become head of the casting shop and Grandpa ran the night casting shop [roughly in 1910]. There is a great picture of Willie in a derby and three-piece suit standing at the casting shop door with Grandpa, while Chan Goss [Chauncey, the son of the then president of the mill], and others with aprons, blackened faces and some in darkened long underwear, stand like peons at one side."

By the end of the 1880s, the wider region was awash in new manufacturing profits. The Naugatuck Valley was producing 85 percent of the brass in all of America, including finished buttons by the millions, skillets, hinges, lamps, fasteners, picture hooks, kettles, artillery shell casings, and you name it. In the space of about 35 miles from Torrington to Derby, some 50,000 people worked every day in this industry. The rising profits – and rising competition fomented by the creation of the American Brass Company in 1893 – could have only helped John Stephen Monaghan at each pay review. Also helpful must have been his friendship with the Goss family who by now more or less completely controlled the Scovill Manufacturing Company.

Congressman Monagan offered some fascinating visions from around this period, some of which arose from memories passed on to him by his father and grandfather himself. Many of his recollections were included in his 2002 memoir *A Pleasant Institution – Key C Major*." He [my great-grandfather] was strong as an ox and had enormous hands. He could handle animals skillfully. He always retained some characteristics of the farmer and I remember him, with his love of neatness and order, criticizing Connecticut farmers for leaving rakes or harrows or other equipment out in the weather to rust," JSM observed.

"He dressed nattily with silk shirts, a stick pin in his tie, a sizeable ring with an incised onyx stone and a gold watch with a gold chain and guard. As a hand caster working near a charcoal fire, he was black at the end of the day and had to clean up at home since the factory offered no facilities. After soaping and rubbing vigorously, he would dress and dash a little violet water on a handkerchief before he came downstairs. His hair would be parted in the middle with wings swept back and his full mustache curled at the tips on occasion." Quite a figure for the son of a man so destitute he had to have his way paid out of Ireland!

JSM continues: "He wore a prince nez to read the newspapers which he studied assiduously. He was well informed on public questions and pondered them deeply. He was a bit of a dandy, but with a core of iron underneath the surface. He was beloved and respected by the men who worked with him, including Chauncey P. Goss, Jr., known as 'Chan,' the son of one of the owners of the Scovill factory."

Note that Chauncey Porter Goss (Sr.) had risen from treasurer of the originally strictly Scovill-family-controlled mill to a director of the company in its major reconfiguration in 1888. That was apparently the year that my great-grandfather John was first hired, perhaps by Chauncey himself, to take over much of the revamped casting department at the core of its prodigious production lines. It is impressive that John would become fast friends with the scion of the next generation of this powerful Goss family.

Congressman JSM further observed about John: "He seemed to have no close friends – and working mostly at night, as he did in later years, did not contribute to socializing. In the morning after he had cleaned up, he would have his breakfast of soft, runny eggs, toast and coffee with a lot of sugar and milk. He would then go to bed and sleep until mid-afternoon. In good weather, he would dress and then go out to sit on the front porch in a rocker, chew his tobacco (Trumps) and greet passersby. The tobacco chewing was a habit deriving from the casting shop where cigarettes were not in general use, smoking was verboten generally, and impractical, in any case, because of the need for the caster to have his hands free to handle and pour the pot of molten metal. The ladies of the family deplored this "filthy habit," but this was JS's only vice and they did not dissuade him. Inside he had a spittoon on the floor by his rocking chair."

The Nolans in Connecticut

In late 1888 my great-great grandparents Patrick and Mary Nolan, then in their seventies and weary of the harsh life in upstate New York, had left their farm behind and finally followed in the much earlier trail of their daughter Ann Nolan with my great-grandfather John to Bristol. As noted, several other Nolans had long since made the move on their own, including their oldest son, James. Anna's one-year-younger brother Thomas Nolan had arrived by about 1876 and taken up work at the Lamp Burner Shop. There he befriended an Irishman named James Smith, a former Bristol copper miner, who introduced him to his daughter Elizabeth. The two were married in 1877 and had five children. Patrick and Mary's daughter Catherine Nolan would marry a Thomas Joseph Miller in Bristol in the late 1880s, as cited. In 1897, the father Patrick Nolan passed away in Bristol at the age of about 71 and was buried at St. Joseph's Cemetery there. With that, all ties to Bangor, New York were severed. A series of foreclosure notices regarding the Nolan farm began appearing in the spring and summer of 1900 in a very local Franklin County news sheet called *Facts and Figures Brushtonian*. Under the heading **Foreclosure Sale** on August 1, 1900, for example, one sees that the couple's Franklin County mortgages are being foreclosed against what appears to be their own daughter Margaret Nolan, now aged 44. The amount involved totals $994.80 and it includes the title to not only their 55-acre North Bangor farm, but two other parcels of agricultural land just to the north in Fort Covington – 135 acres in all.

At about this point most of the Nolans in Bristol were also moving down Connecticut's Naugatuck Valley to booming Waterbury. Central to this transition was the fact that my widowed great-great grandmother Mary Margaret Clark Nolan, took up residence at a house in Waterbury at 61 Round Hill Road (on the Naugatuck border and obliterated by later "urban renewal"). In the census of 1900 she is found there, aged 74, with her son William Nolan, now 30, who is working as "a day laborer in in a brass mill." The daughter Margaret or "Maggie" Nolan, now saying she is 42, is working as a milliner and is co-resident. Also in the house was the youngest daughter Agnes, 31, and working at the same millinery company with her older sister. The youngest resident was George Thomas Nolan, a grandson of Mary Margaret Clark in being the 19-year-old son of Thomas Nolan, who at that time was still living in Bristol.

James Nolan, the oldest son and perennial bachelor, had been living for some time in the Spencer Avenue house of his sister Anna and John Stephen Monaghan, but by 1902 and at the age of 51, he too had moved into the Round Hill Street address with his mother and the rest. In 1906 another brass-caster-in-the-making, George Thomas Nolan, married an Alice Moran in Waterbury. He worked for Scovill's for 47 years as a foreman in the casting department. He and Alice had six children including daughters Harriet, Elizabeth and Alice, and their sons James Andrew and Frederick worked at Scovill's. The son Jim worked his way through the ranks to become superintendent of the entire night shift, while developing a number of patents, while the son Fred (1917-1992) eventually left Scovill's to become a foreman at the Benrus Manufacturing Company. No doubt to the consternation of all, their son George Thomas Jr. (1912-1983), opted for the newspaper business. The young lawyer John S. Monagan looked after his affairs on many occasions.

By 1904, the first wave of Nolans on Round Hill Street were joined with a fresh installment in a house a few doors nearby at No. 36, in the form of Arthur and his wife Mary Nolan Devlin and their sons Raymond and Leo. Rapidly, Leo gained a job as a brass sheet cutter at Scovill's, although he later became a plumber at the long-standing Waterbury firm of M.J. Daly. Raymond moved from early work as a tool maker to becoming a silver caster. The father Arthur seems to have died in 1915. That was the year that the youngest daughter of Patrick and Mary Nolan, Agnes who was now 46, married a widower named Frederick Bates.

Adding further heft to the Nolan clan in Waterbury were several children of Thomas, the one Nolan family member who had stayed on in Bristol for some years after the others left. He may have even purchased the former Monagan family home in Forestville. But he and Elizabeth next purchased a larger house at 311 Frederick Street to accommodate their five children. By the time of the 1900 census, Thomas, was working as a "dropper" in the Lamp Burner Shop of Bristol Brass, while his oldest son James Henry, 22, was employed as an electroplater. George Thomas, 16, had just got a job there as a general laborer; and Josephine, 15, was operating a trimming press. Frederick, 13, was still in school. The widowed daughter Mary Ellen Bowen, 20, was operating a foot press; at their side in the same Lamp Burner Shop was Thomas's now 78-year-old father-in-law James Smith, working as solderer and also living with the family as widower. Also in the house was a one-year-old grandson, Albert Bowen, and a niece named Margaret Dooley, widowed at age 18.

Then things began to fall apart for several members of the family. Within a year, James Smith, the father of Thomas's wife Elizabeth, went blind and then died of a stroke on October 15, 1901. The second oldest son, the

149

aforementioned George Thomas, had moved down the valley to Waterbury at age 18 to start his long career with Scovill's. On November 3, 1902, the whole Frederick Street, Bristol house of Thomas and Elizabeth, insured for $2,000, burned down in the middle of the night with the general fire alarm sounded by the squawkers at where else? The Lamp Burner Shop.

The mother Elizabeth died just around this time. Meanwhile, the daughter Josephine had married a man named Willis and moved to Southington. The father Thomas was growing very ill himself. He finally broke down and moved to Waterbury and the comfort of the extended family, taking with him his youngest sons George and Frederick and an insurance payment for his burned house. The 1903 Bristol City Directory listed him as "Removed to Waterbury."

Thomas was clearly under the medical care of my great uncle Dr. Charles Andrew Monagan in Waterbury. In fact, the next solid records for Thomas concern his death on May 25, 1904, while in the Grace Hospital in New Haven. It seems his daughter Ellen Nolan Bowen, who had moved to New Haven a little earlier, had taken her father in for his last months or weeks as he failed from what had to have been cancer. Remarkably, the administrator of this Thomas Nolan's will, recorded on December 14, 1904, in the New Haven District Court, was my grandfather Walter Edward Monagan, newly graduated from the Yale School of Law. Among Thomas's debtors noted in this will, for the amount of $19, was Charles Monagan, M.D.

Around 1910, Anna Nolan Monagans older brother James Nolan bought a house on 231 Orange Street in Waterbury, perhaps in consort with siblings. In the least, his sister Margaret, listed as widowed in that year's census, and the youngest brother William joined him. In reality, this was likely either just a second, side-door entrance to the same house or a separate mail box. The sister Margaret continued to work for some years as a hat maker beside Agnes. William died in 1924 at the age of 57 and was buried back in St. Joseph's Cemetery in Bristol beside his parents Patrick and Mary Clark

Nolan and his sister Catherine Nolan Miller (with Catherine's daughter Lorena buried beside them all in 1930). Mary Nolan Devlin's unnamed newborn who succumbed to Scarlet Fever in 1898 was buried in that cemetery as well. James Nolan, the oldest brother, passed away on September 12, 1933, at the age of 82, while Margaret lived on until 1946. At that point, there were quite a number of Nolans living in Waterbury, with George from Bristol a decades-long presence in the print shop at the *Waterbury Republican-American*. His grandson James W. Nolan became a close friend of my uncle Andy and a very active campaign worker for Congressman Monagan between 1960-1964 and inevitably had Dr. Tom look after (quite successfully) a health crisis for his infant daughter.

A badly faded photograph of my great-great grandmother Mary Clark Nolan (1825-1910) shows her standing before a house with a white picket fence that is identified as Orange Street in Waterbury. That side street lies a few blocks below the colossus of the Scovill Manufacturing Company at the crest of East Main. As previously introduced, Thomas Joseph Miller was the husband of Catherine Nolan, my great-great aunt who died while giving birth to her son Howard Joseph Miller in April 1889. Afterward, Thomas remained living with Catherine's parents Patrick and Mary Nolan for an extended period, no doubt receiving much help from them in raising Howard and the toddler Lorena, born in August 1887. The father pressed on through this distraught situation with an early job in a bell factory, and eventually became a Bristol policeman.

But around 1895, Thomas Miller began courting a 16-year-old girl named Elsie who he married the next year. Thereupon, Miller inevitably moved out with his eight-year-old daughter "Rena" and six-year-old Howard and took an apartment with his bride Elsie, who was not old enough to have finished high school. This had to have been not only scandalous but a domestic nightmare for all involved. Things grew profoundly worse when Thomas Miller died on January 12, 1902. Aged about 14 then, the orphaned Lorena dropped out of school to work in one of Bristol's remaining clock companies, while her brother Howard weathered the end of the eighth grade. Elsie was now 23.

Inevitably, the situation in Bristol unraveled so drastically that Lorena and her brother Howard were also hurried down the valley in 1904. But instead of moving in with their frail grandmother Mary Clark Nolan, they were welcomed for years to come into the Spencer Avenue household of my great-grandparents, who were of course their uncle and aunt – John Stephen and Anna Nolan Monagan. It was the right place to be for these teenagers who had suffered through so much travail. With much care, the teens were put back into school with Rena being placed in the private Notre Dame Academy, which was becoming something of a nest of Monagan girls by then.

Interlude – About that "Monagan" Name

In the midst of these major changes the Waterbury Monaghans strangely began spelling their name in a seemingly entirely new way, with the rendering henceforth to be known as "Monagan." Generational lore had it that the change was this core family's invention, most likely concocted around 1898 at the instigation of the daughter "Kitty" Monagan who was dabbling on the Hartford stage (and who did constantly fiddle with her first, middle and last names, plus twiddling with various line ups of her initials).

However, there is plenty of evidence to show that this explanation falls short. Indeed, various references in the *Waterbury Democrat* concerning school essay readings and song recitals by the younger sister Helen, born in 1878, clearly indicate that the family began spelling the last name as **Monagan** by at least 1895. As noted, this was in the manner adopted about 20 years earlier by certain relatives in Franklin County, New York. For example, we know that the last will and testament of Artemis Monagan used the new spelling in 1877 (when he was calling himself "Artimus"). Later, Arthur Monaghan was having himself referred to in the *Malone Palladium* as early as November 1886 as being a "Monagan." Much earlier in Massachusetts, Owen Monaghan may have been similarly experimenting at various stages. But the real force behind this name change to Monagan in Waterbury may have actually not been Kitty or Helen but their mother Anna Nolan Monagan. She went back and forth between calling herself the youthful "Annie" versus "Ann," having dropped "Anna" by the wayside, and she seemed quite determined to show how "with it" she was at various times. She also championed an attempted reinvention of her Nolan maiden name as "Nolen." Whether she thought this distinctive and "smart," or truer to some quaint entry on an early census form, it is impossible to say. She later saw to its redeployment on remakes of her parents' Bristol graves. She appears to have been a serial name changer.

This penchant for incessant name-fiddling seems to speak to a love of theatricality by my great-grandmother Anna. Whether she was putting on airs due to the family's evolving social status or just enjoying the odd lark of Irish irreverence, she appears in some remarkably stagey apparel in a number of old family photographs. It feels as if she was sometimes wishing to certify that she was a free spirit reborn. By this point of course, a great many second-generation Irish immigrants to America were actively trying to establish a new kind of identity for themselves, partly to prove they had fully "arrived" and were no longer downtrodden "bog Irish" by any measure now.

The Monagan family was also absorbing other influences regarding "h-dropping," including newspaper reports from afar. Just examine the *Plattsburgh* [N.Y.] *Sentinel* as far back as April 15, 1894, when that newspaper from the north made this reference to a likely daughter of one of the Arthurs: "Miss Monagan and her invalid sister, who have spent the winter here residing in the Hayes cottage, returned to their home in New York last Wednesday." In June 1898 the *Catholic Journal* (from Rochester, New York) mentioned a "Winnie Monagan" in the smart college town of Ithaca.

As they settled into their new spelling, John and Annie Monagan by the time of the 1900 census were clearly running a robust and welcoming house at 15 Spencer Avenue. Though now 54 years-old, John was still hard at work as a brass caster. But he had also found time, beginning by 1895, to serve as a delegate from the First Ward to the Waterbury City Council, a role he would honor for about a decade. In other words, the family's involvement with the political life of Connecticut fatefully began then, seeding its continuance through four generations. Resident with John and "Annie" still in 1900 were Mary Agnes or "Minnie," 29 and perennially single; Charles, now 27 and possessed of a newly minted medical doctor's degree from the University of Pennsylvania; William, learning to be a caster of brass par excellence like his father; Helen, 22 and a devoted primary school teacher; Anna, 20, and a stenographer who also gave regular musical performances about town. Also on hand are Walter, 18, and Bernice, nine (plus James Nolan). Meanwhile, Catherine, 25, is in Hartford, living out her greatest name change of all.

Remaining Monaghans in Malone

As John and Anna's life in Waterbury evolved, their connections with New York's far north were petering out. There is scant evidence of much traveling back to Franklin County there. Generally speaking, the Irish were becoming expert at throwing off their pasts by these days anyway.

The only documented visit to Waterbury by John's Stephen Monagans older brother Edward occurred around 1893. This is odd, since all that was needed was to get on a Vermont Central train in Brushton and make a couple of changes later, bringing one down to Hartford and then Waterbury at the cost of a few bucks by the end of the day. By the sounds of a family story retold by the Congressman JSM, Edward did make this journey at least once. But he might as well have been plunked down on the Champs-Elysees. Apparently, when arriving in Waterbury he cut the figure of a rural bumpkin with his heavy work clothing, rugged boots and generally bewildered air. This all became a huge embarrassment to the upwardly-mobile daughters of John and Anna when in the course of this visit, he arrived late for Mass at Waterbury's gleaming new Sacred Heart Church – a temple in its opulence to the rising Irish middle class. When trying to slip in a back door unobtrusively, Edward instead found himself stumbling onto the edge of the sacred altar and making a complete fool of himself.

The story was clucked over for years by Anna's daughters, and evidently the great-great uncle never returned to Waterbury. One has to wonder if he might have been by now lost in drink, or somehow permanently dazed by his experiences in the American Civil War. He died on February 18, 1900, aged 55, and was buried beside his mother and father in the St. Augustine Cemetery in North Bangor, New York. The sizeable gravestone honoring all three must have been paid for by John Stephen Monagan, my great-grandfather, so one assumes that he made it there for the funeral.

Meanwhile, the fading of Arthur Monaghan (who reverted back to that spelling) was signaled several times by the *Malone Farmer*. Arthur's final death notice there on December 30, 1908, was a celebration of an entire way of living that Andrew Monaghan had also once known only a few miles away.

"Arthur Monaghan, one of Malone's aged and respected residents, passed on Thursday, as a result of shock. He had been in poor health for a number of years, being seriously afflicted with rheumatism and used two canes in getting about. Mr. Monaghan was a farmer by occupation and made a success of it until obliged to retire on account of lameness when he moved to this village where he has since resided. He was a good citizen and a man of ready wit who always had something bright to say to amuse and please a friend and many there be who will remember him for his good substantial qualities. Mr. Monaghan was 84 years of age and is survived by his wife, six sons and four daughters. These are John of Seattle, Wash. and Frank, George, William, Lawrence, Mark, and Alice of Malone; Mrs. Elizabeth Bruso of Malone; Mrs. James Donoghoe of Minneapolis, Minn. and Mrs. Walter Lagan of Portland, Oregon. Also one brother Hugh of Prince Edward Island. The deceased was born in Ireland and came to Prince Edward Island in 1841, going later to Boston. He married and settled in Lowell, Mass. where he resided until 1856, when he came to Malone and located on the farm which he occupied for so many years."

Arthur Monaghan's obituary was vital in pointing this researcher on to his brother Hugh's intriguing story on Prince Edward Island, as reviewed earlier. But his passing was another major lessening of the family's presence in Franklin County. Although the links were fading, the young John Monagan eventually took a wonderful jaunt with his father Charles and aging grandfather John Stephen down memory lane with stops around Andover and Lawrence, Massachusetts and the North Country of New York.

X.

CONNECTICUT-MADE MONAGANS

Mary Agnes and Charles

In Waterbury, the next generation began making quite a mark for themselves as the twentieth century took hold. The oldest of John and Ann's children, **Mary Agnes**, but called "Minnie," received her secondary school education in Bristol and then worked in Waterbury for some years before studying nursing in Bridgeport. She was a deeply caring and strongly motivated young woman and became a nurse in the rapidly growing Waterbury school system, which was something of a pioneering role at that time. In this capacity she offered the first line in school health care for hundreds of impoverished Waterbury children, a great many of them the products of immigrant families living in crowded and terribly unhygienic households. Her unshakeable dedication to this role was remarked on for years.

Referring to the older siblings about this time, JSM's memoir continues: "It may be that the family assumed a "lace curtain" tinge with the move to Spencer Avenue, some distance from the greenhorns of the "Green Road" or the "Abrigador" [arch working-class Irish districts]. Minnie had gained her nursing diploma from Bridgeport Hospital. My father had received his M.D. Walter was about to go to Holy Cross and Yale Law School. Kitty worked as a secretary for John Cassidy, a lawyer [his grandson was my high school classmate] Anna studied stenography with Harry Post [the founder of a local business college] and worked at the Manville Company office. Professor Bonn, who gave her piano lessons, many years later told me what a beautiful girl she was. Helen, slim, fair, handsome, with light blue eyes went to Waterbury Normal School. So beautiful was she that George Fallon, Jack Smith's great uncle, when clerking at Fallon's Drug store at the "Junction" at South Main and Scovill Streets used to dart out and raise or lower the awning just to see her go by. Bernice was the youngest and attended Notre Dame Academy... This was the high-toned Catholic girls' school run by the Congregation de Notre Dame where the girls were taught very rudimentary French, painting on China, water colors, and playing the harp."

The oldest son Dr. **Charles Andrew** (1872-1931), JSM's father, at first developed a flourishing general medical practice in Waterbury – and worked with his sister Minnie in tending to ailing children in the schools – before somewhat specializing in obstetrics. Though prosperous, popular, and

The young doctor Charles Monagan.   His bride Margaret Mulry.

handsome, he continued to live with his parents John and Anna until the age of 38, when he finally met his true love in Margaret Mulry, 25, the beautiful young daughter of a New York banker. His story will be rejoined later.

JSM's idea that the second sister **Catherine Elizabeth** (born in Bristol in 1874) had simply plodded along as a legal secretary in Waterbury misses the story by a wide mile. Perhaps this was because the larger tale was considered very scandalous and was possibly not revealed to the next generation. Kate had been an aspiring actress with a flamboyant personality and ultimately fell long out of favor with her sometimes stern older sister Minnie. She moved to Connecticut's capitol city of Hartford with its thriving theatrical world around 1893 as a single young woman aged only eighteen. This move may have even been made with her mother's blessings for her to become an actress, since Anna sported a fair amount of theatricality herself. Kate's independence ultimately came with a heavy price, however, and her return to Waterbury was not a happy one.

The second son of John Stephen was my great-great uncle **William Henry** (1876-1946). His name managed to combine the intriguing Henry link to the Monaghan family's deep past, and the name of his uncle Owen's first son in North Andover. Unlike his siblings, this William showed little zest for the academic side of things. Instead, he gravitated to his father's visceral world where one's achievements were measured in the pouring out of huge vats of molten metal amidst a backdrop of exploding fire, rather like some setting in a Norse myth. William worked at his father's side and was so thoroughly taught to master the art of brass casting that he became the boss of the entire daytime casting operation at Scovill's, when it was the dominant brass manufacturer in the world. Around that point, **Howard Miller**, having moved into the Monagan residence on Spencer Avenue as a young teenager, was soaring off on a new trajectory of his own within the Scovill company. He eventually became a plant manager at the center of Scovill's organization even as it climbed toward employing 17,000 workers during World War I. Meanwhile, the first cousin James Nolan had risen to become a senior foreman. It was as if this extended family were taking over this mighty enterprise from the ground up and helping to generate millions of dollars of wealth for the Naugatuck Valley in their own wake.

By 1900, Chauncey Porter Goss, Sr., had become the president of the Scovill Manufacturing Company. His heir apparent in Chauncey, Jr., undertook a long apprenticeship in the casting department under the tutelage of both John Stephen and William Henry Monagan so that he would develop a strong hands-on feel for the beating heart of the business. In fact, Chan and William Monagan became close friends. They served in the same company of the Connecticut National Guard when young and shared in some outrageous gags. William on January 19, 1904, married the talented singer Elizabeth Lawlor, and although childless, the couple were fixtures in Waterbury's social life for years.

My Grandfather Walter

My grandfather Walter Edward Monagan was demonstrating extraordinary promise in these years as well. In 1899, the then 18-year-old wrapped up his four years at Waterbury High School with great aplomb. He was secretary of the debating club and the commencement speaker at his graduation. He also appears to have had the highest marks of anyone in his year.

Congressman Monagan characterized his uncle Walter this way: "Walter, originally known as "Ed" from his middle name after his father's brother, was a very different type... He was a student and much quieter than Willy. He looked most like his father and, although taller and slighter, had the same fair coloring, sharp features and blue eyes... He went on to Holy Cross College, the Jesuit college in Worchester, Massachusetts [where he graduated with honors after completing his four-year course in three years]. He then went to Yale Law School and was called by the later Chief Justice Maltbie [of the Connecticut Supreme Court], a classmate, about the most brilliant student in their class."

At Holy Cross, Walter was a varsity basketball player with his exploits often noted in the *Waterbury Democrat*. He was also the manager of the baseball team. He graduated third in his class there in 1902, despite having leap-frogged an entire academic year. He was again made a commencement speaker, with his speech addressing the meaning of Catholicism as he saw it and entitled "Pope Leo XIII and Modern Thought." According to the *Waterbury Democrat* of June 19, 1902, he spoke before an audience of 3,000 "with consummate and oratorical finish."

Walter was one of only 22 students admitted to the Yale Law School in 1902. Despite racing through that three-year program in two years, as was his hyper-intellectual style, he became the Salutatorian (second in the graduating class, which would have included everyone else with three years of study against his two) and was mentioned as the recipient of the Law Prize on the front page of the *New York Times* in June 1904. His young friends then included the future doctor Michael J. Lawlor, a Moran, Henebry and the future lawyer John Cassidy – each representing Waterbury families that would be closely linked to the Monagans for decades. As a young man,

Walter served for four years as Waterbury's Commissioner for Education and for six years as a member of Company G of the Connecticut National Guard (alongside his brother William and Chauncey Porter Goss, Jr.). At different times, he also served as Waterbury's representative in the Connecticut Legislature (circa 1910- 1911), president of the Waterbury Bar (the legal association), "Exalted Ruler" of the Waterbury Elks Club (a playful title later also bequeathed to my uncle Andy), and "Grand Knight" of the Waterbury Knights of Columbus.

Walter when in the Connecticut National Guard.

The Butlers and McKeons

On April 5, 1910, my grandfather Walter Edward Monagan married **Mary Elizabeth Butler**, the daughter of a William Butler from County Kilkenny in Ireland, and another stepping stone in this family's past. Kilkenny was a veritable land of Butlers with at least 359 Butler households present in the county in the 1820s. The name Butler derives from *bouteiller* in French for "wine stewards," but the Butlers much earlier became widely known as gentry who became widespread across Ireland following the Norman-Anglo invasions. Heavy concentrations of Butlers clustered around Limerick, Tipperary, and Wicklow, but the heaviest of all were found around the family seat at Kilkenny Castle. Today, there are some 9,000 people sharing the Butler name in Ireland.

According to the United States Census of 1900, my great-great grandfather William Butler came to America in 1848, or at the height of the Famine – and in this record he also indicated that his date of birth was in June 1836. But at other times he suggested that his birth was closer to 1838, or even 1839. The best guess is that he was born on May 8, 1836, to a Patrick Butler and Margaret Brennan of the townland of Castlecomer beside the River Barrow in the northwest of Kilkenny. But there was a William Butler born in the county's southwest to a William and Celeste Butler in the settlement around Windgap to the county's southwest on July 1, 1837. Thanks to a particularly focused line of research by my aunt Marjorie (Monagan) Kelly, it seems clear that his family immigrated to New York from Liverpool on board the ship *Henry Clay*. This was a true three-decker Famine ship of 1250 tons, and though nearly wrecked in a calamity off Manasquan, New Jersey in March 1846, she was salvaged and returned to Liverpool's immigration runs.

There were likely several Butler siblings already living in Connecticut before this migration. A "Frank" or more likely Francis Butler stood foremost. In **From the Old Sod to the Naugatuck Valley,** Janet Maher explored several older potential siblings named Michael James (1819-1869), Anna (Maher) (1820-1892), Patrick (1822-1864), Julia (1823-1897), and Margaret (Leary) (1829-1892) who all died in nearby Naugatuck. The fact that they are in some cases almost twenty years older, and a step removed from the northside of Waterbury (though essentially over the next hill) suggests that they may have been step-brothers and sisters of my great-grandfather William from an earlier marriage.

William Butler, often called "Willie," was naturalized as a U.S. citizen in Waterbury on March 30, 1859, which made him ripe for service in the incipient American Civil War. In 1860 he was living in a Waterbury boarding house at the age of 22 and working as a "tinner" or tinsmith. He first married an Ellen "Finigan" or better "Finnegan," aged 21, on February 10, 1862. On November 8, of the same year, like clockwork from the first connubial night, they had a daughter named Elizabeth. He may have next served in the 25th Regiment of Connecticut Heavy Artillery, but the relevant documentation has been inconclusive.

In any case, his wife Ellen gave birth to a son William on November 3, 1864, but he died the next year. Then on April 8, 1866, the couple welcomed a daughter named Mary. A Francis James ("Frank") followed in February of 1868. Next came a Julia W., who was born on March 20, 1870 (an earlier Julia had died at birth). This matches with the likely namesake Julia from Naugatuck mentioned above.

The Waterbury city directory of 1869 shows that William was still working as a tinsmith at that time, with his family residence at the intersection of Union St. with 93 North Elm. In 1870. By 1871, his apparent mother Mary (Margaret Mary) is listed as a widow and residing with him on North Elm. William himself had by now shifted into the employ of the A.B.H. Company – a plumbing and heating outfit – while another brother named Frank is working as a carpenter. In all, William and Ellen had seven children, with the last being a daughter Ellen born on March 4, 1872 (according to notes from an old Butler bible as taken down by my father). The mother may have perished during that last delivery. The daughter Ellen, called "Nellie," appears to have married years later a John H. Judd from that influential Waterbury-area family.

Not long after losing his first wife Ellen, and while raising five surviving children on his own, William Butler met and in 1876 married a 15-years younger woman named **Sarah McKeon** (a.k.a. McKeown). Sarah was born in Drummaul townland, County Antrim in northern Ireland in August 1850, and most recently had been living next door to William and his brood on North Elm Street. In 1852 she had immigrated to New York at the age of two with her 29-year-old mother Margaret (Wallace) McKeon.

Margaret and her daughter Sarah departed for America on one of the fastest packet ships running from Liverpool to New York, the three-masted, square-rigged 2,000-ton Isaac Webb of the Black Ball Line. Long, sleek and sharp-lined at 188 feet, but only 40 feet across at the beam and yet with nearly 10,000 yards of sail, she wore the striking looks of an early clipper ship built to fly across the Atlantic at speeds earlier sailors could only dream of. Artists painted the *Isaac Webb* as a thing of beauty from the moment of her launch in 1851 and continued to do so for years on end.

The Isaac Webb was much loved by artists, but most Irish traveled in much rougher vessels.

The Isaac Webb could transport as many as 460 passengers at a time in trans-Atlantic journeys of less than three weeks. For the Mckeon mother and daughter in steerage class there would have been little comfort, however, and the half-nauseating diet of yellow meal, ship's biscuits, and bread scouse would not have helped. Nonetheless, Margaret and young Sarah made it to the Port of New York on May 30, 1853.

The first movements of the widow and child are difficult to trace. Their initial destination may have been to New Haven, where there were living a cluster of people by that uncommon last name. As many as three John McKeons resided there – a grocer, a laborer, and a seaman – and one of these made his way 20 miles north to become naturalized as a U.S. citizen in Waterbury in 1856.

Partly because the name, also common as McKeown and proffered as "mik-ow-AN," was so difficult to pronounce, it was often turned into McCann and other "Irish-lite" permutations, making it a challenge to track back through time. There are references to a mason John "McCuen" living at first on the West Road in Waterbury in the 1860s, and seemingly followed by several brothers. But the fundamental reason for an impoverished Irish widow to hurry north to Waterbury from New Haven with her toddling daughter had to have been the ample work on offer for women in the mills. We do know that a Margaret McKeon remarried some years later to a James McGrath in Waterbury on July 28, 1866. By this point Sarah would have been 16.

This Sarah must be considered the same as the young woman identified in the 1870 census in Waterbury as Sarah "McCann," aged 20. To put it bluntly - *there is no Sarah McKeon identifiable anywhere in Connecticut otherwise.* This Sarah McKeon is stated to be working as a domestic servant in the North Main Street home of none other than the aforementioned Chauncey Porter Goss. In 1860 Chauncy, Sr., had been hired as a bookkeeper at the then modest but rapidly-growing Scovill Manufacturing Company. By the year 1900 he became president.

Chauncy Porter Goss's residence was a handsome Queen Anne Victorian-styled house at the top of North Main Street with impressive turrets, a wrap-around porch looking over sloping lawns, and expansive downstairs dining and drawing rooms. The elegantly brocaded wallpaper therein must have been a chore to dust. But it is a strange fact that my great-grandmother Sarah McKeon as a young woman 150 years ago was doing such work on a live-in basis for the Goss family.

The young Sarah McKeon did not remain long in the house of Chauncey Goss, however. Instead she found a room at 7 Camp Street (just off North Elm) and went to work at making brass buttons, probably at the button division of Scovill's or else at the Waterbury Button Company. Before long she caught the eye of my widowed great-grandfather William Butler. The couple were married in January 1876, when Sarah was 26 and William was 40.

William Butler was by now prospering as a plumber with a new residence on 209 North Main Street – which was about to become one crowded place.

With Sarah McKeon, William had five more children beginning with a William Joseph, born Nov. 28, 1876; and George Henry on September 17, 1879. Next on January 11, 1882, came **Mary Elizabeth Butler**, who would marry my grandfather Walter Edward Monagan. Then on May 21, 1884, followed my great aunt **Anna Louise Butler**, who taught for years with such excellence and passion at the Woodrow Wilson School that she was made principal in the mid-1940s. She also long reigned as a semi-matriarch of the Monagan household at 84 Euclid Avenue in

Sarah McKeon in her later days, Euclid Avenue.

Waterbury. Aunt Louise lived until April 4, 1972 or just under 86 years – despite being an absolute chain smoker. She had a younger brother named Augustine who was born in August 1891 and evidently named after the month of his arrival, but who died at the age of 10.

By the late 1860s, William Butler had developed a very profitable plumbing business that was based at 61 South Main Street. He would have needed to work hard to support his very large family until his death in 1905. His younger wife Sarah lived on until 1921.

Their first son together, William J. who was born on November 28, 1876, knew much sadness. His draft registration card in 1917 clearly shows him to be working as a supply clerk at Scovill's, with his nearest close kin being his mother Sarah then resident at 84 Euclid Avenue. He does not seem to have had a wife. It seems likely that he is the same William J. Butler who next shows up working in accounts for the Bristol Brass Company where he gained statewide notoriety in June 1924 for embezzling $1800, enough to have merited significant jail time. In the census of 1930 he is found living alone at age 54 in an upstairs room in the Young Men's Christian Association or YMCA in downtown Waterbury, one of dozens of similar lonely male souls inhabiting these dorms above the downstairs swimming pool and basketball court, where I always felt somewhat nervous to visit as a young boy. On July 10, 1930, William made his way to the YMCA camp on Bantam Lake near Litchfield, Connecticut. At some wooded spot along the shore he took off his clothes and wandered out until he was well over his head and drowned himself.

A very different story was that of the next brother, George Henry Butler, born on September 17, 1879. He married an Anna Theresa Kelly after beginning working around 1900 at the Waterbury Manufacturing Company (the core business being brass buttons). He remained there for 46 years before retiring as a manager of production. He and Anna had four sons, the first being Reverend George W. Butler, who was born in 1909. At the time of his father's death in 1951, George was assistant pastor of St. Brendan's Church in New Haven. But he became pastor for 21 years after that at the Sacred Heart Church in Suffolk. He ended up as pastor emeritus of the St. Dominic's Church in Southington and from there found his way to attend and sometimes preside over a number of our family rites of passage in Waterbury.

The next son was Attorney Francis Joseph Butler of Waterbury, for some years executive director of the Waterbury Housing Authority and long serving as clerk of the United States Superior Court in Waterbury. After serving as a warrant officer in World War II, he married a Lucy Hanlon and lived until Feb. 9, 2001. The other brothers were Edward A. Butler, later of Cherry Hill, New Jersey, and William. Born on April 21, 1916, Edward Aloysius served as a captain in the Army during WWII and as a comptroller for the giant bearings manufacturer SKF industries. He and his wife Margaret had five children: Katherine Perloff, John, James, Cary Garrison and Shannon Rodefeld. At the time of his death in 2003, there were 14 grandchildren.

William J. Butler, called Bill, worked for years in the sports department of the *Waterbury American*, the hometown newspaper with which my extended family was so involved for decades. Bill with his always effervescent wife Helen (Conway) were for decades fixtures in my family's life – including my aunt Margie and uncle Andy. They were classic citizens of the older Waterbury, with Bill first joining the *Waterbury Republican* (the paper had dueling names from its morning to evening editions) immediately upon his graduation from Crosby High School in 1936. But just before America's joining World War II, he enrolled in the Army Air Force and served in the South Pacific until 1946. Then he came home and was promptly asked to cover the town's new minor league baseball team, the "Waterbury Timers." Much earlier there had been semi-pro teams with names like the Brassmen, Brasscos, Finnegan's, and Waterbury Spuds.

Surely a career highlight for Bill was his coverage of the Aug. 7, 1947, exhibition game of the mighty New York Yankees visiting to play the lowly Class B "Timers" (named after the town's fame in watchmaking) before a crowd of 9,000 at Municipal Stadium, just a holler from the Windsor Street where I grew up. Talk about ways the region's Irish could make good! The starting pitcher was none other than the heavily freckled Frank "Spec" Shea, also called "the Naugatuck Nugget" since he was from that town just down the road. In fact, the whole Naugatuck school system was shut down for Spec Shea's debut in the Bronx that April 14, under the assumption the entire town would attend. The Naugatuck Nugget was a "phenom" and lost narrowly to the famous black breakout baseball star Jackie Robinson for the

American League Rookie of the Year in 1947. That August 7 in Waterbury (with Joe DiMaggio benched for injury) his catcher was Ralph Houk, the later Yankees manager. Alas, Class B Waterbury lost 8-0. One can be certain that the Waterbury mayor John S. Monagan, along with many other family members, was on hand.

In any event, though the Waterbury Timers fizzled out in 1950, Bill Butler went on to cover most every major sporting event in Connecticut. He was made the sports editor-in-chief in 1967 and remained as such until his death in 1981. Many times when I visited Municipal Stadium as a young teenager to watch the likes of Waterbury's AA affiliates of the San Francisco Giants and Pittsburgh Pirates, Bill Butler could be seen perched in the small press box at the top of the stands, watching over the proceedings with a hawk eye.

William and Sarah McKeon Butler's third child was my grandmother Mary Elizabeth, born in 1882. She worked for several years as a school teacher before marrying my grandfather Walter Edward Monagan on April 5, 1910, in a ceremony that was little publicized. The couple must have been weathering disapproval from John Stephen and Anna Nolan Monagan since their first move was into the household of Mary's mother Sarah Ann McKeon Butler, then 60. But she in turn would soon settle into the house they bought at 84 Euclid Avenue.

The Monagans at Spencer Avenue

The marriage of my grandparents Walter and Mary Elizabeth got off to a profoundly sad start. Indeed, their first child Joseph was born only seven weeks after the wedding, on June 1, 1910. To a staunch Catholic family ever keen on polishing its hard won middle-class veneer, the prospect of a bride with a large "baby bump" while making vows in a pristine white linen dress would have been scandalous.

Likely, the marriage of Mary Louise Butler and Walter Monagan was hush-hush. The couple's "honeymoon" seemed to entail a long stay in Philadelphia where their newborn son was placed in the St. Vincent House orphanage there. This was run by the sisters of St. Vincent de Paul, also known as the "daughters of charity." One of those looking after him, and perhaps the head nun, was a "Sister Euphemia." Sadly, the baby died from acute gastroenteritis after living only 1 month and 8 days, as certified by the death certificate signed by Sister Euphemia on July 9. That certificate named the parents as Walter. E. Monagan and Mary Butler of Waterbury, Connecticut.

It is possible that Sister Euphemia in Philadelphia was an associate or even relative of Anna Nolan's younger sibling Martha Elizabeth Nolan (born in 1865 and originally called "Lizzie") who was accepted into the Sisters of Mercy in Hartford, Connecticut on July 17, 1900. (See New Haven's *Morning-Journal Courier* the next day.) That order, in which she became "Sister Mary Justina," had a special devotion to caring for orphans.

In December 1929, Anna Monagan's granddaughter Marion Ann Marks (daughter of Helen Monagan and Fred Marks) would enter the same order at the age of 21. She may have been inspired to do so and possibly even taught in school by her great aunt Sister Justina, since the Marks moved to Harford early on. Marion took the religious name of Sister Joan Marie. Following in her mother Helen's footsteps she became a teacher, serving in Catholic schools across Connecticut and Rhode Island for decades. There are several photographs showing the late middle-aged Anna Nolan Monagan, my great grandmother, posing with visiting nuns in their starched habits and cornetts, with Mary Justina in one wearing what appears to be the garb of a Mother Superior. A Sister Margaret Loretta and Regina Vincent are also pictured in this series, and these could well be other nuns within the family, possibly from the Mulry side, as they are photographed outside the home of Charles Monagan and his wife Margaret Mulry Monagan.

At the time of the 1910 census my great-grandparents Anna and John Monagan, himself now almost 64, were living still at 15 Spencer Avenue in Waterbury, and presiding over an ever more dynamic family. Later that year my grandparents Walter and Mary Butler Monagan purchased their own home at 84 Euclid Avenue and the next year welcomed in a son named **Walter Edward Monagan, Jr.**, my beloved uncle who lived for 97 years. At this point, Anna and John's oldest son and perennial fixture at Spencer Avenue, Dr. Charles Andrew Monagan finally fell in love with the 25 year-old Margaret Mulry in New York and began making plans for marriage in early 1911. Mary Agnes or "Minnie," the oldest daughter and school nurse, was still single at 39 and holding tight to her room at Spencer Avenue. So too was Margaret Bernice Monagan, the youngest at age 18, as she finished up her studies at Waterbury's *Académie du Notre Dame.*

James Nolan, Anna's brother, had moved out several years earlier to take up the aforementioned Round Hill Street residence with his family. Very early in 1904, the then 27-year-old second son William Henry Monagan had moved into an apartment with his new wife Elizabeth Lawlor. My great-grandmother immediately set to filling up his vacated space at Spencer Avenue by hurrying her orphaned Bristol niece "Rena" (Lorena) Miller, 16, and nephew Joseph Howard Miller, 15, into the household. These were the children of Anna's younger sister Catherine Nolan Miller. The two became like a new daughter and son within the family. My great-grandfather quickly landed Howard a job at Scovill's – at which he altogether flourished. Rena was slipped back into the flow of high school at the family's favorite Notre Dame Academy, where the youngest daughter Bernice would have been enjoined to smooth the troubled cousin's way forward.

A particular upheaval had descended upon the house around 1903 with the return of the second oldest daughter **Katherine Elizabeth** Monagan or "Kate" – at the moment going by the name of Elizabeth Gregg – from her broken marriage to a George Gregg in Hartford. That couple's world had altogether fallen apart. Kate had found steady enough work as a legal secretary back in Waterbury, but she and the straight-ahead Minnie seem to have often locked horns. This intriguing story will be told shortly.

The Legacy of Helen Monagan Marks

The next sister, **Helen** Monagan, born in Bristol in 1878, would also make her way out of town. Helen had been the first daughter to be enrolled at Notre Dame. There she stood out as a flamboyant essayist and polished singer of classical lieder and hymns. She also may have been the first, around 1895, to insist that our Monaghans drop the letter "h." The old Waterbury newspapers hold dozens of references attesting to Helen's cultural contributions about town at this time, while indicating that after graduation she quickly became an esteemed teacher at the Clay Street School. She also was a beautiful young woman, with light blue eyes and thick waves of auburn hair.

Helen "Nellie" Monagan in her wedding dress.

Delirious love with Fred Marks in Ridgefield, 1906.

Great-grandfather John Stephen feeding the geese.

Ann serves coffee.

While in her mid-twenties, Helen fell in love with a young go-getter named Frederick Lamont (for his mother) Marks, recently returned from a couple of years in New York City. His father George B. Marks was the co-owner of an adventurous emporium on South Main Street called Ziglatzki-Marks that specialized in art supplies, cameras, gramophones, picture frames, and imported draperies and artistic wall paper. Fred was handsome and full of enthusiasm and the couple were married on November 28, 1905, in Waterbury's grand new Basilica of the Immaculate Conception. With his charm and infectious optimism, Fred was welcomed into the family with open arms. Pregnancy followed swiftly, yet Helen and her husband clearly spent much of the next summer with the rest of the Monagan family on a farm the parents rented in Ridgefield, Connecticut for a long holiday.

For Helen and Fred Marks, this appears to have been a wondrous time. A photograph of them there absolutely epitomizes the thrill of young love. They seem to spend certain nights in a tent on a field above the farmhouse. Toward this the oldest sister Minnie is seen in another photo advancing with a pot of coffee. The father John Stephen looks very happy tending to some geese. Everything seemed to fall together for the family in that shining summer of great ease. But before the year ended Helen's first-born child John died at birth.

Fred Mark's welcome into the family is made manifest in the *Hartford Courant* of Sept. 4, 1908, report on the registering of a new millinery shop in Waterbury called **F.L. Marks & Company**, Incorporated, with premises at 109 Grand Street. My great aunt Mary Agnes Monagan is listed as the purchaser of 198 of the corporation's first 200 shares in the total capitalization of $5,000. A single share was awarded to my grandfather, the lawyer Walter, who was made the business's nominal president. The single remaining share went to Fred Marks himself, who was named secretary and treasurer. My great-grandfather John Stephen Monagan was the incorporator, effectively making this business a family gift to young Helen and Fred. This same year of 1908 the couple had a daughter named **Marion**.

Despite a heavily advertised grand opening and all the best hopes, the business fared poorly and may have been subleased as early as 1909. Its overwhelming shareholder Mary Agnes Monagan finally filed for its bankruptcy in 1912 (see *Hartford Courant*, Aug. 23, 1912). Whether the business failure was fraught with any acrimony is unknown. Over the following years, Fred continued to work in store sales, with an emphasis on wall paper and home interiors. Some such opportunity (and the presence of an extended Marks family there) drew the couple to relocate to Hartford in late 1911, shortly after the birth of their son Frederick Lamont Marks, Jr. The father Frederick worked for a succession of companies until starting a Marks-McQueeney Wallpaper Service on Main Street in 1922, but that partnership was dissolved in 1926. From around 1930 to the mid-1940s he was the lead salesman for a New Haven wall paper firm named H.M. Hodges.

Late in the same decade the son Fred Jr. apprenticed to a New Haven outlet of the burgeoning new overhead garage door business (as did his first cousin Arthur Owen Nelson, Jr., son of my great aunt Bernice Monagan). In 1929 and at the age of 21, Helen and Fred Mark's daughter Marion joined

Happy by the lake, circa 1915. L to R, Helen Monagan Marks, Charles Monagan standing above Marion Marks, Walter Edward Monagan, Bernice, and roughly 70 year-old John Stephen.

Autumn hill climb, possibly Ridgefield. John Stephen is flanked by wife Ann to the left and Bernice to the right.

Also at the crest were young Marion, her aunt Minnie behind, and Bernice and Kate Monagan Gregg.

The core family. Front row: Mrs. Helen Marks, John S. Monagan, Anna Nolan Monagan, Mary Agnes Monagan. Back: Atty. Walter Edward Monagan, Mrs. Bernice Nelson, Dr. Charles Andrew Monagan, William Henry Monagan.

No longer the little girl. Marion in the early 1930s as Sister Joan Marie, with her brother Fred. Photo courtesy Kristy Horstkamp.

The family gala celebrating the golden 50th anniversary of John Stephen and Anna's marriage on November 18, 1919. Front left to right: Charles Andrew Monagan (second son of Walter), John Stephen Monagan (son of Charles), Walter E. Monagan, Jr., Fred Marks Jr., Thomas Monagan (son of Charles), William Monagan (son of Walter). Second row L to R: Helen Monagan Marks, Mary Agnes "Minnie" Monagan, Marion Marks, John Stephen Monagan, Anna Nolan Monagan, with grand-daughters Ann Nelson (daughter of Bernice) and Margaret "Peggy" Monagan (daughter of Charles). Third row: Fred Marks, Walter Monagan holding son John S. Monagan III, Charles Monagan holding daughter Mary, Lorena Miller, Bernice Monagan Nelson. Back Row: Elizabeth Lawlor Monagan (wife of William Henry Monagan), Mary Butler Monagan (wife of Walter), Howard Miller (brother of "Rena"), William Henry Monagan, Arthur Nelson, Margaret Mulry Monagan.

the Catholic Order of the Sisters of Mercy with the goal to devote her life to serving the poor and uneducated, especially women and children. As a nun she took on the name of Sister Joan Marie and taught with a passion at a dozen different schools in Connecticut and Rhode Island. She was the first child to be born to the third generation of Monagans in Connecticut and this made her a pet child throughout the family. A number of old photographs show this little girl in various guises of childhood delight, such as crawling between the legs of aunts and uncles or climbing to a big

Ridgefield hilltop with her proud grandparents. She is prettily dressed front and center with her brother Fred Jr. at the family gala on Spencer Avenue on November 18, 1919, in honor of my great-grandparents' 50th wedding anniversary. After her transformation into a nun in 1929, Marion, or Sister Joan Marie, was photographed on several occasions, beaming very happily, while visiting her grandmother in Waterbury, prior to Anna's death in 1932.

As told in a wonderful letter in the Appendix, Frederick and Helen's great-granddaughter Susan Marks Roberts remembers many cherished family visits as a little girl in the 1940s when meeting her aunt and grandmother Helen. Susan was on the scene, unfortunately, when Helen Monagan Marks was more or less given her death prognosis from stomach cancer when aged about 70.

In 1951, Fred L. Marks, Jr. started his own business in the field of his New Haven apprenticeship, which he called The Overhead Door Company of Hartford. By this point he had three daughters with his wife Irene Larson Marks. The oldest was a Patricia Ellen born on September 27, 1936, whose first marriage in Milford, Connecticut in 1954 was to a Howard William Padowitz. Performing as a ventriloquist as a teenager with a dummy named "Snafu", he supported himself later as window dresser, while working as a magician and comedian on the side. But he also was subject to extreme depression and the couple divorced in the early 1960s. With a new wife, Padowitz moved to Miami where he found his way to regional stardom as a flamboyantly costumed figure called "Ho Ho the Magic Clown" and was a regular feature on a hit TV show called *Skipper Chuck's Popeye Playhouse Show*. This show directly inspired the later nationwide CBS Network children's program, cult classic and shameless imitation by Paul Reubens called *Pee-wee's Playhouse*. But things went sour domestically and one morning Ho Ho shot at but only grazed his second wife Janet, who was divorcing him, on May 23, 1974, before taking lethal aim at himself.

Patricia Ellen Marks must have thanked the stars above to have been well away from Ho Ho. In time, she met a far more stable, but interesting figure named Rosaire Joseph Daigle, a building inspector in Southbury, Connecticut of French Canadian extraction who was also an inventor on the side. The couple married in 1986 (following his divorce) and apparently having a child together, and made their home for years in Hudson, Florida. Patricia died there in 1910, 14 years after her second husband passed away.

The daughter Susan, who has been very helpful in this family history project, arrived next. She herself first married an Italian-American from Ansonia named Frank Maisano, with whom she had a son Mark and daughter Dawn. But they were later divorced, and she remarried to a James Roberts and they have been together for many years. The youngest sister Kathy married a Peter Menold of Milford on Feb 17, 1968, with whom she has two daughters, Jennifer (Daly) and Kristy (Horstkamp).

But the girls' father Fred Jr. early on divorced Irene Larson and left her to raise the three without him. He instead remarried to a Grace Platt, with whom he had a son named Bradford William Marks. His Overhead Door Company thrived but eventually Fred Lamont Jr. was diagnosed with advanced cancer and his spirits grew bleak. On April 4, 1971, he took his own life at his home in Portland, Connecticut. Very sadly, this son of Helen Monagan Marks left eight grandchildren behind, as well as his sister the nun Joan Marie, who would nonetheless keep seeking to inspire young people for years to come.

But the Overhead Door Company of Hartford was clearly a lucrative operation and Fred Mark's son Bradford W. Marks quickly picked up the pieces and long ran it as a steadily expanding business. His son Bradford W. Marks, Jr., a great-grandson of Helen Monagan and Fred Lamont Marks, Sr., was born on July 4, 1963, and lives in Cromwell, Connecticut with his wife Karen. The younger Brad Marks has overseen the still flourishing company through its most recent decades.

Anna and Bernice Monagan

The two youngest daughters of my great-grandparents were **Anna,** born in 1880 and named after her mother, and **Marguerite Bernice** born in 1891. Anna had been a winning student at Notre Dame, and a gifted musician who brightened the whole house with her playing on the living room grand piano – another extraordinary accoutrement for a brass caster and former Massachusetts very young laborer to acquire. After graduating from Notre Dame, Ann learned stenography at the Waterbury Business College,

Anna Monagan.

and then landed a secretarial job with the E.J. Manville Machine Company. Various newspaper references suggest that Anna's generation often went to dances together, whether at the Knights of Columbus (the nationwide Catholic fraternal association in fact started in Waterbury), Waterbury's Talma Club, or various other functions. One newspaper item refers to her cutting the rug at a lakeside dance in Trumbull in 1902 with her big brother Walter Edward, and one Mary Butler, who must be the same as Walter's bride nearly seven years later. There are indications from scribblings on the back of old photographs that the family may have rented a summer cottage in Trumbull near either a Canoe Brook Lake or Pinewood Lake – both now private communities. Anna had lovely, distinguished features, as seen here.

Fate, alas, was not kind to the young Anna Monagan. Despite these glowing early summers, tuberculosis, still rampant in the U.S., fell upon her in early 1907 and she died back in Ridgefield while staying with her big sister Minnie, who had nursing work there. The funeral was in Waterbury on June 8, 1907.

Bernice, youngest of the family, was a different story. Born in 1891, she too attended Notre Dame and is referenced often as giving her own charming piano recitals in that citadel of the Waterbury Irish Catholic middle-class.

Bernice, probably at Spencer Avenue.

Katherine, Helen, and Bernice.

Lake outing around the time of Bernice's marriage.

Among the family's new generation, Bernice must have been a bit indulged, since she was the youngest of the Monagan sisters. Bernice had fine features and soft brown eyes and a whimsical twist at the end of her thin lips. This is all evident in the photographs taken at the time of her wedding on May 13, 1914, to Arthur Owen Nelson, then a foreman at Scovill's. He later became the tax commissioner for the City of Waterbury. Some of the wedding's attendant celebrations were held near a large Connecticut lake in the hills, possibly Warramaug a dozen miles north of Waterbury.

Out of this wedding there emerged a photograph of singular beauty. Helen is at its serene center, and Bernice to the right nests toward her lovingly she is in fact wearing the same wedding dress Helen did in her marriage to Frederick Marks a decade earlier. To the left, Katherine Elizabeth, in her late thirties now, softly leans toward Helen as well, and despite all the travail of her own last decade, she projects great warmth. Those two older sisters, Kate and Helen, would not be photographed together again until about 1947, close to the time of Helen's death.

Bernice Monagan and Arthur Nelson had five children in rapid succession. The first was an Ann Marie (1916-1996) who married a Kenneth Beckham Watts on May 26, 1943, when he was about 30 and she 27. By then, Ann's husband had already been off to World War II and back. He had also started his own tool and die company on East Aurora Street at the base of Bunker Hill – Waterbury was still blessed with countless expert machinists working as subcontractors for the mills then. The couple lived on Highland Avenue.

The next child of Bernice and Arthur Nelson was a daughter named Helen who died in infancy in 1918, perhaps from the horrendous influenza epidemic then ravaging the planet. The son who followed next, Arthur Owen Nelson, Jr. (1919-2007), was an interesting figure. He joined the U.S. Army in November 1940 and kept at it for five long years. As the subsequent Korean War loomed, he re-enlisted on Nov. 14, 1949, and also saw that conflict through to its finish in 1953. He eventually settled into a long career as a draftsman with the Dynamics Corporation of America in its Bridgeport division and married an Eileen Murphy of Waterbury.

Bernice Monagan's daughter Jane Margaret Nelson was born in 1921. On June 5, 1941, Jane married yet another Waterbury tool and die maker named Howard Burton Gaunt, and they had three sons – Howard Burton Gaunt, Jr., Peter, and Jeffrey – as well as a daughter who married a Redding. The couple, Jane and Howard, eventually retired to the St. Petersburg, Florida area. The last of Bernice and Arthur Nelson's children was the most scholarly one, Charles Gerard Nelson, named after Bernice's oldest brother. Like nearly every other male of his time, Charles Nelson was sucked into World War II and in his case served as a U.S. Army reconnaissance specialist in Europe. With the help of the G.I. Bill, he obtained a B.A. and Master of Arts at the University of Connecticut and then earned a Ph.D. in literature at the University of Michigan. In the middle of all this he married Ann Culhane of Waterbury in 1946 and quickly had three sons: Charles Gerant, Jr; Thomas; and Mark Arthur. In 1951 the whole family packed off for Europe on the *Queen Elizabeth* so that he could study Medieval German literature in Germany and Innsbruck, Austria. He was a most congenial man and a professor of German literature for years at Tufts University in Medford, Massachusetts, my alma mater. There we briefly met from time to time when I was a young man – alas, too otherwise pre-occupied to better explore our common ancestry.

Sadly, my great-aunt Bernice died quite young on March 16, 1932, although her husband Arthur lived on until 1948.

William Monagan's Rise and Fall

The second son of John Stephen and Anna Monagan was William Henry and he was born in Bristol in 1876. His middle name appears to be a further acknowledging of the family's Henry ancestors, whether deliberate or subliminal. It is possible that the first name of William had to do with the conjectural brother of Owen and Andrew Monaghan named William who died in New York City in 1875. William himself clearly believed he was named after an important predecessor since in multiple city directories in later life he referred to himself as "William Monagan II" – among them in Waterbury 1914, and New Haven in 1937 and 1941.

As noted, William had a different inclination than the academically driven Charles and Walter (plus Minnie) and artistically encouraged younger sisters. William was instead drawn to his father's intensely physical world, his wrestling with the elements as it were. William, called "Willie," seems to have fulfilled his high school career in Bristol by the time the family moved to Waterbury. He then went directly to work at Scovill's casting shop under his father's watchful eye. He obviously was tutored to an exacting level and became a foreman while still in his twenties. Moreover, when Chan Goss, the son of the vast company's eventual president, was sent to the casting shop for an apprenticeship, it was none other than William Henry who was assigned to stand by his side. The two became fast friends.

While in his thirties, William was made superintendent of the entire daytime casting operation at Scovill's, while his father John reigned over the nights. But once the whistle blew at shift's end, William wore his rising responsibilities lightly, at least in his younger years. He was evidently a great man for parties and dancing with the ladies at the impromptu "hops" and formal galas thrown by the Knights of Columbus and Waterbury's Talma Club, where almost every single name of the attendees was Irish. While enrolled in Company G of the Connecticut National Guard with my grandfather Walter Edward Monagan, he got his name into the newspaper for pulling outrageous pranks against the company commander – who was none other than his buddy Chan Goss. The newspapers mention him running off to the earliest automobile races, and in August 1908 renting a sizeable early motorboat with his friends to cruise Long Island Sound as far as Newport and Block Island, just when his cousin Rena (Nolan) Miller was staying for a fortnight with about a dozen young females like herself, including more Nolan cousins.

On January 19, 1904, "Willie" had taken the hand in marriage of one Elizabeth Lawlor, a daughter of a large Waterbury Irish-American family of similarly rising success. Elizabeth's brother went to both Holy Cross and Yale Law with my grandfather Walter. Elizabeth was a fine soprano singer and her name is mentioned in performances across Connecticut for many years. Her repertoire ranged from sentimental favorites like "Come Back to Erin" to classical Schubert lieder. Many decades later my parents were still warmly associated with this extended family.

William and Elizabeth Lawlor Monagan bought their first house in the hillside Waterbury district called Brooklyn, which was comprised of a colorful mix of Lithuanians, Poles, Irish, and Italians. Although the couple never had children, they were a constant presence at family gatherings. Willie was obviously a popular guy, and a superb golfer. By 1916 (or earlier) he was admitted to the Waterbury County Club, which was a leap into the inner sanctum of Waterbury's old Wasp hierarchy. But it appears that none of the blue bloods had a golf game to compare with Willie Monagan. The Goss family may have been involved with the new membership.

After all, in 1910, when aged 34, my great uncle William Monagan had been made the head of all daytime brass casting at Scovill's – which at that point had about 9,000 employees. The diligently trained son of John Stephen must have received a whopping raise in reaching that level, since by the end of the year William and his wife Elizabeth took up rooms as full-time residents in the swank new **Elton Hotel,** facing the town's two-acre tree-lined central Green. This colonnaded beaux-arts structure, which still proudly stands, has a large history. On the site before had stood the landmark "Scovill House" inn – originally built as one of that illustrious family's residences until a terrible fire in 1902 razed it and some 40 surrounding buildings. Wealthy families like the Scovill's and that of John S. Elton, the founder of the rival Waterbury Brass Company, responded by pouring in money to create a far grander replacement, which was called the Elton Hotel. The place affected a high style and made money from the moment it opened in 1904. The lavishly corniced and marbled entrance way opened to multiple restaurants and ballrooms and a gleaming tap room. Upstairs the residential suites offered brocaded wallpaper and every possible amenity, including the brilliant new idea of bed-side telephones. The Goss family and their friends (with servants) took up several of the most expansive suites. And five decades later

The Elton in its glory days.

Waterbury was booming then.

John Fitzgerald Kennedy essentially would wrap up his campaign to become president of the United States of America by standing on that Eltons Hotel's balcony with Congressman John S. Monagan at his side and calling for tens of thousands of the intensely Catholic town's citizens to vote for him.

Around the time that William and Elizabeth took up residence in the Elton, money was not a big issue for the upper echelons of the Scovill Manufacturing Company – for the world had fallen in love with brass. California had seen its "Gold Rush," come and go. But Waterbury was still in the throes of its "Brass Rush" and this was spinning off wealth every which way. In the closely held, family-styled Scovill business, top performers were well rewarded indeed. Thus William and Elizabeth managed a luxurious cruise to Bermuda in November in 1913 – a favorite destination, by the way, for the Monagan family in general for a number of years.

Once World War I started in 1914, the clamor of America's allies for brass shell casings and other military goods immediately generated many millions of dollars of new business in Waterbury. When the U. S. began gearing up for its own 1917 entry into the Great War, things took off to a new level. Scovill's kept throwing together new production facilities until there were at least 100 buildings in its complex. As my cousin Charles Monagan noted in **Waterbury: A Region Reborn,** "During World War I [Scovill] was to manufacture some 2 billion brass cups for cartridge shells, 443 million bullet jackets, 21 million time-fuses for shrapnel, and 19 million 75mm shell cases, just to name a few items." Long lines of newly arriving immigrants from Italy and Lithuania in particular queued before the employment window every morning – and often got hired on the spot. Scovill's by this point had 17,000 workers and was running flat-out 24-hours a day. The whole Naugatuck Valley was working at the same fever pitch. The biggest and most feverishly growing rival, the American Brass company, had its own 16,000 workers and sold $1 billion in goods to the war effort.

By this point Howard Miller, the nephew of Anna Nolan Monagan, living still in the Monagan's Spencer Avenue house, had attained a position of considerable power beside William as a superintendent of operations for all of Scovill's workings. His charge was to maintain a constant seamless flow of production across the sprawling complex. Meanwhile, other Nolans, as well as Bernice's husband Arthur Owen Nelson, also had their shoulders hard to Scovill's great industrial wheel. My great-grandfather John Stephen seems to have eased out of the night casting operations by around 1913. But he must have often been overcome with pride with this mind-boggling display of family progress from its past of great destitution.

The end of World War on November 11, 1918 found William Henry and Elizabeth Lawlor Monagan still very thick with Waterbury's swell set at the Elton. Elizabeth's singing must have added pzazz to many parties, and William cemented many friendships through his gift of humor and great flair at golf, which he obviously honed even further at the Waterbury Country Club. For several years he represented the club and Waterbury in general as an elite player at the Connecticut state golf championships. Meanwhile, the Elton's panache was only growing. Before long, it was advertised as the perfect place to begin what was called the "Ideal Tour," with stops at similarly grand hostelries in Manchester, Vermont; Boston; Lake Sunapee, Mount Washington, and so on. The famous American writers F. Scott Fitzgerald and James Thurber variously stayed at the Elton before long.

The Elton was also becoming even more desirable as a full-time residence. It was managed by the Judd family, who owned a large chunk of nearby Middlebury, and it was home to at least two Goss couples – George, the vice president of Scovill's, and his wife Estelle; plus William and Mary Goss. Sherwood Roland and his wife (from generations-long friends of the Monagans) were other residents – he would effectively manage the city of Waterbury at various points. Physicians and property developers lived there too. Some of the residential suites had sufficient space to house personal servants in their suitably distanced rooms somewhere down the hall.

But a whisper of unease began to spread around Waterbury at this time. With the end of World War I, the soaring demand for brass products fell back considerably, even as Scovill's became locked in ever deeper competition with the constantly expanding, and frenetically innovative American Brass Company. That outfit kept gobbling up major brass competitors as far away as Wisconsin and upstate New York, where in 1917 it acquired the 5,000-employee Buffalo Copper and Brass Rolling Mills. Then in 1922 a bomb effectively dropped on Waterbury when the massive conglomerate of the Montana-based **Anaconda Copper and Mining Company** bought out the entire holdings of American Brass Company. Controlling both the raw materials that make brass and half the final production capacity for that alloy in America, Anaconda had the entire industry between its teeth and set to fixing prices and dictating the terms of supply wholesale to the farthest reaches of the brass industry. Suddenly a much lesser player, the Scovill Manufacturing Company panicked. In the face of such a ferocious new competitor, the company initiated a top-to-bottom analysis of its old school, chummy ways of doing business. A new class of efficiency experts, who the workers called "hatchet men," were brought in by John Goss in a desperate push to ramp up mechanization, combined with slashing labor costs by eliminating hundreds if not thousands of jobs. Great golfer he might be, but

William Henry Monagan was one of those who came out on the short end of this company-wide revamping. The verdict appeared to be that he was overpaid, too close to management, and a relic set upon older ways of making brass. When the beans were all counted, Willie Monagan, the once bosom buddy of Chan Goss, was given his walking papers.

Perhaps a gentle separation was initially attempted. According to various city directories William and Elizabeth were still enjoying the swell life at the Elton until late in 1922. Also William may have been doing some brass casting work on the side in Bridgeport by 1919. The Goss's could have even helped with that. Then in 1923, William found a new job as a "superintendent of casting shops" at an unnamed enterprise in West Hartford. But that stint was short-lived, and things seemed to unravel further. Maybe he was falling behind technologically. What's clear is that the couple next moved to New Haven where William became part owner of a coal supply business – which also failed. But Elizabeth kept at her singing as a much admired soprano across the state. Of course, by 1929, the Great Depression had hit and with that crisis businesses were failing by the tens of thousands across the land.

A year or two later, the New Haven city directories were showing William to be "working in a credit department." Next, he was in "insurance and real estate." Maybe Waterbury – which he could get to in under an hour when he wanted – had left a bad taste. It must have helped that also living around New Haven was his sister Helen Monagan Marks. Finally, William shifted jobs yet again to become a "turn key" or warden in the county jail in nearby Hamden. Give him credit, for William was rapidly promoted to superintendent of the entire facility while in his 60s. He died on March 7, 1946. His widow Elizabeth moved back to Waterbury in 1955, where she had a large extended family all along.

The Millers and the Monagans

Soon after William Monagan moved out of 15 Spencer Avenue, his place was taken by Anna's orphaned niece and nephew from Bristol, Lorena and

Joseph Howard Miller. Happily, this duo became all but sister and brother to the rest and stayed on for years.

Lorena's travails have been discussed – her mother Catherine Nolan dying at a tragic childbirth in 1889, the father Thomas Miller latching on to a gal half his age in 1895, only to die prematurely himself in 1902. Lorena had dropped out of school when her aunt "Annie" decided, with John Stephen's blessings, to invite her and her brother to come live with them in Waterbury in early 1904.

This regrafting of a splintered family into a new whole worked out remarkably well. At Waterbury's Notre Dame Academy, Rena was given every opportunity to rediscover a level of promise and opportunity that had been stolen from her life so early on. She became an outstanding student, and the following year Lorena finished second in her class and was asked to give the salutatorian address at her graduation on July 23, 1906. Considering what the girl had been through, one can imagine the swell of pride that had to have been felt not only by her aunt Anna, but also her 81-year-old grandmother Mary Clark Nolan who was living nearby on Round Hill Street with her son James. Just two weeks after this, according to the *Hartford Courant* of July 6, my great-grandfather John Stephen Monagan was whisking Rena off with two of his daughters for an extended holiday, of which and he wanted people to know. "The Misses Anna Monoghan [sic] and Lorena Miller, Mrs. F. L. Marks [meaning the newly married Helen Monagan], and J.S. Monoghan have left for Ridgefield where they intend spending the summer," the item read.

Lorena Miller, Ridgefield 1906.

In the autumn, Lorena landed a job as a stenographer at Waterbury's Colonial Trust bank, a very desirable entry job for a young woman of that era. Things were going so nicely that the *Hartford Courant* of July 28, 1909, named Lorena as being among a pack of thirteen young Connecticut women, chiefly of Waterbury, who were about to spend two weeks on holiday together on Block Island for a great lark. Among the group was a Patience Miller, likely a cousin from the remaining clan in Bristol. As noted, "Willie" Monagan and a crew of male friends rented a flash motorboat on the Connecticut shore then and stopped off to meet the young ladies. The 1910 census showed that Lorena's brother Joseph Howard Miller, though only 21, was already a "foreman in a brass shop."

Rena and Howard Miller lived at 15 Spencer Avenue for nearly the rest of their lives. In the early years, Lorena was listed in the Waterbury city directories as a stenographer, but her responsibilities in the bank increased steadily. Howard rose rapidly to become a "superintendent of operations" at Scovill's, a powerful plant manager. Neither ever married. One curiosity is that on the eve of America's entry into World War 1, with German U-Boats ranging wide, the still single Lorena set off on March 12, 1917, on a leisurely holiday break to Cuba, island of rum and hot sun. Port records in New York on April 6, 1917, show her – now 28 years-old – arriving aboard the cruise ship *Morro Castle* from Havana, and affirming that she was born in Bristol, Connecticut.

Howard Miller, amidst caskets.

Snapshots From Waterbury's History

North Main Street in its heyday.

Noonan's "Café" across from Scovill's and run by our
Windsor Street neighbours.

Scovill's origins were in buttons – millions of them.

Civil War buttons
from Scovill's.

Fourten million brass shells were launched at Verdun.
The name of Waterbury was well accounted for.

After that, Lorena simply settled back into everyday life in the Monagan household on Spencer Avenue. But at the census of 1920, she took to calling herself "Marie." She was also promoted to Assistant Trust Manager in her bank, while serving as a notary public with her own office on West Main Street. Finally her listings in the Waterbury city directories stop in 1928 when she may have even moved to Manhattan for reasons completely unknown. It was there in any case that she abruptly died at the age of 42 on March 22, 1930. But she too was buried in St. Joseph's Cemetery in Bristol beside her mother Catherine Nolan Miller and Nolan grandparents Patrick and Mary. When all is said and done, Lorena Miller's brother Howard was another puzzling figure. He obviously was a young man of considerable ability who soared through the ranks at Scovill's. Congressman Monagan would later describe him as "practically the de facto ruler of the mills." He seems to have been given an exemption from military service in WW I due to his importance in munitions manufacturing. Various photographs indicate that he was quite close to Charles and Walter Monagan through all these years. But he seemed to have led a quiet, retiring life, without ever making a splash on the Waterbury social scene. He too died young, at the age of but 41 in 1932, the cause unknown.

The Mystery of Kate Monagan Gregg

There was one other new resident in the Spencer Avenue household in the run up to 1910, and this was the second daughter Catherine Elizabeth Monagan, who was born in April 1874. Her story and that of her mysterious husband George Gregg has been saved for last because it is extraordinary. Catherine, who quickly became known as Kate, was clearly born with stars in her eyes. In 1893 and when only 18 years-old, she said goodbye to Waterbury and took a room all by herself in the Connecticut state capital of Hartford. Though only 32 miles north, this to her was a far more glamorous place due to its numerous theatrical and musical venues at that time. Above, all Catherine adored the stage, and some said if you could make it in Hartford with a big opening run, you might land on Broadway in a nonce. There strangely does not seem to have been much resistance offered by my great-grandparents. Note that in certain historic family photographs, my great-grandmother "Annie" sports a slightly hilarious look and has an outlandish touch in dressing that suggests she comported herself with a theatrical flair. Perhaps she too once had dreams of the stage. She may have even had a musical gift and sung around the house, since at least three of her girls were keenly interested in music, and William Henry married a polished singer in Elizabeth Lawlor. The more one examines things, Anna seems to have been the person who orchestrated much of the family's social evolution. She and John were clearly a dynamic duo, two very exceptional people in many regards, who together rose into a way of living that could never have been predicted from their humble roots.

Pragmatically, Hartford was simply not very far away from Waterbury and in that first year of Catherine's move her mother knew she would have enjoyed the protective eye of her older brother Charles, who was finishing up at Trinity College there. His star performances on the college's baseball field would have also provided a pleasant occasion for many short train journeys for the family to come up from Waterbury and perhaps enjoy a picnic with their young daughter, too.

Hartford at the time was a fairly bustling city of 80,000, and not short on affluence. Lovers of the performing arts had the Majestic Theater, Poli's Vaudeville House, the Bon Ton Burlesque, and Apel's Opera House to choose from, along with many side venues for amateur and professional troupes alike. So many national touring companies and major New York theaters adopted Hartford as a place to polish up their newest developing productions that a truly grandiose playhouse called the Parson's Theater was opened in 1896. Compared to Bristol or Waterbury, Hartford was another world back then, classier and swanker and with direct links to the "Big Time" of New York.

The 18-year-old Catherine's first success was to land a day job as a stenographer. But she was chasing the theater from the start. She certainly had some affectations, among these being a penchant for fiddling with her and our family's names. My aunt Marjorie Monagan Kelly has suggested that this was the daughter who pushed hardest for an upgrade of the historic "Monaghan" name to a more modern (to her ears) "Monagan." She turned her name Catherine into Katherine while she was at it, then became "Kittie" and next "Kittie. I. Monagan." Was that her burlesque name? In the Hartford city directory she morphed into "Monagan, Kate I." and with the "I" perhaps after some stage name. Whether this "I" was for Irene or Iphigenia or something else, no one knows. This was possibly another Kittie concoction.

Along the way, Kate fell in love with a dashing young man called "Georgie" Winslow Gregg, Jr., whose father George was a prominent Hartford businessman and popular character about town. Katherine's beau no doubt also had much charm to go with his good looks. His father George owned the premier carriage dealership in the city, and raised his own thoroughbreds, including one called "Idol" who had hit it big as a racer and sire. The father also owned a modest Sumatra-leaf tobacco farm within the city limits, which was a nice extra asset since that Connecticut River valley crop was prized worldwide.

"Georgie" Gregg was an only son and a hothouse flower. He was certainly an avid and flamboyant denizen of the local theaters, both in performing and working backstage, whether in set design, lighting or construction. In this world George Gregg, Jr., seems to have been living and spending large. As early as 1895 the *Hartford Courant* noted that young George, 21, was training a mighty race horse of his own. In 1897 he was violently thrown by a colt and broke his collarbone, and "Georgie's" injury made a splash in the Hartford Courant. But almost everything the parents Alice and George did jumped into the press, even when the father called reporters with outlandish stories just for fun. He was a prized raconteur at the Gentleman's Driving Club.

Ultimately, Catherine Elizabeth Monagan – Kate – married young George in nearby Farmington, Connecticut on November 17, 1898. Strangely, there does not seem to have been any newspaper articles about the event. Perhaps the affair was kept modest due to the Gregg family's mounting but very hidden financial difficulties. Or maybe there was something else to hide since the Greggs had otherwise sought attention from the Hartford press for many earlier years. Their house at 165 Capen Avenue, where Kate immediately took up residence, was a stately affair with eleven large rooms with many bay windows, multiple porches, and several outbuildings, including a six-stall horse barn and a substantial carriage house. In addition to the newlyweds, the 1900 census reveals there also to have been resident a daughter named Florence Elizabeth Gregg, aged nine, who was either physically handicapped or emotionally troubled or both.

The best of times, the worst of times. A charming beachside photograph of the newly married couple was taken around 1899-1900 from the relatively close resort of **Block Island**, Rhode Island. The picture includes both intimates and a couple of outsiders who squeezed in just for the fun. There are two main props – a donkey cart, and a giant teddy bear – that were the stock and trade gimmicks of a particular roving Block Island photographer beckoning in subjects for his next shoot for a number of years along "State Beach," as it is called now. To the right of this jocular group stands my great-grandmother Anna in a sort of Japanese silk pants suit – this is quite a flamboyant presentation and possibly reflects some new production at the recently opened Block Island theater, since touring vaudeville acts were a constant summer presence along the Rhode Island shore in those days.

Sitting atop the donkey is a youngish couple who are possibly William Henry Monagan and his eventual bride Elizabeth Lawlor. But the main fascination lies in a handsome, chuckling and mildly epicene young man with a bow tie lolling in the sand beside both the donkey cart and the giant teddy bear. This has to be "Georgie." Touching at his shoulder is a lovely, buxom young lady in an elegant white lace dress – by all lights Kate Monagan Gregg. Behind her on the actual donkey cart are two other women in white lace – possibly Minnie and Helen but the likenesses in this slightly hazy photo do not clearly come across – and beside them are a couple of what in Ireland are called "notice boxes" (people who stick themselves into things where they don't

A vision from old Block Island, with mother Anna in kimono, Georgie Gregg (?) holding teddy bear and Kitty at his shoulder. Possibly William Henry Monagan on the donkey.

belong). The essence of this photo may well be tied to a new act appearing at the theater at the center of the little Block Island village of New Shoreham that had been converted from a roller-skating rink in 1897. Or maybe George and Kate simply called for a big party the summer following their wedding. This fun-loving young couple were certainly prized company in Hartford for a little while. The *Hartford Courant* of February 11, 1901, paints a winter scene of especial elan. A fresh snow had fallen the day before, prompting scores of young gallants to join together for a rollicking series of horse-drawn sleigh races through the central Bushnell Park and its adjoining streets. George Gregg, Jr., no doubt with Kate at his side, was featured as a singular swell in the crowd, with the journalist hinting that he had a few $50 bills to wager on whatever best bets caught his eye – this was no "chump change" for that era. And why not, since the writer noted that "Georgie" Gregg, Jr., happened to be featuring his own stunning race horse named "Rex Nutwood."

At this time the city directory said that Kate was employed by the family business as a buyer of fine carriages or their accoutrement, and George Jr. was doing whatever was his role as his father's "clerk." It made no mention of the countless hours he was devoting to his true love, the stage. The real story was that the father was failing both physically and financially. Worried about a looming lawsuit and mounting debts concerning his fine big house, he had quietly transferred ownership of his business jointly to George Jr. and my great aunt, now legally "Katherine I. Gregg." This would appear to be her fourth name change since 1893.

In what seems to have been the final execution of a carefully crafted plan, George Jr. and Katherine together filed for bankruptcy on the last day of 1901. Kate listed her assets as totaling a not-so-swanky $159.00, while George Jr. declared that he had $416.30 to his name. (Not a lot when bragging about making $50 bets on a lark.) Nonetheless, George and Kate kept living beyond their means. Ultimately, the father grew gravely ill in April 1902 and died within three weeks. The newspapers were told that the wife Alice Burt Gregg was too ill to attend her own husband's burial in New Britain. This could have been either physically true – since she too died before long – or psychologically so.

The Gregg family legacy kept crumbling. By November the big house was put up for sale. But there were no takers, and the following May of 1903 the banks foreclosed and drove the family into much humbler quarters. Acrimony festered. George's mother Alice Burt Gregg was by now suffering from cancer, and abandoned Hartford around 1905 for Long Island City, New York. She simply left her two children to fend on their own – one the spendthrift George, the other, the daughter Florence, some special kind of mess. The daughter Florence was clearly troubled and must have contributed to the rancor. She was soon enrolled semi-permanently into the nearby "Newington Home for the Incurables," whether for physical or psychiatric reasons or both.

The mother Alice died in the Bronx, New York on February 11, 1907. Her will was spiteful, specifying that everything she had left was to be bequeathed to institutionalized Florence alone. To George (and thus also to Kate Monagan) all she offered was deathbed absolution from his various debts to her. That is not a mother's kindest possible parting. All this travail had to have hastened the end of the marriage of the once fun-loving young thespians, my great aunt Kate and her possibly binge-drinking George. There was no child to bind them. Kate Monagan gave it all up and moved back to the family homestead in Waterbury, even though her oldest sister "Minnie" had a way of casting a very stern eye upon her. Around this point in time, Kate insisted on being called Elizabeth.

The whole scene with husband George must have gone strange. His erratic sister Florence Gregg alleged years later that upon institutionalizing her he said he wanted to throw away the key. George later swore this was not true. But he seems to have cracked up a little, too. From the historic Block Island photograph and many later signals, and the basic trajectory of the rest of his life, one is given to wonder whether he fled from his marriage because he realized that he was not actually meant to be very heterosexual at all.

What certainly did happen is that George left Hartford and his marriage by at least 1907 to work as a stagehand with the company of **George M. Cohan**, America's most celebrated song writer, actor, and producer all rolled into one. The star of stars, George Cohan was called "Mister Broadway" and his hit songs came by the dozens – among them "Yankee Doodle Dandy," "You're a Grand Old Flag" and "Over There!" He was an American icon and George Gregg chose a life of constant touring back and forth across North America to work with his company rather than be constricted by wife or children or any responsibility beyond himself.

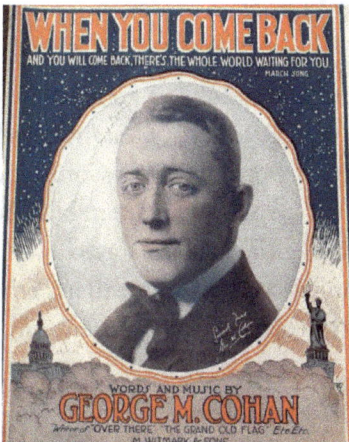

A brilliant songwriter and showman, George M. Cohan was one
of the most famous Irish showmen of all time.

Because Hartford's theatrical scene had been so splendidly active in these years, George Gregg would have enjoyed numerous opportunities for meeting the great George Cohan himself, as well as his stage production foreman. In 1906 and 1907 alone, Cohan's company ran at least five new productions through Hartford. These included *Little Johnny Jones* at Parson's Theater on Christmas 1906, *Running for Office* at the Hartford Opera House in February 1907, and at Parsons's in October 1907. One way or another George Gregg had to have personally met George Cohan (occasionally rumored to be homosexual himself, but with no evidence). The rest was history and consigned to it also now was his marriage to Catherine Elizabeth Monagan, with all her spellings.

The heart-broken "Kate" thus retreated alone to the Monagan family house at 15 Spencer Avenue around 1903. She landed a job soon enough as a stenographer with the lawyer John Cassidy. Year after year she stuck to this lonely role, while possibly receiving occasional communications from her mercurial husband who kept traveling the land with the great George Cohan and his "Yankee Doodle" band. She evidently never made any attempt to divorce her own "Georgie," but of course that prospect remained anathema to Catholics a century ago.

But Catherine did step out for at least one great hurrah around the third week of October 1915 when she treated herself at age 40 to a great getaway cruise to Bermuda. She stayed for at least five weeks on that pleasant island. She is listed as Katherine (with a "K") E. Gregg, born in Bristol, Connecticut, when disembarking from a luxury liner called the *SS Bermudan* in New York on November 29, 1915. Five weeks seems a long time to have stayed away at this cold time of year all alone at this age, unless there was more to it. Perhaps she was even embarking on some kind of trial reunion with her husband?

According to the Waterbury city directories, Kate stuck around at Spencer Avenue for at most two more years after that. But then she hied off to New York City, as far as the family knew then or still does now. For whatever reasons, she did not appear at the family gala honoring her parent's 50 years in marriage on November 18, 1919, where practically every single other relative was on the scene. So what happened? My aunt Marjorie, now 100, does remember Kate appearing at her parents' Euclid Avenue house and settling into a long talk alone with her mother one time in the late 1920s, when Marge may have been only six or seven herself. "I got quite interested because she had arrived in a taxi, which nobody did in Waterbury back then," Margie recalled. "What we heard was that she was looking for money after trying to visit her sister Minnie at Doctor Charles's house on Cooke Street. But Minnie wouldn't even open the door over there. So she came to my mother next." At this point, the desperate Kate Monagan would have been over 50 years-old, so this is not a pretty story.

Within a few years of his initial stage touring, George Gregg began facing some terrible new challenges. That's made clear via his World War I draft registration card as made out on September 12, 1918, in Wheeling, West Virginia. He declares his employment to be as a "field manager and time keeper" at the weird new community called **Nitro, West Virginia**, which was then producing 100,000 pounds of high explosives a day for the U.S. war effort against Germany. The registrant's entries indicate that George (with the spot-on middle name of Winslow and hailing from Connecticut) is now "blind in left eye and deficient in right eye." This sounds as if a test batch of Nitro's nitro blew up in his face, although late-onset blindness can occur for other reasons.

The idea is purely speculative, but one wonders if Katherine Elizabeth Monagan might have at this time tried to be a soothing presence in George Greggs life once again. Perhaps it was at his side that Kate remained during the family's historic reunion in 1919. However, in the census of 1920 George appears on West 24th Street in Manhattan residing with dozens of mostly men in a place called the Cotton House, while working as a "foreman," presumably of a stage crew. Kate Monagan Gregg is not a co-resident, although she too is thought to have been somewhere else in town.

But the story gets stranger still. By this point George's sister Florence had finished up at a state trade school after years at the "Newington Home for the Incurables" and was finally off on her own. In the late 1920s she fell in with a wealthy older man named Mylan Agustus Stafford who owned several properties around Wethersfield, Connecticut. They were married in 1929 when Florence was 39 and Mylan was about 70, but this relationship had no chance. The *Hartford Courant* of February 21, 1931, explained: "A divorce was asked by Mylon A. Stafford, 72, of Mansfield from Florence Gregg Stafford of Hartford on the grounds that the defendant was an imbecile. Mrs. Stratford strenuously contests the charges. Stafford has been married twice before." The divorce was approved and Florence was awarded alimony of $10 a week.

Later, at the age of 80, Mylan killed himself with three cyanide tablets. By then Florence Gregg had remarried to a parking lot attendant named Harry Clifford Jones of Glastonbury. The two were church-goers, with Florence often attending Christ Church Cathedral (Episcopal) in Hartford. There her prayers were answered. On December 23, 1946 Florence was stunned when a policeman knocked on her door with her brother George, now completely blind, at his side. It had been nearly 40 years since they had last seen each other. Florence burst into tears, exclaiming "I have a brother!" Led by the policeman, the three began singing Christmas carols into the starry eve.

All of this back story has arisen from the recent discovery of various items in an upstate New York newspaper called the *Ticonderoga Sentinel*, which helped to pinpoint George W. Gregg, the former Hartford scion, as living hermetically in the slightly artsy community of **Schroon Lake** in the late 1930s and 1940s. This was not far from other historic Adirondack resorts like Lake George and Lake Placid that had long hosted top summer theater. The *Ticonderoga Sentinel* of February 20, 1941, had noted that he was in hospital, apparently for a last-ditch eye operation. The same paper of June 3, 1943, ran this small story: "Have you seen the good looking belts and leather pocket books that George Gregg is making to sell? George has been taught to do this by a teacher of the blind and is being taught to read Braille. Doc Lyons will display them for him."

George, also now a regular church-goer and a passionate choir singer, clearly sensed that his time on earth was ending, and he wanted to gain closure with his sister, whose whereabouts remained quite unknown to him. As things played out, on November 11, 1945, George inquired about an unfamiliar voice he heard singing at that Armistice Day's church ceremonies. He was told that this belonged to a visiting Connecticut State Trooper named Frederick Feegle who was a friend of the minister, Reverend Frederick Errington. George asked Reverend Errington if the trooper might help locate his long-lost sister in Connecticut, but what made this task a hard challenge was that Florence's name had changed at least twice via marriage, first with the aged husband with the cyanide tablets, second with the parking lot attendant. Finally, the long-awaited word of her location surfaced over the phone. Then, just before Christmas in 1946, the Reverend Errington drove George to Connecticut and with the Trooper Feegle thereupon assuming the lead, the three found their way to the front door of Mrs. Florence Gregg Jones in Glastonbury and stood side-by-side singing carols of joy as she opened the door to that remarkable Christmas encounter. Their astonishing reunion and catch-up time together continued for five days. But alas, by the next January, George Winslow Gregg was dead.

Whether Katherine Elizabeth Monagan Gregg, Georgie's bride of 1898, had any contact with the former Hartford idol in his last years is not known. The Adirondack newspaper articles make no such reference, and the last and very iffy written record pointing to this long lost aunt suggests that her days possibly ended in the Bronx, New York in March 1952. But the story does have one beautiful extra twist. An astounding mid-to-late 1940s photograph of Helen Monagan Marks has recently been forwarded by Helen's grand-daughter Kristy Menold Horstkamp. It is wonderful because of the nearly identical looking woman standing close to Helen, who is similarly at least well into her sixties. These two are absolutely sisters. The visiting sister here cannot be Bernice, who died in 1932, or Minnie, who died in 1938. That leaves only one choice, which is Katherine Elizabeth, who in say 1947 would be aged 70. Yet here she has reappeared for one last joyous reunion with Helen, who was by now growing gravely ill and died in 1949. It is a very touching picture of sisters reunited at last.

Sisters reunited at last, circa 1947.
Helen center, Kate right. Courtesy Kristy Menhold Hortkamp.

Helen and Fred Marks in their later years.

XI.

GENERATIONS CHANGE

Euclidean Monagans

As the twentieth century's second decade unfolded, my grandparents Walter Edward Monagan and Mary Elizabeth Butler were busy filling up their three-story house at 84 Euclid Avenue with a new generation of Monagans.

Theirs was one of the more pleasant districts of Waterbury's northside. Named after the ancient Greek mathematician who is considered "the father of geometry," the tree-lined **Euclid Avenue** was thus proportioned along neat lines, with a small triangular parklet in its midst. At this house my grandparents would raise seven children, beginning with my uncle Walter Edward Monagan, Jr., who was born on June 12, 1911, and was destined to become a Yale-educated lawyer just like his father. On April 7, 1913, there arrived a second son named William Henry. Next was the debonair Charles Andrew or "Andy," born on December 31, 1915. On March 6, 1918, my father John Stephen Monagan arrived. He would eventually take to calling himself in formal situations John S. Monagan III, to help stave off confusion. Next, came a trio of sisters: Louise Ann in 1920; Marjorie in 1922; and Joan Marie in 1928.

In addition to raising this large family, my grandfather Walter Monagan was a busy man professionally from his earliest days after graduating from the Yale Law School. He rapidly forged a partnership in the leading Waterbury firm that became **Carmody, Monagan and Larkin.** Numerous references to his formidable presence in the law courts can be found in the Connecticut newspapers from this era. In addition to his services as Waterbury's Commissioner of Education, beginning when he was only 25 years-old, he also became a representative in the Connecticut State Legislature, and was elected a secretary for the Knights of Columbus, a key social group for the Waterbury Irish. In 1912, the *Norwich Bulletin* reports that he presented the keynote speech to the region's annual Holy Cross alumni gathering at the Hotel Taft in New Haven. At different times, Walter was president of the Waterbury chapter of the alumni of Holy Cross College, president of the Waterbury Bar Association, and "Exalted Ruler" of the Waterbury Elks Club.

Walter's law firm maintained offices at 153 Chestnut Avenue. Like everyone, he had to fill out a standard questionnaire in 1917 as part of his registering for the U.S. military draft. Then 35, he had already served six years in the Connecticut National Guard as a sergeant and explained that he had certain limitations: To wit, he could not drive a car, motorcycle or boat; operate a wireless; understand telegraphy or navigate. But he said he could ride a horse and handle a team of them.

Congressman Monagan (who would later work for my grandfather Walter) in his memoir recollected that Walter "developed into one of the outstanding lawyers in the state. He was extremely active as a trier of cases and his questioning and somewhat sardonic mind made him a formidable cross-examiner. He worked hard in preparation and, as an example, knew exactly the distances in the courtroom from bench to sheriff's stand and from jury box to witness stand." The latter sounds like the recipe for a born courtroom performer.

The 1920s were a time of considerable upheaval in the United States, beginning with the spreading of tremendous labor unrest, including in Waterbury where the increasing mechanization of the brass mills, and resultant elimination of countless jobs, provoked several mass strikes. The social fabric was twisting under many contradictions and extremes by now. The supposed total ban of alcohol sales under the Volstead Act was supposed to have become the national gospel by 1920. But in the cities, and maybe in the Elton Hotel when curtains were drawn, this was an era of startling new freedoms, and provocative new dress and dance styles – a.k.a. the "Roaring Twenties." The prohibition act was evidently regarded as something of a joke by my grandfather and probably about everyone he knew. Through long associations with Waterbury's Knights of Columbus and Elks Club, bootleg beer and liquor was undoubtedly steadily available through these years.

Even more profound change arrived in 1929 in the form of **The Great Depression**. That thunderous blow to the world's economy began in the United States with the stock market crash of "Black Friday" on September 4, 1929. Before you could say "Wall Street," banks began to fail by the hundreds while unemployment rose by a factor of 600 percent. Businesses of all sizes collapsed and the industrial output of the U.S. dropped by a whopping 46 percent. New investments in most everything dried up across great reaches of the country. For nearly a decade, millions of people scraped for even marginal employment and many among the swelling underclass effectively gave up hope. But at long last, the pendulum swung back and a great economic rebound began to take hold in America around 1937.

In truth, the Depression never hit Connecticut remotely as hard as it did the American South and West. In particular the Waterbury Monagans seemed to skip away from its path. Even as the nation struggled as a whole, my grandfather Walter appears in the 1930 census as presiding over an 84 Euclid Avenue household that now included yet another personal servant. And he clearly indulged himself now and then in the forbidden "Satan's Brew." An immigration report from the Port of New York in August 1931, for example, shows Walter and Mary returning there on the ocean liner *The Majestic,* which ran back and forth to Halifax, Nova Scotia from New York as a fabled "booze cruise." Prohibition may have long and ridiculously reigned on "dry land" but once you got offshore in 1931 all that changed, and Halifax made its name as one of the great party destinations of the time. Further, the White Star Line's Majestic lived up to its name in its every fitting. Weighing in at 56,551 tons and powered by multiple express turbines, she was said to be the largest steamer in the world, and boasted lavish palm courts, gilded bars and restaurants and a first class lounge fit for royalty. Winston Churchill was one of many famous people later to cruise on board this ship.

In July 1936 another record from the Port of New York reveals my grandparents' fresh return from a gala vacation clear across the Atlantic. This was on board the *RMS Virginian,* sometimes called *The Virginia* and more often the *SS Drottningholm,* as it was an ocean liner making trans-Atlantic crossings for that Swedish-American line. Maybe it was about then that Walter's career had reached its pinnacle. Or maybe this trip was just a lavish celebration of some very handsome returns realized from earlier investments in the likes of the Perkdell Holding Corporation of Waterbury and the Electric Merchandise Company of New Milford (the forerunner of the Connecticut state electric utility).

Charles Monagan's Family

After gaining his medical degree from the University of Pennsylvania in 1898, Charles Monagan returned to Waterbury and became a general practitioner, while developing a specialty in obstetrics. However, he found it sufficiently difficult to gain access as an attending physician to the then "waspy" Waterbury Hospital that he joined with other young Irish Catholic doctors to try to devise a new alternative. Their solution was to band with the Sisters of St. Joseph of Chambery to create a new Catholic hospital called **St. Mary's** in 1907. That institution grew dramatically over the next decades and has long since thrived as a teaching hospital for the Yale School of Medicine. I myself was born there.

As noted, John and Anna Monagan's oldest daughter Minnie was a pioneering force in advancing in-school health monitoring and nursing in Waterbury, where many children were still growing up in crowded tenements. Charles was the attending doctor for many years to this vital health service; and as Waterbury's Commissioner for Education from 1907-1911, my grandfather Walter Monagan helped create its initial framework.

A popular man about town, Charles enjoyed leadership positions in several of Waterbury's civic and social clubs. His military draft registration questionnaire in early 1918 revealed that he weighed 190 pounds and was precisely 5 feet, 8 and ¾ inches tall and could still handle a team of horses. However, his first son, the Connecticut Congressman, made it clear that his father by then adored a classic Packard roadster. Acquiring such a "hot rod" early on, he must have made heads turn when driving down Waterbury's thoroughfares.

But it was not until February 14, 1911, that Charles married at the Church of St. Francis Xavier in Manhattan a 13-years-younger Margaret Mulry, a beautiful daughter of an Irish-American family that had prospered in the banking world close to there. It is interesting that Charles chose as his best man his cousin Howard Miller, rather than either of his brothers. That same year he and Margaret moved into a sizeable house at 64 Cooke Street, just a few minutes above the town's central Green, and a short walk from Fulton Park. There the couple had six children, beginning with John Stephen Monagan, the future politician, who was born on December 23, 1911. He was followed by a sister named Parthenia on May 22, 1913. She lived but five years, dying on May 23, 1918.

On November 29, 1915, the couple next had a son named Thomas Mulry Monagan who grew up to become a beloved Waterbury pediatrician. Then came the daughters Margaret Mary on June 28, 1916, and Mary Elizabeth on December 13, 1917. Margaret or "Peggy" never married and spent most of her life in New York City. Mary Elizabeth graduated from the College of Mount Saint Vincent in 1938 and worked as a teacher before marrying the outdoor advertising maven Richard Murphy, who was a much admired Waterbury personality.

Sadly, Charles's wife Margaret died from the global "Spanish" flu epidemic soon after the birth of a third son, Charles Andrew, Jr., on January 22, 1920. The infant also shortly died as well. With astonishing compassion, Charles's sister Mary Agnes, the school nurse, almost instantly moved in to help her brother look after his distraught and deeply needy four surviving children. To this supreme sacrifice "Aunt Min," as they called her, would devote the

215

Dr. Charles trying out his fabulous new motor car with a young fan looking on.

final 18 years of her life. Mary Agnes managed not only to bring a sustaining stability back into this household, even while carrying on with her own very demanding career, but to light a spark in each of her young charges. JSM recalled years later, "She gave up everything for us." But he as the oldest appears to have locked horns with her for a while when in his late teens. His memoir conveys what it was like to be young in Waterbury in those years with considerable charm, and more than a little self-effacement. He also vividly describes a poignant road trip that he joined in around 1926 with his father and grandfather to Andover and Lawrence, Massachusetts and then on to Malone and Bangor, New York. They must have sought out the aged McGowans, if alive, and some other old farmers of Franklin County.

Doctor Charles's Cooke Street household had its quirks. He was said to work from early morning into the night each day in answer to the huge demands of his medical practice. Maybe out of guilt, Charles did a lot of "soft parenting" and even kept an open account for the kids to have access to treats on request at a shop across the street. As a high school student in the 1920s, the son JSM was allowed to hold rollicking jazz practice sessions at home for his "Monagan Melody Men" led by his hot trumpet, even as his father was examining patients in a suite across the front hall.

In addition to pursuing his musical hijinks, the young John Monagan was a champion swimmer at the state high school level and again at his next stop at Dartmouth, where his academic concentration was as a literature major. He subsequently took an LLB degree from Harvard Law. John's first years of practice in the late 1930s followed under the sometimes gruff guidance of the formidable trial lawyer who was my grandfather Walter Edward Monagan. By now John's younger sisters Margaret and Mary had made their way through Waterbury's Notre Dame Academy and were finishing college. Thomas Monagan was just wrapping up his medical studies and preparing for a career as a pediatrician. All in all, "Aunt Min" had done a very impressive job. It was good that she did so, since doctor Charles Monagan died in 1931 when only 58 years-old. Mary Agnes Monagan kept the household together for another seven years until her own death in 1938, at age 67.

John and Anna Monagan's Last Years

My great-grandfather John Stephen Monagan did not retire from brass-casting until around 1913, and no wonder. Family photographs suggest that he remained remarkably fit into these later years. At the time of his daughter Bernice's wedding in 1915, he remained so spry that he was photographed comfortably sitting on his haunches in the old Irish country style of relaxation, no longer seen at any age in America (or Ireland) today. He and Anna clearly enjoyed pulse-quickening hill climbs and other outings with the younger generation. They both look to be faring remarkably well at the time of their great 50th anniversary celebration in 1919. By this point they had a dozen grandchildren-with about a half dozen more to follow.

**John and Ann, back on the golden anniversary
day of November 18, 1919.**

John Stephen nursed a mischievous side from early on. Thus in the census of 1920 for Ward I in Waterbury he seemed so irritated by the questionnaire that he tetchily said that his name was "John Q. Monagan." He was now aged 73, and Anna this time said she was 67. Also resident were Howard Miller and his sister Lorena, who was trying out the name of "Marie" then. Lorena never married and stayed put in the Spencer Avenue household until nearly the end of her life. Additionally resident in 1920 was a servant named Lester Rice. Howard seems to have lived right there until his passing on February 16, 1931, when still in his early 50s.

Anna was deeply religious and treasured visits from the family's nuns. On the left she is at Cooke Street with a Sister Margaret Loretta (left) and beside Minnie to the right is a Regina Vincent – both likely Mulry's.

Elizabeth Ann Monaghan Allen was the first child of Owen and born in North Andover, Massachusetts in 1840. Here she is seen with her grandchildren around 1919.

The family may have by now acquired an additional investment property in the North End. Another listing in the 1920 census shows that extended Sullivan, Boch, and Garren families were resident in a separate dwelling owned by a John Monagan of that distinctive spelling then.

Curiously, my great-grandfather availed of a Civil War pension, despite beginning his service only at the very end of that terrible conflict. John Stephen died on November 1, 1928, just shy of attaining the age of 82. An insignia in honor of his military service stands beside his grave. My great-grandmother Anna Nolan Monagan died on December 9, 1933, having reached the age of 81. By that point she had lost two daughters (Anna and Bernice), and two sons (Charles and Thomas), and several grandchildren. But there gathered around many grandchildren now to mourn the passing of their so very warm-hearted and ever resourceful and imaginative grandma.

John Stephen and Anna in the late 1920s.

XII.

WORLD WAR II

As the Great Depression began to fade, the fourth-generation of the Monagan family in America were coming of age. Naturally, during the 1930s they would have heard about the Nazi seizure of power in Germany in 1933, the horrors of the Spanish Civil War (1936-1938), and the atrocity-ridden Japanese invasions of China – all of which served as stark foreshadowings of the coming cataclysm of World War II. But in Waterbury and across America, most young people were not terribly concerned at first, so keen was the new generation's appetite to be left to their own bright hopes far from these troubled faraway lands. However, all that began to change utterly once Hitler invaded Poland in 1939 and the next year unleashed his blitzkrieg across northern Europe. In America, the process of militarization now took on a frenetic urgency. Then on December 7, 1941, the Japanese struck at Pearl Harbor and America's entry into the global war proceeded the next day.

Walter Edward Monagan, Jr., Military Lawyer

My grandfather's oldest son Walter (1911-2008) attended Holy Cross College in Worchester, Massachusetts, just like his father and three younger brothers to follow. Then Walter Jr. attended Yale Law (again like his father), graduating in 1935. Along the way, Walter took several summer breaks to Block Island where he played the drums, beside his brother Andy on vocals and piano, in the cavernous waterside bar called Ballard's. Inevitably, Walter went to work in the Waterbury law firm of my grandfather, Walter Edward Monagan, Sr. But this arrangement lasted for only two years, perhaps because the father could be a hard task master.

In the summer of 1938 Walter Jr. married a New Haven-born woman of many talents named Mildred Aubrey (1913-2007). A graduate of

Middlebury College in Vermont, Mildred was well read and keenly observant, while active in amateur theater and dabbling in painting. The couple's fancy Pelham, New York wedding was presided over by a duet of priest cousins – the Reverend Vincent Mulry of New Jersey and the Reverend George Butler initially of Waterbury. Mildred was attired in "a gown of white silk net and Chantilly lace." A newspaper report continued, "The gown, a Mainbocher adaption [i.e., Parisian couture], was fashioned with a square neckline and the sleeves were puffed and shirred full at the elbow... She wore a fingertip length veil." Shortly thereafter, the couple left Waterbury for Philadelphia where Walter had been hired as a legal representative of a major insurance company.

On September 1, 1939, Germany unleashed its *Blitzkrieg* against Poland and the following spring its forces stormed across northern Europe, while its "Axis" ally Japan rampaged through successive conquests across the Pacific. These events swiftly transformed the lives of this next generation of Monagans along with almost everyone else in North America. But often forgotten now is the remarkable truth that, for those who were not killed or maimed, these epic crises also engendered accelerated responsibilities and opportunities for countless young Americans – many perilous, but some not.

Well before America entered the war, Walter, who had served in the U.S. Army Reserve since 1936, was called into active duty on September 19, 1940, in the Army Military Intelligence Corps as a Second Lieutenant. He now became the chief security and public relations officer for the huge **Frankford Arsenal** in Philadelphia. This facility grew into a city unto itself with 22,000 employees tasked to manufacture the lion's share of all the small arms ammunition for the American war effort – many millions of pounds of it every month.

Walter was rapidly promoted to the rank of Captain and then Major (years later he became a Lieutenant Colonel). Eager for overseas service and confident of the coming Allied victory, Walter enrolled in 1944 and 1945 in crash academic courses in Michigan, Virginia, and Illinois in both military governance and the rudiments of Japanese language, culture, and law. For Walter the Allied victory created intriguing new opportunities to see the world as an intelligence officer and legal adjudicator of the endless issues of military occupation that followed. Soon after the Japanese capitulation on August 15, 1945 (fewer than 10 days after the nuclear bombing of **Hiroshima and Nagasaki**), Walter was dispatched to Tokyo and then to Seoul, Korea. There he became a leading legal officer for the new military government, and a liaison officer with the 25th Soviet Army then occupying the northern half of the Korean peninsula. His wife Mildred came to join him following a gut-wrenching crossing of the Pacific to Yokohama and then to Korea in October 1946. She had many the trying domestic experiences in post-war Seoul and her observations are vividly expressed in a letter in the Appendix.

In October 1947, the couple returned to Tokyo where they remained until 1952. Walter was initially involved as a civilian there, working as a U.S. State Department lawyer in the Allied administration of occupied Japan. For a year and a half his duties were focused on the strategically important Ryukyus or "Nan sei" chain of islands sweeping 775 miles from southern Japan to Taiwan. Then the Korean War broke out on June 25,1950 when communist North Korean forces launched a devasting assault on South Korea. American, British, Australian, and New Zealand forces soon joined the fray, while "Red China" poured in over two million of its own troops. Walter was called back to active service in the U.S. Army as an intelligence officer. When the war finally ended, he and Mildred managed to sail by ocean-liner from Japan to France and from there began a leisurely tour of western Europe – where he would ultimately be very happily stationed as a war claims administrator for the next decade.

William Henry Monagan, Navy Gunnery Commander

The second son of Walter and Mary Butler Monagan was William Henry Monagan, an uncle who brandished a twinkle in his eye through all of his 100 years on earth. William graduated from Holy Cross in 1934 and then briefly worked as an insurance agent in Waterbury before enrolling at Georgetown University's School of Law in Washington, D.C. He started his long career in government service with the Department of Justice as a fingerprint technician, perhaps as a student's part-time or summer job, but he was quickly promoted after gaining his Georgetown law degree in 1940. On February 25, 1941, William married Dorothy Lee Hewitt of Baltimore, Maryland, and they had two children, Kathleen in 1942, and Robert in 1948.

As America's involvement in World War II intensified, William joined the U.S. Navy in September 1943 at the rank of Ensign and became a commander of various Navy gunnery crews on merchant marine shipping. His responsibility was to guard against the constant menace of German and Japanese submarine and aircraft attacks upon vital supply convoys. This service took him to such distant shores as England, Italy, Africa, Panama, New Guinea, and the Philippines.

My uncle William's son Bob, now 72 himself, recounted years later that his father weathered four extremely perilous armament supply convoys through the Arctic Ocean to the Soviet Union's ports of Arkhangelsk and Murmansk at the peak of the conflict. Speaking at a small family reunion in sunny Florida in early 2022, Bob said that memories of

William Henry Monagan as a young naval officer. Courtesy Bob Monagan.

Young William and his bride Dorothy.

Walter and Mary Butler Monagan in 1941, about a year before her death, with William and Dorothy.

the infamous screeching of German Stuka dive bombers hurtling out of the sky and blasting away at these ships gave the genial father nightmares for years to come. His father's worst memory was of watching the very next ship ahead obliterated and vanishing with a gurgle into the abyss before his eyes, since it held his best friend in the Navy then. In a few minutes, he glided over the spot where there was nothing left at all. On a happier note, Bob, 72, and my brother Jim, 75, a day or two later latched onto a parasailing thrill ride that lifted them side-by side 450 feet into the air and yelping below the clouds with only dive-bombing pelicans, not Stuka dive bombers in sight.

After the war, my uncle William Henry Monagan returned to the Justice Department in Washington, D.C., and worked for some years in the Attorney General's office as a senior analyst, and then chief of the administrative records division. He ultimately retired in 1972 as a department chief. Until well into the 1970s he remained keenly active in the naval reserves and was ultimately promoted to the rank of Lieutenant Commander. Although his beloved wife Dorothy pre-deceased him in 1995, William continued on with much grace (and many golfing outings) for years, his life heartened by his six grandchildren and 11 great-grand-children. He ultimately died in 2013 at the age of 100 and was buried with full military honors in Arlington National Cemetery in Virginia. The ceremony, attended by many family members, included an honor guard and horse-drawn caisson, and a bugler whose solemn playing of taps was followed by a 16-gun military salute.

Charles Andrew Monagan, Navy Airforce

Walter Monagan's third son, born in 1915, was Charles Andrew Monagan. His middle name was certainly a tribute to my great-great grandfather Andrew Monaghan, who was very likely to have been in full named Charles Andrew. In any case, my uncle was almost universally known as "Andy" although he was sometimes jocularly referred to as "C. Andrew."

Andy possessed a natural elan and great bonhomie. His trademark zest was already apparent in the eighth grade when he won a citywide contest for reciting with his own special grandiosity the soaring Gettysburg Address of Abraham Lincoln. He had an easy sense of humor and self-confidence helped by his good looks. After graduating Holy Cross with a Bachelor of Science in 1936, Andrew worked for years in sales for the Scovill company, an almost inevitable melding of his talents when considering the family's history.

But on March 4, 1943, when aged 27, Andy's number came up and he enrolled in the U.S. Navy as an Ensign. He was first sent to Jacksonville, Florida where he trained as a navigator for the Navy Air Force transport and supply fleet (there was no distinct U.S. Air Force yet). Andrew was deployed to the South Pacific while American marines were launching one bloody island assault after another as they moved ever closer to Japan. On May

1, 1944, he was promoted to Lieutenant, Junior Grade, thanks to making countless landings on remote and sometimes perilous island airstrips to bring vital supplies to the marines and sailors who had been locked in terrible conflict on the ground and at sea.

The Allies' victory over Japan was announced on August 15, 1945, but Andy stayed on in the Pacific until May 1946 to help in the supply of the American forces of occupation. He was promoted to full lieutenant in this period. Upon returning to Waterbury, Andy resumed his work as a regional salesman for Scovill's for another 15 years, before relaunching his career to become a teacher. He was a fabulous entertainer who loved to find his way to any party's piano where he played and crooned all kinds of standards from the great American songbook. But he was in no hurry to marry – that is, until one Seena Lerner Bernbach came along in the early 1970s and changed his life.

John Stephen Monagan, Lieutenant Quartermaster

Though the last-born of Walter Edward Monagan's sons, my father John Stephen Monagan was the second of his generation in Waterbury to enroll in the U.S. military as the country drew ever closer to joining the war. John graduated from Holy Cross College in Massachusetts in 1939. With his "head for figures" my father had enjoyed regular employment in Waterbury's banks during the summers.

After Holy Cross, he landed a job as an accountant/treasurer for the Northern Brewing Company in distant Watertown, New York, apparently through a college classmate whose family owned the business. My father considered this to be one of the most carefree periods of his life. When about 70 years old and in declining health, he made his way alone the 400 miles from Waterbury to Watertown as if to revisit his youth one last time. There wasn't much of familiarity left by that point, alas.

In the summer of 1941, Germany's forces were sweeping across Russia with the goal of seizing Moscow, as the Japanese had just whipsawed across

Southeast Asia. This was when my father was inducted into the U.S. Army as a Warrant Officer on August 11, 1941. He served in a long training period at the army base of Fort Devens in Massachusetts, whence his letters home aired many complaints. These focused on the 5 a.m. wake-ups, incredibly tedious drills, and especially the army's inability to come up with boots to fit his giant size-13 feet so that he could proceed into some more meaningful duty elsewhere. Ultimately, he got his footwear and was transferred to the U.S. Army Airforce base of Tyndall Field, Florida. There he served as a Lieutenant Quartermaster, an important role in this frenetic staging ground for the American invasions of North Africa and Italy and the massive build-up already underway in England.

Due to very serious ulcer problems, my father was never sent into combat abroad. However, in this same period he met my mother Helen Hope Hurst, who was then working as a secretary for the army brass at the same Tyndall Field. Born in Charleston, South Carolina on January 14, 1918, she possessed a lovely southern drawl and a huge vivacity that had to have been attractive to "Jake" as my somewhat self-conscious father was called. Her mother was a Helen Marie Deasy from an arch-Irish-Catholic family from County Cork that moved to Cincinnati, Ohio in the late 1860s. Her father Harris Hurst was a Texas-raised rogue of the Old South, and an extraordinary character whose youthful adventures included a serious

My father John Stephen Monagan.

228

go at silver mining in Oaxaca, Mexico. He also sold some of the earliest tractors in Canada, gilded brass cash registers in Charleston, new-generation typewriters in Louisville, lumber in a plant he bought in Chattanooga, and managed (briefly) an early French film company's attempts at expansion into North America. My mother Hope's family included prolific writers – Hawthorne Hurst, John Shirley Hurst, and the novelist Mary Deasy – and a nationally celebrated classical music singer on CBS Radio, Helen (Deasy) Nugent, one of the top female vocalists in her day. Opposites attract, as they say, and Jake and Hope were married in a humble chapel at Tyndall Field in Florida in December 1943, and not in Connecticut as planned, very much because of my father's worsening ulceritis. He ultimately underwent

My mother Helen Hope Hurst taking dictation from a Capt. Case circa 1943.

major surgery and was given a medical discharge from the army in March 1944, after 31 months of continuous service. Following his recuperation, the couple moved north to Waterbury. My father first worked there for the international accountancy firm Barrow, Wade, Guthrie & Co, while "Hope," as she was always called, was using her outstanding secretarial skills with a local law firm. A few months later my oldest brother, Stephen John Monagan, was born in Waterbury on September 14, 1944.

John S. Monagan, Mayor of Waterbury

My father's first cousin of his identical name, John Stephen Monagan, born seven years earlier in 1911, was given a medical exemption from military service in World War II since he had undergone a massive operation for intestinal cancer in 1939. This was an extraordinary medical success story that added 65 years to his life. A very popular young lawyer about town, he was elected to Waterbury's Board of Aldermen (city council) in 1940, and then was elected Mayor of the city in 1943. Over the next two years he was a frequent presence at the train station wishing Godspeed to departing young recruits, and welcoming veterans lucky enough to be returning home. When the war finally ended, John Monagan was at the forefront of several of Waterbury's gala parades and celebrations. Suave, handsome, self-confident and always impeccably dressed, he was dubbed "Waterbury's most eligible bachelor." But in these years John resided with his sister Margaret in a spacious, high-ceilinged apartment on the avenue named after Waterbury's most important innovator – Israel Holmes – and where my brother Philip Harris Monagan maintains a law practice to this day.

XIII.

POST-WAR RENEWAL

Another Generation Starts

The 1950s have often been hailed as the peak of the American dream, being a time of huge enterprise and irrepressible optimism, when many middle-class Americans in fact believed in the possibility of nearly unbroken economic progress ahead for the rest of their lives and their children's to come. By this point, almost all reference to the horrors of the Famine and their ancestors' subsequent immigration travails had been exorcized from the everyday talking of Irish-Americans in Connecticut. The huge optimism afoot was helped by the fact that nearly eight million World War II veterans had newly received either free college educations or advanced training programs under the **GI Bill** and they were all itching to make their own mark upon a spectacularly growing economy. Unemployment was minimal and business opportunities seemed legion. For America in the 1950s was making and exporting worldwide all manner of wondrous new things – Chevys and Ford roadsters with soaring fins; passenger jets by the thousands with swell lounges; miraculous medical devices; and of course tens of millions of astonishing color television sets that could beam in the era's programs of constant good cheer – from *Leave it to Beaver* to *Father Knows Best* and Jackie Gleason's *The Honeymooners*. The other thing that America was making was babies – so many millions of them that this generation was called the "Baby Boomers. "

The 1950s were generally very good years for the Monagans of Waterbury, Connecticut. My father John S. Monagan III, or "Jake," had returned from Florida with his new bride Hope and quickly landed work as an accountant, while my mother soon gave birth to their first child **Stephen John** Monagan on September 14, 1944. However, some acrimony with his increasingly difficult father Walter prompted John to undertake a diversion for several years to Hartford. There my brother **James Edward** Monagan was born on November 21, 1946, and my sister **Nancy Hope** Monagan on February 17, 1948. But Waterbury was where my father craved to be and in the late 1950s, he landed a position as treasurer at the **"Timex"** Corporation in Middlebury, just over the town line. For a century this enterprise had been known worldwide as the **Waterbury Clock Company** as a producer of vast amounts of inexpensive watches. (Thus the provenance of the baseball team the "Waterbury Timers.") But after going corporate, it was renamed in 1944 as Timex. After its wartime years of making bomb fuses, the company sought a new image and turned back to mass producing affordable wrist watches in astonishing numbers. By the 1950's end, one out of three wristwatches on the planet was being made in Middlebury, Connecticut. Through half of this decade my father was stationed in the central accounting office while the company was selling 3 million watches a year.

It was during this time that I was born on September 18, 1952. My brother **Philip Harris** Monagan, the future attorney, came along on September 17, 1959. With the family's numbers growing, my parents in October 1952 moved us all into a five-bedroom house, built around 1900, at 24 Windsor Street in Waterbury's rapidly growing Bunker Hill neighborhood. The seller was my father's first cousin, Dr. Tom Monagan, the pediatrician who with his bride Margie Kehoe had already had seven children by then and desired a bigger house. At 2,100 square feet, 24 Windsor Street was hardly small, however, and it came with an ample side yard with a grove of hefty oaks that were excellent for the more daring climbers and hoisting rope tire swings. Best of all was the grand old red barn out back with a cupola on top of its sizeable hayloft – a future redoubt for all manner of childhood play.

The extended family gathered together there even at that very first Christmas, and who knows who slept where.

Jake and Hope Monagan with their newborn son Steve, 1944.

The Story of Bunker Hill

The history behind this house at 24 Windsor Street merits its own digression, since it is emblematic of certain transitions beginning in places like Waterbury and across America at the end of the 19th century. Though only a couple of miles north of one the more heavily industrialized urban centers on the East Coast, Bunker Hill somehow lolled for generations in a separate world. For the longest time, the area had but one dusky road with some scattered dirt tracks angling off into its various farmsteads and woodlands. Through most of the 1800s, there were only a few families to be found on all

233

Christmas on Windsor Street, 1952. Front row, L to R: Hope Monagan holding yours truly; Nancy Monagan; Joan Monagan Clinton holding Maureen and Gail; Mildred Aubrey Monagan, my brother Jim before her; Big Aunt Louise Butler; Kathleen Monagan (later Porter) beneath her; Little Louise and Margie Monagan Cetta, with my brother Steve before her. Back row, L to R: My father John S. Monagan; John Clinton; Joe Cetta holding Bobby Monagan; grandfather Walter Edward Monagan, then about 70; uncles William and Andrew Monagan standing behind Dorothy Hewitt Monagan.

of Bunker Hill, and they were mostly prominent landholders with scant Irish blood among them – their names including Newton, Block, Warren, and Woodruff. Several of these old-line Yankees led dual lives, making substantial side-money through inter-marriage or quiet investment in the brass industry just down the valley. Gradually though, this Bunker Hill set began to latch on to the economic expansionism of the age and banged together new enterprises of their own, such as a sawmill in Oakville and a Bunker Hill syndicate's American Suspender Company of Watertown.

At the foot of this sprawling but very gradually rising hill lived a William Brown, born in 1804. He had long owned several hundred acres of rich lowlands along the juncture of the Naugatuck River with the Steele Brook as it meandered down from Watertown. He also owned 73 acres of woodlands with a thick cluster of these ruffling up into Bunker Hill. A son had title to 50 acres of woodlands more. William Brown was so enamored of the beauty of all this that in 1870 he hired a regionally acclaimed artist to paint the entirety of his holdings. This was done in the dreamy style of the Hudson River school, as if the heavy industry in the opposite direction did not even exist.

Brown's Meadows, by Samuel Scott.

The Waterbury Civil War veteran Ira Edwin Clough was another Bunker Hill farmer with lands bordering a crossroads known as Clough Brook, just across from today's Kaynor Technical School. His house may have been the grand 5,600 square-foot Victorian built on the Watertown Road in 1883 just beneath my family's eventual home and bordering the initial one-room Bunker Hill School, a catapult's toss from the back of our barn. A former brass caster himself, Edwin Clough was killed by the kick of one of his milch cows in January 1894.

Somehow into this mix there relocated one William P. Jarrett, a youngish go-getter with a zeal for selling insurance and making money wherever it might beckon. To him it was plain to see that Waterbury's growing middle-class might become keen on moving to Bunker Hill, if ready-made lots and new houses on brand new streets could be neatly cut out of the old woodlands. Around 1896, a syndicate led by Jarrett bought up a big swath of land in the area and rapidly began clearing the woods, laying out streets, and starting construction on various new homes. A detailed map of Waterbury from 1898 shows that a then house-less thoroughfare from an upper plateau to the bottom of the hill, named Windsor Street, had already been laid out. Jarret, who by now had a substantial downtown real estate office, was a great promoter. For at least a decade he called the whole area "Morningside"– as if to say the dark aspects of immigrant history could all be cast off for a new life here. He told the *Waterbury Democrat* that the workmen landscaping "Morningside" were amazed at the numbers of Indian arrowheads they kept uncovering – his subliminal message being that the place was also deeply rooted in time.

Dr. Tom Monagan and the Baby Boom

The seller to my parents of the house at 24 Windsor Street was my father's first cousin Thomas Mulry Monagan. By the of end of World War II, he had been promoted to Lieutenant Commander in the U.S. Navy. But rather than being discharged from service after the capitulation of Germany, he was sent off in the summer of 1945 again on an extended deployment with the *USS Zenobia,* a new naval cargo and medical supply ship named after the minor planet Zenobia 840. The American ship's name essentially being a tribute to the Greek god Zeus must have led to much head scratching and many jokes on board. Following the Zenobia's return to port on April 1, 1946, Dr. Tom rejoined the family in Brooklyn, and was honorably discharged. Meanwhile, Tom's sister Mary Monagan Murphy had been then keenly scouting for a house for her brother in the vicinity of her own amiable neighborhood in Waterbury's Bunker Hill. Matters in this regard became more urgent when a third child, Thomas, was born in New York on July 30. Within a month, Dr. Tom acquired the comfortable old house, built around 1900 with its red barn on 24 Windsor.

At this time, Dr. Tom quickly set up his nearly permanent doctor's offices on 195 Grove Street, where his broad desk was said to be always topped by a jar of brilliantly colored lollipops. With his deep gravelly voice and huge smile, Tom made an instant positive impression on Waterbury's new "Baby Boomer" parents, especially because children of all ages and their mothers too loved this man. His medical practice flourished from the get-go. Meanwhile, Tom's family was growing at a phenomenal pace.

Dr. Tom's godson Charley Monagan, the long-term editor of *Connecticut Magazine* and author of many books, recalled recently, "He was a wonderful common-sense doctor, probably a lot like his own father. Mothers liked him and trusted him completely and this was a time when kids were multiplying like flies. In the beginning he made daily house calls. Whatever you were of age or background, you never doubted that you had his full attention. He was just beautifully fixed on people. He liked a good laugh, a beer, a cigarette, and a New York Giants game on Sundays. He was an avid golfer. Of course much of his time was devoted to being a father as well... All of his children went to private school [the girls all went to Notre Dame] and college and he presided over ten weddings. My father often referred to him as a saint."

On Windsor Street Tom and Marjorie had a third daughter named Barbara in 1948, a Christine in 1950, and the next year the twins Jane and Elizabeth. By the time the house sold to my father in September 1952 (a month that saw the birth of Bernadette or "Bunny"), Tom and Margie already had seven children. The pediatrician's family next moved into a large, characterful house on 146 Pine Street, closer to the town center. There they had yet four more children – Mary, Sheila, Carolyn (called "Kiki), and Bernard or "Ben."

Tom's oldest daughter Gretchen Monagan Sterling fondly remembered how expert her mother was at running this formidable household, with chaos averted by her mastery of every little detail to come her way. "Our mother was the quiet center of our family. She made sure that we went to Confession on Saturdays and as a family to Mass on Sundays and Holy Days. She was always there when we came home from school. On the kitchen wall she had a calendar that charted all of our piano lessons, tennis matches, swim meets, and dance classes. We got to all of these activities on time. We sat down to a family dinner every night... Mom squeezed fresh orange juice in the morning and cooked us oatmeal in the winter. She somehow always had the materials on hand for our school lunches every day." Drawing on her training as a registered nurse in New York, for many years Margie Monagan headed the Waterbury Day Nursery and served as a director of volunteer services at St. Mary's Hospital.

Jane Monagan Marrone, who lives in Darien, Connecticut with her long-time husband Sam and has been immensely helpful on this project, shared some reflections on the earlier ways of Waterbury. "When Dad was really young, he kept a diary. He went to Mass every day, serving as an Altar boy [with tips then for weddings and funerals]. He would write how much money he had made in the upper left hand corner of the page. I remember that one day there was an entry for $20.00 and the next day it was $8.00. With all that he went and purchased a bicycle!"

Jane continued, "I do always think of the cultural separations in our town. The heavily Italian Brooklyn district comes to mind where we would go to get their delicious bread and donuts. Near the Jewish synagogue across town on Cooke Street we had dresses made for some of our weddings by a woman who had a number tattooed on her arm which signified she had been in a Nazi concentration camp. But she made such beautiful dresses and how they fit!"

Eleven children of Thomas and Margie Monagan married and produced a great many new descendants of their own, while spreading their genes across a number of states. Only three still live in Connecticut – Jane Monagan Marrone in an old sea captain's cottage on the Five Mile River in Darian, her sister Ann Monagan Noonan in Naugatuck, and the youngest child Ben, who lives in Middlebury. Somehow, the parents made sure that the family flourished as a closely knit group. In fact Tom brought together the entire family – even the son Ben, although he was only in utero – to his 25th reunion at Dartmouth in May of 1961. There he and Margie were awarded a Schwinn "bicycle built for two" as the class prize for having more kids than anybody else from his graduating year of 1936. After receipt of

The ultimate Baby Boom. Tom and Margie Monagan got their kids in line to celebrate their award for being the best reproducers from Dartmouth to graduate from *1936*.

this marvelous contraption back in Waterbury, Tom and Marge staged a wonderful family photo for the *Dartmouth Magazine*.

Dr. Tom passed away in 2005 after an extended battle with Alzheimer's. His wife Marge had died several years later. Their twelve children with 11 spouses (and one "life partner"), 29 grandchildren, and 27 great grandchildren, are all living.

Marjorie Monagan and Joseph Cetta

World War II profoundly transformed the lives of nearly everyone who lived through it, as the story of my Aunt Marjorie further underlines. During most of the war, she studied literature at the Catholic, all-female Trinity College in Washington D.C., even as her brothers and cousins were shipped off to various military bases or far-off duties around the world. In the summers, Margie worked in Waterbury's wonderful Bronson Library and after graduating she returned to work as a reference librarian there. A few years later she became the librarian at Wilby High School. For four summers she attended Columbia University in New York in order to complete a master's degree in library science. In short, she was an exceptionally dedicated and professional librarian.

It was in this period that my aunt met her future husband Joseph Michael Cetta, a U.S. Army veteran and recent graduate of the University of Connecticut now working as an eighth-grade teacher in Waterbury. Joe had enlisted in 1943 almost immediately after graduating from Crosby High School. Following the D-Day landings in northern France the next year, he saw heavy combat.

To Margie, Joe must have seemed an exotic at first as his family hailed from the deep south of Italy, specifically from a town called Avellino not far from Naples. Thousands in Waterbury shared a similar heritage since Italians poured into the city at the end of the 19th century and decades to follow. Today, roughly 25,000 of the city's total population of 110,000 claim Italian heritage.

Joe Cetta's father "John" (Giovani) came to America in 1906 at the age of nine in hand with a not much older half-sister. The two somehow made their way to meet with other relatives in Waterbury. Upon his World War I draft registration on February 22, 1917, Giovani was working as a barber. He became a naturalized citizen soon thereafter and marred a "Katie" (Concetta) Di Napoli, who was several years younger, on November 23, 1923. Her parents Charles (Carlo?) and Anna both came from the beautiful province of Puglia (and reportedly met at Ellis Island). They had in all six girls and one boy, Concetta being the oldest. As time went by, the family expanded and reconfigured throughout a four-story house with a front porch on each level – a "four decker" in the local parlance – at 22 Cossett Street in the city's heavily Italian North End. John Cetta rented rooms at No. 20 and that must have been how he married Katie, who was born on the 4th of July in 1906 and wanted to be American through and through. In the next-door house, Concetta and Giovanni – Kate and John – had five children. Joseph Cetta, born in 1924, was the oldest.

Joe Cetta was a highly popular student at Crosby High School, where he played both basketball and football. On July 14, 1943, just a month after his graduation, he enlisted in the U.S. Army. After basic training he was enrolled in a special Army program at Brooklyn College that was never completed. Following the massive D-Day landings on June 6, 1944, and with the heavy casualties sustained in the continuing action, the U.S. Army had to feed in replacement soldiers by the thousands. Around the point when the allied forces stalled in the Ardennes in Belgium at the onset of winter, Joseph Cetta became one of those replacements. This was the region where there commenced on December 16 the Germans' last-ditch onslaught of 200,000 men and 1,000 tanks in the so-called "Battle of the Bulge." The epicenter of what has been called the greatest battle in American military history lay at the crossroads of **Bastogne,** which became completely encircled and subject to round-the-clock assault from December 20 to 27, 1944. Joseph Cetta was deeply involved in that terrifying conflict, which carried on and on in later envelopments and did not see the Germans routed from the Ardennes until January 25, 1945. Joe Cetta weathered heavy combat. Evidently in the preceding weeks' fierce skirmishes in the "Low Countries" he was sent out with a patrol across a river on a raft into German controlled territory. He later mentioned that he was the only one to come back alive.

After the German capitulation on May 8, 1945, Joe returned to Waterbury. He then enrolled in New Britain Teachers College, which later became part of the Central Connecticut State University. Following graduation, Joseph Cetta became a devoted teacher and baseball coach in the Walsh primary school in Waterbury. It was around then that he met my aunt Marjorie Monagan.

Joe Cetta, greeted by his mother with a medal on his chest – plainly he's no longer 17.

As the relationship grew, Joe Cetta inevitably brought Margie home to meet his family. Alas, "Papa" DiNapoli – Joe's maternal grandfather who had first worked at the Waterbury train station – could say little due to his still limited English. But he beamed with approval and hurried out to the garden to cut off a fresh rose to present to the young Irish-American lass as a welcoming from his heart. With the romance of Joe Cetta and Marjorie Monagan came a blending of two of the great immigration threads in the making of both Waterbury, Connecticut and America. There was surely excitement and some extra scrutiny in the air when Marjorie Monagan exchanged the vows of marriage on December 27, 1952, with her beloved Joseph. My aunt also fell in love with Italian culture, history and cuisine. On October 28, 1953, she gave birth to her black-haired bambino Catherine Marie – probably named after Joe's mother.

Alas, tragedy struck within a few months when Joe, who had survived the mortal perils of World War II, was diagnosed with leukemia, which ultimately saw to his final passing in a New Haven hospital on May 6, 1954. Marjorie and Cathy moved back to the family household on Euclid Avenue, which at this point still included a varied cast of characters. These included my aging grandfather Walter, retired from the practice of law, and widowed since the death of my grandmother Mary Butler Monagan on July 10, 1942; plus the third oldest son, the still arch-single Andy, and Margie's always gentle but learning-impaired sister, born in 1920, my aunt "Little Louise." She was called that because also co-resident was Walter's sister-in-law, my never-married great aunt Anna Louise Butler – called by us kids "Big Louise"– a very long-serving teacher and school principal. This then was a fairly eccentric Irish-American household, which Margie was crucial in holding together for many years. This role must have been very trying at times since my grandfather Walter Monagan was becoming increasingly difficult with age. This once utterly brilliant man held on until August 8, 1961, when he died of cancer at the age of 79.

Even a child visiting that Euclid Avenue house could see that one of its festering problems was tobacco smoking. Indeed, the 1950s in America could have been called the "Decade of the Cigarette" – since the furious smoking was going on in those years by almost everyone at any office, factory floor, weekend party, or even lakeside picnic. At 84 Euclid Avenue, my great-aunt's substantial bedroom resembled an opium den, as she puffed away furiously on her cigarettes while attacking her intricate jigsaw puzzles and extraordinarily long games of solitaire. The ceiling directly above her table went yellow from the smoke, almost like an omen in a classic noir film. Though this was a strongly Catholic household, the one person who could be most counted on to show up in church every Sunday was my uncle Andy, the handsome and slightly devilish party man who found his most fulfilling joy in belting out hymns to the Lord.

All the while, though, the open-hearted DiNapoli's of Cossett Street never let my Aunt Margie and her daughter Cathy out of their warm hearts. Every week for years on end, the mother and daughter joined in the family's great Sunday feasts, and these two very different family lines remain close to this day. My aunt Margie became a wizard at Italian cooking and her daughter Cathy, long a science teacher and assistant headmaster until her recent retirement from a much respected preparatory school in Falmouth, Massachusetts, has been pleasantly conflicted about her cultural identity ever since.

As a high school librarian, Marjorie at least had her summers free and in 1959 managed a great get-away to Europe on the huge Cunard White Star cruise liner the *S.S. Mauretania*. Her paramount destination was Paris to meet up with her oldest brother Walter and his wife Mildred – still juggling the legal fall out from World War II – with that couple then joining her on an extended continental tour. On the voyage across the Atlantic, Margie made lifelong friends with a most serendipitous group from the remote Franklin County, New York crossroads of **Brushton,** only a mile or so from the 19th century farms of Andrew and Owen Monaghan. As of this writing,

Still setting a certain Irish tone in Waterbury – late 1960s?
That's Margie left and brother Andy just beside.

Marjorie is enjoying her 100th birthday with continuing alacrity and wit in Naples, Florida.

Joan Monagan and John Clinton

Born in Waterbury on August 2, 1928, my aunt Joan Marie Monagan was the youngest of Walter and Mary Butler Monagan's seven children. Ever amiable and inquisitive from her earliest years, Joan was another of the family's gifted students. She served as editor-in-chief of her school yearbook in 1945 at Waterbury Catholic High. Therein she was lauded as being "pure in her affections and noble in her aspirations" by the assistant editor Anne Brophy. The Second World War had just ended when she went off from Waterbury to Trinity College in Washington, D.C, right after her sister Marjorie had finished up there. Joan was arriving at the nation's capital at a time of great euphoria following the Allies' August 15 declaration of victory over Japan, which drew the final curtain on World War II. Legions of exhilarated young servicemen were suddenly everywhere back in America, enrolling for free in colleges across the land, and with money always jingling in their pockets – all thanks to the G.I. Bill.

Joan must have been asked out often, but the man who most captured her interest was a passionately idealistic young Georgetown University student named John Clinton. His story – their story – is inspiring. It begins with the birth of John Clinton's father John Francis "Jack" Clinton in Boston in 1878, who was followed by a brother William. The toddler and infant then contracted such severe cases of the German measles in 1880 that both were made permanently deaf. However, at Boston's Clark School for the Deaf, Jack and William learned to both lip-read and persevere with incredible determination. In high school Jack played football and ran track. He also quickly displayed superior talents as a cabinet maker and set up his own high-end furniture business – while also serving as an instructor to others. Inwardly driven, he disdained sign language as a somehow soft and indulgent way out.

In the mid-1920s Jack Clinton met a younger deaf woman named Gertrude Denner, a German baker's daughter and seamstress born in Cambridge, Massachusetts. The couple married and on February 14, 1927, had a son they named **John Brooks Clinton,** my uncle in-law-in-the-making. My aunt Joan was obviously moved by the profoundly arresting stories of his upbringing. I myself once asked John what happened when he cried as a baby and thrashed around in his crib with his deaf parents incapable of hearing him. He explained that each night as he was settled in his mother would tie one end of a long skein of string around his tiny thumb and then tie the other end taut to a ring on her own finger as she lay down to sleep in her bed across the way. Thus she could sense her infant son's every toss and turn in the night.

Coming from such an extraordinary background, John Clinton learned a lot about human grace. Quietly but powerfully Catholic, John always maintained that he, with parents who could not hear a word he spoke, was uniquely blessed. The family house was in the Jamaica Plain section of Boston, and in 1940 John enrolled in the Boston English School, a top Boston high school, whence he graduated in June 1944. This coincided with the D-Day invasion.

John promptly enlisted in the U.S. Navy on September 1, 1944, although aged just seventeen. As it happened, he was based "state-side" until June 1945. Then he was shifted to the newly commissioned aircraft carrier the *U.S.S. Champlain,* which was assigned to ferrying American troops back home. John was discharged in March 1946 and entered Georgetown the following autumn, where he soon met my aunt Joan at a weekend party.

The two young idealists began to date and somewhere down the road talked of marriage. In 1949 Joan graduated from Trinity College and returned to Waterbury, while John returned to Boston for the summer. There, John fell desperately ill and after much probing was diagnosed with tuberculosis – still a widely killing disease – and confined to an indefinite stay in intensive care. Ultimately, he needed to have part of one lung removed. This was major surgery and required extensive after-care. During this long ordeal, Joan took many train trips to Boston, where she stayed with the deaf but deeply loving parents of her fiancé, while attending to John's bedside. That Joan was helping keep their son alive must have been clear to the parents.

In the end, John did recover nearly miraculously and was released from hospital after almost a year had passed. The couple were finally free to celebrate marriage in the Basilica of the Immaculate Conception in Waterbury on July 29, 1950. They settled into a public housing apartment as John completed his Bachelor of Economics at Boston College, where he graduated in 1952 "with great distinction." In the next year (with the first children Maureen and Gail under wing), he completed a Masters at Harvard's Graduate School of Public Administration. In 1953 he landed a junior management position with the federal government back in Washington and the family moved into an apartment in Alexandria, Virginia.

John first worked within the U.S. Bureau of the Budget (Office of Management and Budget today), an agency charged with oversight of myriad entities reporting to the President (then Dwight Eisenhower). Eloquent, deftly incisive, and intensely idealistic, but blessed with a wry sense of humor, John Clinton rose quickly through the governmental ranks. After John Fitzgerald Kennedy was elected President, he was drafted in 1962 into the inner Kennedy White House staff to help in vetting the finalists for the highest ranks of the administration, including future cabinet members. The

Joan and John at their son Jim's 1974 wedding to Audrey Sue Lemon.

assassination on November 22, 1963, of this beloved president was crushing to him, but John remained in the White House long after the ensuing inauguration of Lyndon Baynes Johnson. He next worked until 1966 with the top brass of the Air Force. Then he moved into the newly created Department of Housing and Urban Development (HUD) and grew deeply involved in the Model Cities program, including helping to manage a major federal initiative in creating entirely new communities from scratch. The family kept growing – ultimately to include nine children – and changed residences in 1965 from Annadale to a lovely stone house at 802 Hillwood Avenue in **Falls Church,** Virginia. All could somehow still be packed into an oversized car or two for Sunday Mass, the odd North Carolina Outer Banks or Delaware shore holiday, or visits all the way to Waterbury, Connecticut. With an unswerving devotion to what he believed was right and good, John weathered many shifts in the political tides until he left HUD in 1985 to work with an advocacy group called the Senior Executive Association.

John believed – almost as an extension of his passionate Catholicism – that it was government's responsibility to help the less fortunate move forward and create a new "commons" for society in general. Despite the constant commotion of a house with children running wild everywhere he turned, he read widely and could talk knowledgeably about almost anything.

John's widow, Joan is also an extraordinary communicator, ever concerned about the well-being of others, and affectionately turning any failing conversation with her great wit and irreverence toward some more amusing next stage. She has never tired of gently noting the proud achievements of her many offspring (and their spouses and grandchildren) who she has managed to surround with unfailing love. Joan has always been incredibly devoted to the extended family, showering hospitality upon every arrival no matter the hour or the occasion. One treasured memory is of the family converging in great numbers on a beach house Joan and John were renting on Cape Cod in about 1959. Appearing on the scene was a nearly complete line up of Joan's siblings and their spouses as well as eight visiting children, on top of Joan's

Joan and John at the Outer Banks.

own six young kids at that time. There was a running kids' party by the beach and the juvenile bedlam grew so complete that the rickety front door got knocked clear off its hinges. Other hostesses might have lost it right there, but not Joan. Instead, she invited a couple of us kids to stay for another week, so much did she love children.

At countless distant family milestones, Joan and John found a way to appear, even if it meant driving for hours to Connecticut with a car loaded with kids. She herself has continued to host regular gala family reunions at Falls Church, even when easing into her nineties. At my daughter Laura's 2015 wedding to Rohan Geraghty in Kinsale, Ireland, Joan was there at the age of 87 (with her daughters Maureen and Gail and grand-daughter Grace).

Today, Joan's house in Falls Church remains an iconic gathering place, in part because most of her nine children and their various spouses still live close by. Alas, John Clinton, who suffered an earlier heart attack, died in 2003 at the age of 77.

A Clinton family holiday around Cape May, New Jersey circa 1985. Front row: Joanie, Gail, Maureen. Back row: Neal, Tom, Steve, Paul, Andy, Jim.

Peggy Monagan of Greenwich Village

Dr. Charles Andrew Monagan, my grandfather's oldest brother, had with his wife Margaret three daughters in addition to the sons John and Thomas (as well as the short-lived infant Charles). The first, born in 1913, was named Parthenia. She died as a little girl on March 23, 1918.

The second daughter Margaret Mary Monagan, but always called "Peggy," was born on June 28, 1916. She too went to Notre Dame Academy and then attended the College of Mount Saint Vincent in the leafy Riverdale Section of the Bronx. A free spirit, she had to have been another of this clan wanting to become a writer, since after moving back to Waterbury she first called herself a "journalist" in the city directory of 1940. By then she had moved into a flat on 42 Holmes Avenue with her lawyer brother John, who would serve as Waterbury's mayor from 1943 to 1948. This of course was the period when the huge war effort was followed by euphoric victory celebrations, at

250

which she marched in the lead of at least one major parade with John.

By 1947 Peggy Monagan was calling herself a "bookkeeper" and evidently growing itchy as the post-war excitement died down. After her brother married Rosemary Ann Brady in Bayonne, New Jersey on May 23, 1949, the apartment was let go. Peggy's response was to say goodbye to Waterbury and move into a rent-controlled but spacious apartment in a brownstone on 43 W. 9th Street in New York's bohemian Greenwich Village. Charley Monagan, the oldest child of the former Mayor, was her godson. The long-term editor of *Connecticut Magazine* recalled years later, "I loved her because she was smart and very droll and funny and always gave me a small birthday check." But she "smoked like a chimney," he added.

Margaret took on a long-term job at a New York printing company that specialized in children's books, including the works of Maurice Sendak, the famed author/illustrator of children's classics like **Where the Wild Things Are** and **In the Night Kitchen.** In that capacity she was able to present her many nieces and nephews with first-run Sendak posters that they treasured forever after. Though Margaret never married, she made frequent trips back to Waterbury to stay with her sister Mary Monagan Murphy's family and convene also with Tom Monagan's ever-growing brood.

Margaret's niece Gretchen, who lives with her husband Bill Sterling in Massachusetts, remembers other details. "Peggy was very wise and funny, and she had a very special cat called Rosie. But she especially knew about birds and their individual calls and she introduced me to all kind of species, which began my life-long interest in birds. When I turned thirty, she sent me a card with a five dollar bill and a note that said, 'To ease the pain.'"

Margaret Monagan kept in touch with the Mulry family and can be found on a Colonial Airlines manifest along with her aunt Mary Mulry on July 23, 1955, departing for Bermuda from LaGuardia Field in New York. The two returned two weeks later via "Idlewild," as JFK Airport was called at that time. Margaret doted on her extended family through the years, but she never moved back to Connecticut until spending her last months with her sister Mary and Dick Murphy in Middlebury while struggling against advancing lung cancer until dying on July 7, 1983.

Mary Monagan and Dick Murphy

The youngest daughter of Charles and Margaret Mulry Monagan, Mary Elizabeth, was born on December 13, 1917. She was only two years-old when her mother died and thus was almost altogether raised by her "Aunt Min." Mary attended Notre Dame Academy and then the College of Mount Saint Vincent, like her sister Peggy. After graduating in 1938, she returned to Waterbury to work as a teacher.

Before long she met the strapping Richard Bernard Murphy who had been a star athlete in Waterbury and received a football scholarship to Georgetown University in Washington, where he graduated in 1934. Dick Murphys father "Jack" had emigrated from Cork City in Ireland all alone as a young teenager in the late 1880s, then ended up in Bridgeport, Connecticut, where he developed an early wall placard-posting business into a substantial outdoor advertising "hoarding" or billboard enterprise which he eventually relocated to Waterbury. In 1937, the son Richard returned to Waterbury to live with his by-now-widowed father and younger brothers at 230 Grandview Avenue and to become a manager of the family's already thriving business.

Dick Murphy and Mary Elizabeth Monagan were married on September 4, 1940. They then moved into a four-bedroom house at 123 Newton Terrace in the Bunker Hill neighborhood. This was two and a half blocks from the 24 Windsor Street house of my childhood.

Newton Terrace was named after Charles Nathan Newton (1811-1892), whose ancestors were among the earliest settlers of Bunker Hill. A prosperous farmer with manufacturing sidelines in Oakville, Charles Nathan Newton grew old with no direct heirs and left his sizeable lands instead to an orphaned niece named Harriet McAuley. A property developer named Charles Curtiss soon swooped in and talked her into selling off these lands in the late 1890s, making way for the Newton Terrace and Nathan Street neighborhood which I patrolled daily on one of my newspaper delivery boy routes of long ago.

The back of my family's red barn abutted this former farm. The turn-of-the-century Newton development was as pleasant as they come, with tree-lined, gently sloping wide avenues sporting handsome houses, most with fulsome verandas and at least four bedrooms. For a growing number of young professionals or machinists and the like who had been flourishing at the edges of Waterbury's still booming brass industry, the draw of the newly opening lands on Bunker Hill must have seemed idyllic, especially when a direct trolly to the city center came into being.

In any case, after moving into their Newton Terrace house in 1940, Mary Monagan and Dick Murphy quickly began to add children, including in 1941 a Mary Elizabeth, called "Mundie"; Catherine Agnes; Richard Bernard, Jr.; and in 1951 Joseph-and a year or two later a son William. But the family thus outgrew the house and by 1952 moved to a larger, and statelier home at 107 Prospect Street, two blocks above the Green and within Waterbury's central district of historic homes, many built for the city's earliest industrialists.

Mary's brother Dr. Tom visited her on Newton Terrace while he was seeking to relocate his family after the war. She clearly was the one who found the house on 24 Windsor Street, which was purchased by Thomas Monagan in August 1946, and then sold by him to my father John in September 1952.

Mary was a dynamic woman who loved reading and had a quick wit and great warmth. She was a devout Catholic and was considered the spiritual leader of this side of the family. Her husband Dick Murphy – for 62 years – was a large personality and became well rewarded for his ceaseless energy since the family business leapfrogged forward in the American post-war economic boom. With so many people constantly driving about in their new cars with soaring fins and flashy chrome grills, roadside billboards had become a very hot means of spreading commercial messages. Dick Murphy set the pace in this business in Connecticut for years.

One sign of his success, and generosity, was that in 1949 he and Mary made as their wedding present to her brother John, the musical former mayor, and his bride Rosemary Brady, nothing less than a gleaming new grand piano. In 1947 Dick and his father John Francis Murphy – "Jack" – then 73, had managed to take a splendid, just-the-two-of-them trip to Ireland. The goal was to visit Cork City where Jack was born around 1875. They returned on the ocean liner the *S.S. America,* arriving in New York on May 27. Jack's grandson Joseph Mulry Murphy, a long-time professor of interfaith studies in the department of theology at Georgetown University, recently recalled, "My father did indeed visit Cork with his father (John F.). He used to tell a story that the two of them were walking the streets of Cork and someone called out "Hello Jack!" recognizing my father after fifty years [and then some] away in America. He was born in Lavitts Quay [beside the River Lee which encircles downtown Cork] and emigrated to New York in 1889 at the age of 13 and apparently alone. He was quite a colorful character and developed the billboard business in Bridgeport." [Joseph himself is the author of many books, particularly on African religious beliefs and practices. As my cousin Michael recently said, "This family should have started its own publishing company."]

As it happens, my own house looks down upon that same Lavitts Quay today. In what would have been the late 1960s, Dick and Mary Murphy and Dr. Tom and Margie Monagan sailed to England on the *S.S. Queen Elizabeth* and from there toured Ireland, likely with County Monaghan and Cork City both on the agenda. Meanwhile, Dick and Mary's eldest daughter "Mundie" at the same time moved back to Newton Terrace with her husband Maurice Smith in a house across from the one in which she was first raised. When the next daughter Catherine was married, she and her husband Thomas Lyons bought a house nearby on Nathan Street in the 1970s. The siblings eventually branched out much further – Catherine to Maine; Joe to teach at Georgetown and travel Africa and other exotic parts with his fascination for the earliest pre-Christian religions; while Mundie stayed local and taught for 40 years at Wilby, Notre Dame and St. Margaret's in Waterbury.

By the late 1960s downtown Waterbury had been experiencing a precipitous deterioration, with employment plummeting with the collapse of the brass industry, and a rising crime rate. The city was also victim to a horrendous evisceration by federal transportation authorities who drove a new interstate highway through its heart and in fact obliterated places like Spencer Avenue and Round Hill Street where my ancestors had once created such a splendid new world for themselves. The old feeling of Waterbury being an enclave of warmly interconnected, even throwback neighborhoods as refuges against the ever more fragmented world was vanishing. Like countless others in the 1970s, Mary and Dick Murphy moved from the city center to the much brighter seeming suburbs that had been untrammeled farmland until of late, their destination being Middlebury.

But all the while, the Murphy Outdoor Advertising Company enjoyed impressive growth under the helm of the son Dick. He oversaw the creation and management of satellite offices in Bridgeport and Middletown, Connecticut and as well as another in Colonie, New York. The company also bought many parcels of land upon which they could erect new advertising at the drop of a hat. They also retained ten trucks and a fixed staff of 25, including Dick Murphy's brothers. No doubt this advertising clout was helpful in some of John S. Monagan's early campaigns for the United States Congress.

Dick Murphy and his family enjoyed many long summer holidays on the Connecticut shore. *The Hartford Courant* of July 26, 1959, noted that the family was ensconced for six weeks in a cottage on Giant's Neck Beach in Niantic, just east of Old Saybrook. The families of the then first-term Congressman John Monagan and Dr. Tom had just visited. The sister Peggy of New York had now come up for a week. The parents proudly noted that their

Is that a lion cub or a dog? Dick and Mary Monagan Murphy seem unconcerned.

daughter "Mundie" was about to enter Marymount College in Tarrytown, New York, while their son Richard Jr. was carrying on at Canterbury, the prep school in New Milford. Within a year or two, the family had purchased a sea-side cottage at Grove Beach Point in Westbrook, Connecticut.

From Middlebury, Marry Monagan Murphy served as a long-term volunteer at St. Mary's Hospital in Waterbury and she remained a devout Catholic all her life. Thus when her second daughter Catherine spent a year of college abroad in 1965, it was at the very Catholic Loyola University's satellite operation in Rome. Of course, Catherine had been another member of the family to attend the very Catholic Trinity College in Washington, D.C. While in Rome Catherine met a Thomas H. Lyons from none other than Euclid Avenue in Waterbury. They were married at Waterbury's Basilica of the Immaculate Conception on August 27, 1966, and then headed off to of all of places Vermillion, South Dakota, close to the University of South Dakota where Thomas was enrolled to become a doctor. They eventually ended up residing in the riverside town of Newcastle, Maine. In time they had three children: Maura, Tara, and Daniel.

In 1978 Dick Murphy's son Richard B. Murphy Jr. took over the family business. Four years later, the massive Gannett newspaper chain and media corporation bought out the whole enterprise. But the elder Dick Murphy remained active in many civic endeavors around Waterbury, including the Chamber of Commerce (of which he had been president) and the Waterbury Park Board. In their "golden years," Dick and Mary Monagan Murphy were able to savor long summers on the Connecticut shore and on Block Island – that generations-spanning retreat for the Monagan family – where their daughter "Mundie" and her husband Morris Smith had a home.

Dick and Mary ultimately moved into a retirement community in Southbury. Dick died there at the age of 92 on July 13, 2003. His wife succumbed three months later, at age 85, while staying with their daughter Catherine in Maine.

Tom Monagan, Navy Doctor in Iceland

Another Waterbury Monagan whose life was profoundly transformed by World War II was Thomas Mulry Monagan. The much loved "Dr. Tom" had a quick intellect and followed his older brother John to Dartmouth, graduating in 1936. He next took a medical degree from Harvard in 1940. He interned at the famous Brigham Hospital there and then went on to do his residency at St. Vincent's Hospital on Mulry Plaza in Manhattan (named after his mother's banking family). A certain Brooklyn-born Marguerite ("Margie") Kehoe was working there as a nurse, and they began to date.

Before the knot could be tied, Thomas was inducted into service and commissioned as a lieutenant in the U.S. Navy on October 1, 1942, at the huge naval base at Norfolk, Virginia. He managed to keep courting Marguerite nonetheless, and they married in New York on February 8, 1943. That November they had their first child, Gretchen, in Norfolk.

Tom Monagan's betrothed Marge Kehoe, at a Queens riding camp.

The young Lieutenant Monagan with his first children.

The young Dr. Tom was next sent off to Iceland, which played a peculiar but important role in World War II. This all started on April 9, 1940, when the Germans swiftly seized Denmark, the then mother country to this remote island territory. The British immediately feared that the same fate could befall the lightly populated Iceland, which lay in the middle of critical shipping lanes from North America that were constantly under attack from German U-Boats. To deny the Germans the opportunity to create even more havoc, a British expeditionary force of 746 marines invaded the island shortly after dawn on May 10 and seized it for Mother England in time for everyone to calm down after a long lunch.

But this remote outpost lay at the fringes of Britain's over-stretched administrative capacity and on July 8, 1941, the United States was asked to take Iceland off its hands. Following the transfer by handshake, the U.S. Navy subsequently built a major airbase outside Reykjavik. Its job was to provide air cover for convoys steaming across the North Atlantic, while serving as a stop-over for the constant resupply of U.S. warships heading back and forth from Europe. By the time Lieutenant Thomas Monagan was posted to Iceland in April 1944, a vast armada of American shipping was being assembled in bases around England, Scotland and Northern Ireland in preparation for the D-Day landings of June 6. Hundreds of medical men and women were being deployed in and around Iceland in advance of that epic assault. The idea was that this would be a halfway station to deal with a stream of wounded and sick naval personnel needing immediate care on their way home.

But the D-Day landings were a triumph, and the Russians stormed into central Europe from the east. The result in time was the total capitulation of Germany on May 8, 1945 – V.E. Day. With that, there was no further need for any American medical outpost in Iceland. So Dr. Tom was sent back to Norfolk, Virginia where on June 10 there followed the birth of his second daughter, Ann Celeste. But on July 10, 1945, he was promoted to Lieutenant Commander, with the implicit understanding that his time in the Navy was not yet done. In August, he was sent off again on an extended deployment with the *USS Zenobia,* a new naval cargo and medical supply ship bizarrely named after the minor planet Zenobia 840, itself a tribute to the Greek god Zeus. Following that ship's return to port on April 1, 1946, Tom was discharged and rejoined the family in New York. Very soon after that, they would all be living at 24 Windsor Street in Waterbury's Bunker Hill, which would become the house of my own childhood a few years later.

The Nolans Post World War II

The Nolan clan were celebrating as well at the end of World War II. George T. Nolan's son Fred is left on the couch holding his son, also Fred and flanked by his mother Alice Moran Nolan and father George T. Photo Courtesy of Jim Nolan.

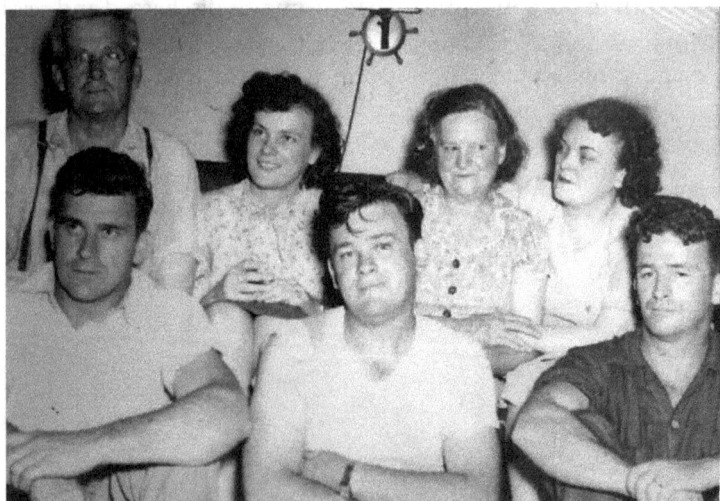

George Nolan, Sr., with daughter Alice (married James Finnegan), wife Alice Moran Nolan, daughter Betsy. Front row: sons George, Fred, and Jim.

George Nolan, Jr., with his sons George 3rd, Jim, and Patrick.

XIV.

OPTIMISM IN THE 1950'S

When Children Roamed Free

The 1950s was a time of all manner of new beginnings, and the new "Baby Boomer" generation of Monagans tasted the thick of this excitement in full. Many pundits have likened the decade to the near peaking of the American Dream. It was certainly a time of overwhelming American confidence in a possibly limitless future (aside from the menace of the aggressively expanding and nuclear-armed Soviet Union). In the U.S., job opportunities were now legion and start-up businesses were flourishing everywhere. On the now "must-have" television sets, adverts ran non-stop for the ever-more-futuristic labor-saving products that were flying into being. In 1955, even my father, as phlegmatic a wage-earner as could be, became so infused with the era's optimism that he summarily quit his solidly remunerative job at the booming Timex Corporation in Middlebury to test the decade's rising economic waters on his own. Despite a house full of kids, he was determined to become a free wheeler and start his own private accountancy practice in a small suite of offices in the Farrington Building overlooking the Waterbury Green.

The 1950s had its own traumas – among them the bloody Korean War and the Civil Rights movement domestically – but it also was a time of almost euphoric American triumphalism. This era was wreathed with a world of weird new inventions and sometimes wildly irreverent new attitudes; witness Frank Sinatra's "Rat Pack" and Elvis Presley's racy hip shaking. However, older ways were still vivid in Waterbury's outlying districts like Bunker Hill. One of my earliest memories concerns a wandering Italian "organ grinder" who appeared every now and then on Windsor Street with his pet rhesus monkey scampering upon his shoulders while he worked a crank-controlled barrel organ for us gawking little kids. From this apparatus the minstrel would grind out his merry tunes whilst the chimp hopped down to earth with a tin cup which he waved before our noses for a few pennies or nickels to be dropped in. It was magical to behold. Every couple of weeks a banged-up old dump truck would groan its way up the hill with the driver shouting, "Rags! Rags! Rag Man!" Then he filled the back payload with discarded clothing and ragged old blankets for a marginally profitable resale to some distant market in the Balkans. There was scant social welfare available in America then.

The greatest thing about this era on Windsor Street was that children were allowed to roam gloriously free. If you disappeared for three or even four hours, that was hardly a worry – so deep was the trust between neighbors. The sense of shared responsibility between families with children of similar ages was so tight it was almost like this neighborhood comprised a small village unto itself. This was also a world of what we kids called "short cuts." So we all knew how to hop over every fence or cut behind every shed or garage unseen to get to where we wanted to go, as if we small ones owned this world.

Because of its barn and sizeable side yard and my parents' easy attitudes, our place became a magnet for layers of kids to glom together every single summer and weekend day – sometimes 20 or so at a go with their various clusters. At times the barn became a free-for-all, with the big kids scrambling in and out of the cupola to staddle the very ridgelines of the roof, just to show they could. There were twin horse stalls at the base of that barn. Over the larger one my sister Nancy presided as a kind of priestess over what she called the "Holy Cross Club" and where she heard regular confessions and offered absolution for most sins. She hung a crimson flag from our father's same-named alma mater against a side wall and created an "altar" over an old door thrown across a pair of saw-horses. Nancy also doffed my mother's black rain coat on backwards so that it might look like a nun's cassock. Eventually, her parishioners rebelled, however. "The club had to be disbanded after the members staged an insurrection and refused to let me hear any more of their confessions," Nancy laughed years later.

The intensity of activity at 24 Windsor escalated as the years progressed. The "haunted houses" that were staged in the barn's hayloft gave new meaning to the macabre. Powerful M80 firecrackers sometimes excited my parents' swift interventions. Snowball fights assumed epic proportions. Massive snow fortresses arose in the side yard, where my brother Jim with his ingenious mind was ceded with some substantial control.

For new schemes, my oldest brother Steve, born in 1944 – and later an Airforce test pilot – devoured the great boyhood-celebrating magazines of the 1950s like *Popular Mechanics* and *Popular Science*. One of Steve's early projects involved creating a catapult with automobile suspension springs affixed to its base in his quest to throw stones hundreds of feet and over the roof of a particular neighbor

The Barn at 24 Windsor.

with woods out behind. After a certain misfire, he was told to cease and desist.

Steve had a genius for making incredible things, which later included a hi-fi set, a hand-pumped (by Jim) diving machine, and a sail boat out of a kit. Given free rein and today's "crowd funding" he could have been building military grade flying drones.

Steve created for me when a little boy an incredible facsimile of a Sioux Indian war shield. The circular frame was fashioned out of pre-soaked willow stalks over which Steve stretched and stitched a canvas cover to maximum tautness.

He studied tribal pictographs and then painted the surface with iconic images of young warriors at battle or hunt. Then two-dozen brilliantly dyed turkey feathers were attached via ultra-tough carpet thread. Next, he made me a war bonnet. With that shield in my hand, I patrolled our yard's perimeter for days wearing nothing but my own loincloth and warpaint from head to waist. I brandished a new bow, also hand-crafted by Steve, in hand and a quiver of arrows slung across my shoulders in case some tribe of children from say Nathan Court might attack. Inevitably, the imagination ran dry and I took to shooting at our many squirrels with absolutely no possibility of success.

Growing up in this kind of world brought many benefits, and some odd challenges. Seeing that I was too little to join the warring big kids in the barn's loft, my father had a teeming truck load of sand dumped at its side to create the ultimate sandbox of any small boy's dreams. The spilling forth of that near avalanche just for me was a moment of unforgettable joy. My retinue of little friends materialized immediately with arms full of prized toy cars and tanks and army men and no one could ever count how many hours of bliss followed in the next years.

The man who delivered this marvelous mountain of sand, John Brophy, was emblematic of this time. He was a Waterbury character and one of my father's early accountancy clients. The Brophys were a still half-agricultural clan holed up in a peculiar hollow that was called "Town Line" since their different fields straddled the confluence of the Watertown, Middlebury, and Waterbury boundaries. Though this nook on the back road toward Watertown lay less than three miles away, it then amounted to another world, with little trace to be seen out there yet of the manicured suburbia eventually to transform so much of Connecticut (and America). Two of John's adjoining brothers worked in the mills and machine shops just enough hours to subsidize their real love of farming.

During World War II John Brophy had risen to the rank of colonel in the United States Army Intelligence Service, so he must have had a sharp mind. But upon coming home, he reverted to a more devil-may-care approach to life. Ostensibly for the fun of it, he also opened his own "luncheonette" on 78 Center Street in the dead middle of Waterbury. This emporium was called "Brophy's Coffee Bar," and was located near the Green. One of the cafe's novelties was slicing hot dogs down the middle so that they could be fried on the grill. This was just not done to American hot dogs at that time.

Lawyers, bankers, and other businessmen like my father constantly made the rounds to Brophy's to catch up on the latest "local intelligence" and Waterbury's in-jokes. And therein Jake Monagan and John Brophy became special friends. Out in "Town Line" on the Middlebury Road, John and the other Brophys were assembling their own legions of kids – one a star jockey – who were all comfortable riding fast horses and tending cows. My father became the accountant for the Brophys Coffee Bar and obviously liked that better than working for Timex and counting its 3 million wristwatches a year. But then again, he seemed to pick up new business everywhere. No doubt this was because he was so flexible and willing to be paid in odd ways such as by sandbox sand, or the ploughing of our driveway after heavy winter snows.

My brother Jim, the salutatorian of his class at Crosby High School in 1968, was another profound influence on my young life. He was incredibly patient with me and intriguingly thoughtful, which are qualities many big brothers do not have. He loved reading, especially history. However, Jim was wildly contradictory as an adolescent and could dabble with danger and mayhem when in the mood.

In winter, a favorite activity for all was sledding since you could fly down the steep Windsor Street at break-neck speeds once the big snows fell. But the mortal danger in that thrill came from the fact you were hurtling straight toward the always fast traffic of Watertown Avenue at the bottom of the hill. And there was no buffer between life and death down there. Every sledder thus became an expert at dragging his feet at the last moment and driving head-first into the huge curbside banks of snow left by the city plows at the bottom of the hill. When your sled was not in perfect control, you just rolled off at the very last minute and prayed fast.

Perhaps it was here when my brother Steve first contemplated becoming a test pilot. Repeatedly racing our sleds at such speeds with our bail-out tricks into snowbanks inevitably led to rivets popping loose and cutting up the rider's clothing. One particular day I remember my mother looking at me in astonishment when I came back in the front door with the third pair of trousers I had cut up that afternoon. Incredibly, she just broke out laughing. Then again, she had to bring me to the Waterbury Hospital emergency room at least five times for various broken bones, head contusions, and the rest. When I was about ten, my newest chemistry set experiment went terribly wrong, this time while making gunpowder in the basement, and nearly blew out the windows of the whole house. I was fortunate that Doctor Rod Good intervened so ably to restore my full eyesight.

Below Watertown Avenue there lay many acres of scraggly bottomlands along the Steele Brook tributary of the Naugatuck River. These hosted a rough baseball field and an area then called the Gun Lots (for shooting clay pigeons and pheasants) and were mostly used for growing corn in the summer. This area was flooded in the winter to create a vast, typically rough public skating surface, but with welcoming bonfires usually roaring out of old barrels by its side (where of course certain parties were passing noggins). It was a euphoric scene with a touch of Brueghel to it on a good day. But I preferred after hurrying through my post-school newspaper route to race down to the frozen flat stretch of the Steele Brook just beyond to practice my new hockey moves and full throttle stops and starts in a deeper peace. You could skate for as long as you wished after dark there since the far bank had a neon lit parking lot beside a factory was that thrummed into the night. In that lonely setting, I imagined I would be a star.

In 1959, my brother Phil, the last of our brood, came along and ably restoked and extended these traditions. He too remembers the incomparable briskness of meeting snowbanks face-first and bringing in whole new groups of children to repopulate the barn. He also fondly remembers the incomparable freedom to roam unsupervised as a child on Windsor Street. "I still dream about Bunker Hill all the time. The neat well-built, imposing houses and every other one full of at least five kids. The hidden cut-throughs behind them, the pass-ways and garages, out-buildings and barns we would sneak into and hide or play or set up command centers for the Fifth Army.

"It was magical and there will never be another place like it. Nowadays, you wouldn't let your kid out to the mailbox. But back then Mom walked me to the first day of kindergarten at Bunker Hill School a few blocks away and that was it, you were on your own. In fact you made the trip four times a day since we came home for lunch. It seemed every front porch was occupied by adults who actually sat there and talked to the gads of children passing by, not a worry in the sky about that then. In a few minutes from our house you got to the penny candy store and right after that the Bunker Hill Pharmacy where you could sneak a peek at the latest comic books until Clyde, the old guy who ran the soda fountain, would shoo you away. It was all so colorful. Four times per day you made this walk and each segment was different, each day. When I tell you that moving away from Bunker Hill (when I was eight) into the wasteland that was the Country Club area was devastating to me, I mean it."

Silly Putty and Wiffle Balls

The surging economy of the 1950s brought along a thirst for new entertainments and inventions of many kinds. For children there was always an excitement in the air, sometimes fed in our Connecticut childhoods by the silliest phenomena. It was in New Haven in 1950 that a young advertising copywriter named Peter Hodgson borrowed $147 to launch a synthetic rubber novelty product that had been discarded as useless by scientists at a nearby branch of the massive General Electric Company. But a blob of the gooey, stretchy, salt-water-taffy-like stuff had the capacity to bounce almost forever. Hodgson had the vision to jauntily name it "Silly Putty," then package it in airtight, bright plastic egg shells, and sell the stuff as an absurd cocktail party joke of a thing. But once he got a mention in the New Yorker magazine, he sold 250,000 capsules of Silly Putty in three days and a craze went wild. My father was an early purchaser.

This was the age of the "Hula Hoop" as well, and he appeared one evening with a car load of these plastic marvels which instantly had my sister Nancy and her little friends gyrating up and down our side yard to keep these gravity-defying things whirling around their waists (or necks, knees, or arms) for half of forever. One fanatic from Australia was recently able to do this for 100 hours straight.

Another amazing Connecticut invention came to life in the early 1950s and this was created by a Fairfield dad named David A. Mullany. In collaboration with his young son, Mullany devised a wondrous plastic baseball with multiple vents that made air flow through it in uncanny ways when pitched with just a little extra wrist-twisting and insouciance. The result was that it could be made to curve, slip, sink, float and leap by an expert ten-year-old as if the batter were facing some astonishing offerings by a seasoned World Series ace. But this ball had other magical assets as well – most importantly, it would break no windows and allowed endless games to be played between just two kids, instead of the 18 required for "real" baseball. A stroke of genius in short. Dubbed the "Wiffle Ball," this invention was ultimately brought to market out of a tiny factory in Shelton, Connecticut in 1955.

My father quickly found his way there and became Dave Mullaney's financial advisor and first accountant. One of my father's most triumphant moments in that role featured his returning to Windsor Street from his first Wiffle Ball business meeting with the backseat of his latest Chevy packed with samples of this new wonder – a very odd accounting fee indeed. Our side-yard's huge popularity as a hub for neighborhood play now shot to the stratosphere. The games that followed went on for hours, day after day. Of course, we drove our neighbors nuts.

My sister Nancy never forgot the thrilling day in 1955 when my father took her down the valley to see the little plant in Shelton where these magical orbs that conquered America were made. It wasn't practical, everyday brass goods but sometimes hilarious new plays on reality that were emanating out of the Naugatuck Valley now.

Another Naugatuck Valley enterprise forged in that era's boundless optimism was the Alcort Company – its game plan being "a sailboat in every driveway." And this was started by two Waterbury friends as a lark. Their main product was a bare-bones sailboat which was meant to be affordable by almost anyone since they sold it as a ready-to-assemble kit, basically containing a 15-foot surfboard-like unsinkable hull with a single mast and nylon sail, simple tiller, and retractable fin-like keel. Probably while knocking on the door for their business, my father bought a "Sunfish" kit which my teenaged brother Steve assembled and painted in a flash. This easy-sailing craft provided years of enjoyment for all of us children on Middlebury's gentle Lake Quassapaug, although my sister Nancy eventually improvised a niche use in sailing just out of my mother's eyesight from her beach chair so that Nancy could smoke one of her menthol cigarettes in sublime, secret peace.

WIFFLE BALL®
Regulation BASEBALL SIZE
IT CURVES!
BAT IT! BOUNCE IT!
SAFE ANYWHERE

XV.

MONAGANS IN THE 1960S

By the late 1950s, the numbers of the extended Monagan clan in and around Waterbury were growing impressively as was the family's name. As noted, Dick Murphy was making quite a splash in the region's advertising industry and he and his wife Mary Monagan Murphy now had five kids in their busy Prospect Street house. My aunt Joan Monagan Clinton would appear in summer visits from Virginia with her husband John with the vanguard of what was to turn into a family of nine children, with the added births of Andrew, Paul, Joan, Steve, Neil, and Tom. Uncle Bill also visited with his daughter Catherine and son Bob a couple of times.

But nobody was topping the prodigal numbers of children being produced by the pediatrician Tom Monagan and his wife Margie in the grand Pine Street house the family had moved into after vacating Windsor Street. By the decade's end they had a total of twelve children – ten of them girls. The boys at either end were Thomas and Ben. By now, Dr. Tom, with his gravelly voice, no-nonsense manner and big crescent smile, was one of the most successful and beloved pediatricians in the city of Waterbury.

The other central figure in this evolving family history was the former mayor John S. Monagan. Handsome and supremely self-confident, he married the New Jersey beauty Rosemary Ann Brady in Bayonne in 1949. Rosemary was born in 1926, and at the age of 18 became a nursing cadet in 1944 to do her part for the war effort. The couple had a succession of five children beginning with Charles Andrew Monagan, called "Charley," who was born in Waterbury on March 8, 1950; and the next year Michael, a musician and long-term teacher of handicapped children now living outside Los Angeles. Mary Parthenia, always called "Parthy," hit the scene in Waterbury on March 21, 1953. A skilled photographer and musician and avid gardener, she has long been a resident of Charlottesville, Virginia. Laura and Susie were born in Maryland in the next several years. In 1958, John S. Monagan campaigned to become a United States Congressman from the Fifth District of Connecticut. The Dartmouth grad won handily. He was quickly identified as a "comer" in the upper echelons of his party and ably represented the district, with its then heavily Irish-American and hugely Catholic base in what would become a remarkable run of seven consecutive terms in the United States House of Representatives. Inevitably, the family relocated to the Washington, D.C. area, and eventually purchased a house in Bethesda, Maryland.

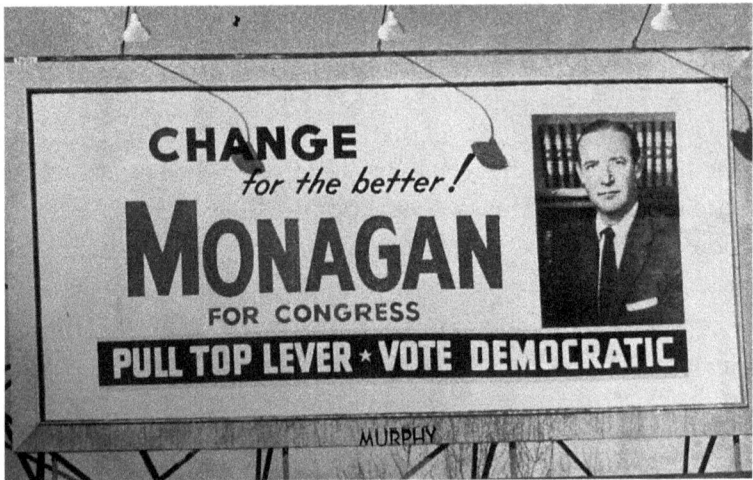

All in the family. A classic Murphy billboard for John Monagan's first congressional campaign in 1958. Courtesy Joe Murphy.

JFK and That Magic Night in Waterbury

One of the most extraordinary moments in the Monagan family's history occurred on the night of November 6, 1960, when John Fitzgerald Kennedy appeared in Waterbury to close off his quest to become the first Irish Catholic president of the United States. Wherever he campaigned that summer and fall, the 43 year-old senator from Massachusetts generated enormous excitement with his ineffable charisma and soaring eloquence. In Waterbury, so close to his neighboring state, Jack Kennedy's appeal ran especially deep. With so many thousands of largely Catholic immigrants having peopled every hillside, here in the Naugatuck Valley he was seen as an avatar of achievement and an icon of hope. But at the end of the 1950s, many Irish-Americans still held on to lingering stories from earlier generations and most still cultivated a sentimental attachment to the land of their forebears. For the Irish of Waterbury, a proud sense of a cultural identity apart still held strong. And now here arose the sudden possibility of an Irish Catholic from the next state becoming President of the United States of America.

John F. Kennedy's decision to come to Waterbury on the penultimate night of his campaign against Vice President Richard Nixon stirred a tremendous excitement up and down the Naugatuck Valley. Waterbury itself was still often claimed to have one of the highest percentages of Irish-Americans of any city in America. But the electoral outcome in Connecticut as a state was thought to be quite up in the air. Assuring JFK that he would receive an adoring welcome in Waterbury – with great press then to redound across the nation – were both the Governor Abe Ribicoff and none other than John S. Monagan, the former mayor who was now seeking reelection to his second term in the United States Congress. So the plan was made for the potential next president of America to wind up his nationwide campaign in the Brass City, with a speech to be delivered on the town Green at 9 p.m., before returning to Massachusetts the next day to await the election results.

By early that night of November 6, 1960, thick crowds were pouring into Waterbury's center. In time, somewhere near 50,000 people amassed. Every main thoroughfare and side street was chock-a-block, and people came out on porches, balconies, and rooftops. The solemnly colonnaded Basilica of the Immaculate Conception was illuminated to shimmer like some monument from ancient Rome – for here in the morning Jack Kennedy was due to receive Holy Communion and thereby reaffirm his proud Catholic faith to America in a showy final flourish to his campaign. The absolute focal point was the floodlit balcony above the entrance to the stately six-story former Elton, renamed as the Roger Smith Hotel. It was decked out in billowing red, white and blue bunting as if awaiting the coming of George Washington himself. Up there would soon be perched at Kennedy's side and above a giant "WELCOME JACK!" banner both Governor Ribicoff and Congressman Monagan. The only problem was that as 9 p.m. came around the one person no soul could see was Senator John Fitzgerald Kennedy himself.

There might be a small delay, it was announced. Okay, alright and no matter, for the mood on Waterbury's jam-packed, two-acre central Green remained electric, maybe even a little tipsy. The brilliant Danish pianist and hilarious showman Victor Borge, famous on late night TV, serenaded and tossed around zany jokes while people sang along and swayed hip-to-hip. But when 10 p.m. came there was still no JFK. And the same was true at 11. A light rain was falling and it was getting ever colder. More warm-up speeches were given, there were many more pleas for patience – and the clock struck midnight. It was getting to be like kids waiting for Santa Claus by now.

But somehow the crowd remained ebullient, with sing songs and chants echoing around the Green as time kept tick, ticking. There were so many interconnected families standing shoulder-to-shoulder together out there – among them many Monagans, Nolans, Butlers, and Murphys – as if it were the party that Waterbury had been waiting to throw for itself for generations. Gretchen Monagan, the oldest of Dr. Tom's children and a senior at Notre Dame Academy, had gotten there early to gain a prime spot. "We had already been waiting there for about eight hours since late afternoon – try to Imagine! We were just freezing but the air was filled with excitement."

Finally, JFK's campaign plane touched down at 1 a.m. in a little airport in Stratford, Connecticut – about 45 minutes south of Waterbury – where 2,500 people had also been waiting for hours to cheer his arrival. One wonders if there were drinks on board, since Kennedy madly proceeded to shake hands with half of this crowd, even though he was hours behind schedule and courting pandemonium.

Now, JFK's motorcade began to roll up the Naugatuck Valley along Connecticut's Route 8, and people were crushing in around it from all sides, wanting to be part of history. The cavalcade feathered its way north through one archly Democratic and heavily Catholic industrial town after another – Shelton, Derby, Ansonia, Seymour, Beacon Falls, and Naugatuck. All along the way thousands lined the road, calling out euphorically. "They were at every crossroads... at two in the morning, they were waiting with torchlights and red flares to cheer and yell, 'We love you, Jack!" the historian Theodore White wrote in his book **The Making of the President:1960.** The progress toward Waterbury, the final exclamation point to Kennedy's tumultuous campaign was achingly slow.

For the thousands of shivering souls left on the Green – "the largest mass of humanity the city had ever seen" wrote the local newspaper columnist Sherman London (with whom I later worked as a young reporter) - the excitement grew feverish. Spotlights were roving through the skies and campaign music blasting, when close to 3 a.m. the motorcade entered Waterbury's outlying streets. Massive cheers rent the air as JFK's limousine stopped beside the Green and he scurried up to the balcony of the Roger Smith Hotel to look out over the thousands below. Stationed at his side was the first-term U.S. Congressman John S. Monagan. "My name is Kennedy and I have come to ask for your support!" belted out the beaming young Massachusetts senator, thereby emotively underlining the fact of his Irishness and eliciting a joyous roar in response. Even at three a.m., the man was counting votes.

This night was history in the making. With its old-line blue bloods and affluent New York suburbs further south, Connecticut had long been a staunchly Republican state in national elections. But that base was being shaken now. Pierre Salinger, J.F.K.'s celebrated press secretary, pronounced that this visit to Waterbury was the most moving point of that entire, remarkable presidential campaign.

The next morning an exhausted Jack Kennedy did go to Mass across the street at the Immaculate Conception, where so many in this Monagan family were married or seen off to the next world. The family connection to John F. Kennedy deepened that much more after he headed off toward a rally in New Haven. A few miles down the road, the whole motorcade stopped at a pre-arranged point around Bethany so that Jack Kennedy could shake the hands again of not just John S. Monagan and Rosemary, but each of their awestruck young children along with the whole sprawling family of Dr. Tom. As Gretchen Monagan Sterling recalls, "John called my father in the morning and told him to take us all 'out east' to see the procession of the cars on the way to out of town. When the cavalcade drove up, John shouted, 'There's my family!' pointing at us. And JFK shouted, 'Stop the car!' We all got to shake JFK's hand. My sister Betsy still has the glove she wore when shaking his hand."

Meanwhile, glowing press reports about this Connecticut visit flashed across the country, and Waterbury may have been one place that in some exquisite little degree helped put John Fitzgerald Kennedy over the top, especially in Connecticut where he won 54 percent of the vote, and in some tangible way, nationwide. Although Richard Nixon, the eight-year vice president under President Dwight David Eisenhower and a very strong candidate (and later U.S. President), lost the national popular vote by the smallest of margins, JFK won his swing states and became the 35th president of the United States. The excitement around the first year of his administration, with his glamorous Jacqueline Bouvier at his side, was called a kind of Camelot, though tragedy of course lurked from the start.

Happy Saint Patrick's Day gathering in Washington, D.C., 1960 on the eve of JFK's run for the presidency. The young Congressman Monagan (lower right), with then senator John Fitzgerald Kennedy (above), and to this right the powerhouse for decades of the U.S. House of Representatives, Tip O'Neill. Also in the top row left is U.S. Congressman Neil Gallagher (democrat, New Jersey), and in bottom row to the left are the Connecticut congressmen Robert Giaimo (left) and Emilio Q. Daddario. Only JFK and JSM will not suffer the indignity of those hats! Photo and details courtesy of Charley Monagan.

3 a.m. on that famous Waterbury night, with Gov. Abe Ribicoff left and JFK.

Congressman Monagan clearly had the president's ear.

JSM in an edgy campaign moment beside the doomed Robert Kennedy in his 1968 run for the presidency, sometime before his assassination by Sirhan-Sirhan.

In a happy moment, JSM's oldest son Michael is left, sisters Parthy and Laura right, then mother Rosemary, little Susan, Congressman John, and son Charles.

The excitement certainly resonated across Ireland. Framed photographs of John Fitzgerald Kennedy were hung almost overnight in front halls in every province, from teeming Dublin tenements to the remotest farms, typically close to a portrait of Jesus Christ's with a tiny electric light flickering within His Sacred Heart. These two gaudy images of what it was meant to be Irish lived side by side for many years to come, as witnessed time and again during my own travels in the early 1970s. But none of these proud Irish people could have guessed that Kennedy's own heart had once been so touched by the distant city of Waterbury, Connecticut and that beating pulse of a family called Monagan.

My Grandfather's Passing

One would have to say that the extended Monagan family enjoyed a string of fine triumphs in these years, when many of the latter-generation figures in this narrative were coming of age. But this was also a time mixed with sadness and the point when grandfather Walter Edward Monagan, the once prominent Waterbury lawyer, finally passed away on August 8, 1961. The cause of death was essentially cigarette smoking.

Walter was the last of his generation to go. The first, some thirty years earlier had been Charles Andrew Monagan, M.D. Also passing away in the 1930s was the youngest sister Bernice Monagan Nelson, and the hugely self-sacrificing oldest sister Minnie. As noted, William Henry Monagan, the brass caster who had once lived it up in the Elton Hotel, had succumbed in 1946. His sister Helen Monagan Marks died a couple of years later. The enigmatic sister Catherine had more or less vanished into New York City, and it remains unknown where and when she died despite considerable efforts to find out. Regardless, the passing of my grandfather Walter was a milestone.

The *Waterbury Republican* ran an editorial in my grandfather's honor the day after his passing that read in part: "Walter E. Monagan was above and before all of what is referred to today in all too often derogatory terms as 'the old school.' Walter Monagan loved Waterbury. He loved its people. And in his associations with the people of the city, whether it was in legal circles or elsewhere, he maintained a very warm and human manner. He thoroughly enjoyed a good argument, purely for the sake of argument. He was never happier than when he had an opportunity to stimulate the thinking of younger and less experienced men. He could – and did – take both victory and defeat with good grace. He was a man utterly without malice, a man of wit and humor, a man of sympathy and broad understanding. His passing leaves a void not easily filled."

At the next year's meeting of the Waterbury Bar (the regional lawyers' association of which my grandfather himself had been a president) the Congressman John S. Monagan read out a formal tribute to his uncle Walter, that was counter-signed by Patrick Healy, the chairman, on June 20, 1962. It read, "None of us who are now old timers at the Waterbury Bar need any reminders of the gifts and skills of Walter Monagan as a lawyer. He was a student by endowment and nature. He had a sharp and penetrating mind, a sure ability to see the exact nature of whatever legal problem confronted him and a swiftness in reducing it to its essentials... he had an astringent but kindly wit. He would shake his head sadly when he encountered anything but the clearest thinking, but he would also praise with pleasure when the praise was deserved. All who knew him recognized his sure command of the law." The letter then went on to cite his many achievements, even though everyone in Waterbury knew he also had his flaws, as do we all.

However, Walter and Mary Butler Monagan produced some remarkable offspring, and one of these who came into his own in this period was my dear uncle Andy.

Uncle Andy and 84 Euclid

Front and center on that historic November night in 1960 on Waterbury's Green was my uncle "Andy" or Charles Andrew Monagan, still then an arch Democrat and a bachelor. Handsome, humorous, and affable, the former U.S. Navy air force navigator could be found many the Saturday night exchanging stories and tickling the ivories at Waterbury's Elks Club, where he was eventually elected to be the "Exalted Ruler." Everyone loved to share a sing-along or beer with Andy – including his younger compatriot and cousin Jim Nolan, from my great-grandmother's line (who has been another helper in this narrative).

After returning from the Pacific in 1946, C. Andrew Monagan resumed working in regional sales for the Scovill Manufacturing Company, to which the family was so long connected. His travels on its behalf sometimes required entertaining overnights in larger cities, notably New York, which he didn't mind. But the fundamental problem was that Scovill's, like the whole brass industry in Connecticut, was by a small twist here and a dramatic turn there inexorably collapsing. Even a salesman with the greatest personal flair could not mask this demise. By the mid-1950s, major product lines were being radically thinned down or dropped altogether at Scovill's as the company desperately sought to cut costs in the face of growing and much cheaper foreign competition. To circumvent Connecticut's relatively high and unionized labor costs, entire branches of the business were being shifted to the American South or overseas. Long gone were the benevolent personal relationships that had so handsomely rewarded the likes of my great-grandfather John Stephen Monagan and his son William Henry and Howard Miller and the rest. With each passing year, the now distant corporate management of Waterbury's once fabled brass industry was growing ever more indifferent to its origins.

Seeing the writing on the wall and plainly wanting a new lease on life, Andy Monagan began studying to become a science teacher. Around 1960 he quit Scovill's to begin a new career in the Naugatuck school system, just a few miles south of downtown Waterbury. Given his social skills at winning people's hearts and curiosity, Andy was a natural and became a director of science education at the City Hill Middle School there.

But Andrew was in no hurry to change the domestic side of his life. At the age of 45 in the house of 84 Euclid Avenue he was still surrounded by his own built-in if eclectic family. Most central to the household was his widowed sister Marjorie Monagan Cetta, my dear aunt who was an innately great cook but who had her skills advanced under watchful Italian eyes. With Margie's daughter Cathy Cetta growing up by his side, it was almost as if Andy experienced the joys of fatherhood as well but with minimal responsibility. His father Walter, my grandfather, was on hand until 1962. Also in that Euclid Avenue house remained my aged great aunt Anna Louise Butler, the formidably sage, retired school principal. Complementing all this was Andrew's sweet but "learning challenged" younger sister also named Louise. My Aunt Marjorie looked after her with consummate grace until "Little Louise" was enrolled in a Southbury care home in the 1970s.

Amazingly, this all somehow worked, partly because Andy himself was so easy-going, but more importantly because Aunt Marge was such an organized and caring person. As much as he loved his nights out, Andy remained an arch Catholic and a deacon and devoted choir singer in his local church. But life is sometimes blessed by a new stroke of fortune from out of the heavens above. Somewhere around 1970, an 18-years-younger lady named Seena Claire (Lerner) Bernbach struck a light in my 55 year-old uncle's heart, and she happened to be of all things Jewish and divorced, both taboos to the staunch Catholic church hierarchy of that time. But Seena was adorable.

To previous generations from both sides the idea of their marriage would have been unthinkable. So it was no surprise that this odd couple could find not a single priest or rabbi in Waterbury who would marry them. Ultimately, some quietly contrarian man of the cloth in Stamford did the job on August 4, 1972.

Seena was the wife no one could have anticipated for the quintessentially Irish bachelor Andy, but the marriage worked out wonderfully. He knew nothing about Judaism but wanted to learn and respected its traditions profoundly from the start. Seena was nearly a foot shorter than my uncle but had a sense of humor just as tall. She was somewhat low-key but cocked an eye in hilarity at the frequent rising of her new husband's stentorian voice. She loathed his early cigar smoking and had to thoroughly eradicate and reinvent his wardrobe but loved him to death. The family welcomed her in unreservedly.

Seena's father Fred Lerner was a prosperous furrier from Middletown, Connecticut and saw to it that she like her brother Arthur attended the University of Connecticut. After graduating in June 1954, Seena married a Dr. Erwin Bernbach from Waterbury whose medical specialty was in podiatry, the long looked down upon study of feet. In discussing this, Erwin sometimes played the Borscht belt comedian-"Podiatrist? I wouldn't

Seena in younger days.

286

have known one if I stepped on him," he said. With Seena he had two children, Faun and Marc. Around 1970 they divorced, and my uncle Andy stepped in.

For 33 years Seena worked as a devoted kindergarten teacher, eventually in one of Waterbury's more racially divided schools. She loved children and people of every stripe, and wonderfully renewed the life of my uncle Andy. The odd couple lived in a spacious house on Marney Drive in suburban Middlebury, with a gleaming grand piano in the living room over which Uncle Andy loved to entertain his dearest relatives or a party crowd. His daughter in-law, Faun Bernbach, born in 1958, was often on hand. She was a thoughtful soul who first married a Welsh photographer named Chris Evans, but then a fellow college teacher named Peter Lucas who was a colleague at the University of Illinois. Faun, director of the Literacy Center there, sadly died from cancer at the age of 47 in 2005. Her brother Marc (married to Doris and father of Abigail and Rebecca) had followed his father into podiatry and they worked together for some years.

Uncle Andy was a much loved crooner

In his later years, my uncle Andrew sold real estate in Middlebury and kept up a very active role as a deacon in the Catholic Church. Seena was a regular congregant at the B'Nai Israel synagogue in Southbury. After a bout of breast cancer in the 1980s, she threw her energy into selling quality prostheses to similarly affected women. The couple were guiding spirits to our family right up until Andy's death in 2001, and Seena's in 2003.

Hope Monagan vs Status Quo

The story of my mother Helen Hope Hurst Monagan bears further telling. "Hope," as she was always called, was born in Charleston, South Carolina on January 14, 1918. She was born to Helen Marie Deasy of Cincinnati, Ohio, whose own Cork-born mother had died of typhus when she was a child, and her father William Harris Hurst of Axtell, Texas. My mother's father Harris was an extraordinary character who was once the toast of Oaxaca, Mexico, where he married my grandmother. The couple lived in more southern U.S. cities than can be listed here. Their sons included Hope's dear artist brother Harris, and the writers Nathaniel Hawthorne Hurst (who published five novels before dying of pneumonia at the age of 24) and John Shirley Hurst, another novelist, who was a city editor for some years at the Washington Post and a communications honcho for the State Department (or CIA) in places ranging from Formosa to Michigan, plus newspapers from Miami to Albany. Hope's brother Paul was another Hurstian raconteur who managed or purchased several bars and hotels along the Panama Canal before dying young of diabetes. My mother inherited the same elegiac passion for travel as her parents – for example, venturing alone to Cuba when she was 23 – and never let this characteristic go.

Even while raising five children in the boisterous Windsor Street of the 1950s, Hope kept trying to make "mad money" on the side, partly to self-fund a variety of long-dreamed of future expeditions – including several excursions to revisit her southern Hurst family. A meticulous legal secretary and expert at shorthand, she had worked for government agencies in Washington, D.C. by the age of 18 (when her father died), and a top law firm in New York City when she was 21. It was in doing similar work for the U.S. Army in Florida that she met my father. A chief client in Connecticut was the Waterbury lawyer and Yale professor, Peter Marcuse, son of the internationally famous philosopher and sociologist Herbert Marcuse. Hope also became heavily involved in the production of a monthly newsletter called the *Bunker Hill News*. Somehow, she managed a trip through the Panama Canal Zone (home to her beloved nephew Paul Hurst, son of her same-named brother) and on

to South America. Ireland, Spain and Italy were later destinations, with my
father invariably preferring to stay home in Waterbury, which he thought to
be the best place on earth.

The 1960s in Waterbury were not quite the era of "women's liberation," a
term whose confrontationalism my mother disliked, anyway. While accepting
a traditional housewife's role, Hope simultaneously kept exploring a world of
new opportunities for women that were arising with the times. She developed
a passion to finally earn a college degree and began taking courses at the local
C.W. Post community college (where she did earn an Associate's Degree).
Hope also set out to overcome her terrible jitters at public speaking though she
was otherwise a hilarious life-of-the-party figure who thrilled in impromptu
skits – as another means of boosting her self-confidence. In the mid-1960s,
she began attending regular meetings of the local Dale Carnegie Society.
With his perennial best seller **How to Win Friends and Influence People,**
Dale Carnegie was phenomenally popular early guru of self-improvement
who spawned a nationwide craze. (The classic Peter Sellers Cold War farce,
*DOCTOR STRANGELOVE – or How I Learned to Stop Worrying and Love
the Bomb* was partially a lampooning of this.)

The foreshadowing was all in place, but it was still to the family's shock that
my mother announced one day in perhaps 1967 that she was ready to run
for a position of authority in Waterbury's government as a member of the
Board of Alderman. To her, it was beside the point that no woman had ever
done this before and that the Aldermen in Waterbury seemed to always be
cagey lawyers or property developers. The idea that a housewife from the
Deep South and with a very modest education would take on Waterbury's
entrenched political system may have seemed outlandish, but that was Hope.
She was an intuitive and original personality, and she simply decided her
moment had come. My mother then developed and began delivering her
stump speech with showy aplomb – just as she had learned at Dale Carnegie
– about her eagerness to take on the cronyism that she correctly saw as
pervading Waterbury's politics. What Hope Monagan was doing was in fact
historic. She campaigned energetically and won handily.

Helen Hope Monagan.

My father John Monagan (left) with friends.

Once in office Hope Monagan was no shrinking violet. She made serious inquiries about the general issue of civic corruption – a Waterbury tradition – and ultimately uncovered a major scandal in the city's out-sourcing of the ambulance service via a system of rank collusion with a company called Campion. She took all this on single-handedly and became much praised in the press for her courage. Sherman London, the political columnist for the *Waterbury Republican-American* adored her. But sadly, despite making such an impact my mother declined to run for a second term. It was all too "nervous-making" was her explanation.

Hope did have a long continuum of (mostly) satisfaction ahead in watching her five children progress into adulthood and marriage, with 13 grandchildren in the offing. Ever popular, she never lost her marvelous sense of humor. Around this time my parents moved from Windsor Street to a newly built home near the Waterbury Country Club, which was my golf-loving father's bastion. In a flash all the character of old Bunker Hill was gone.

However, my father remained intensely industrious, because that was his way and he fretted as our generations' college fees loomed. My oldest brother Steve left first with his acceptance to the United States Air Force Academy in Colorado Springs – an event that transformed his life. My brother Jim next gained acceptance to Georgetown with a handsome academic scholarship. There too he maintained a near perfect grade-point average, despite working long hours on the side to help pay a lot of his own way. From Georgetown Jim followed with a master's in physics from Rutgers. My sister Nancy went on from Notre Dame to Trinity College in Washington (as had her aunts). Later, after years of child-rearing, she earned a Ph.D. in education from Widener University in Philadelphia, allowing her to further her career as a professor of education. I myself went to the Taft School in Watertown, then Tufts University outside Boston and with a year each in London and Trinity College in Dublin. My brother Phil graduated from the University of Connecticut, then received a law degree from the University of Miami. He quickly passed the bar in both Massachusetts and Connecticut.

In the mid-1980s my father sold his accountancy business and for the next several years worked as a financial comptroller for the flourishing Wesson Oil Corporation, started by his dear Windsor Street friend Bill Wesson, and now run by Bill and the lovely "Frana's" son Bob. But in the late 1980s, my father had the first of a series of debilitating strokes, with many thanks to his insatiable cigarette smoking. He worked with impressive determination to regain function after the first one, but the second left him half paralyzed until his death in 1997, at the age of 79.

My mother in contrast remained wonderfully active until almost the very end in November in 2003. Despite all the challenges of her upbringing, people everywhere knew she was special, since a *joy de vivre* was what Hope spread through life.

XVI.

LATER SNAPSHOTS

Uncles and Aunts

Uncle Walter on drums.

Walter Monagan. My uncle Walter, the State Department lawyer, and his wife Mildred were last noted as leaving Japan at the end of the Korean War for an extended tour of Western Europe, before transferring to Washington, D.C. In 1956, Walter was shifted to a series of government positions in Heidelberg, Paris, and London, all involving the settlement of continuing claims for restitution arising out of various lingering issues related to World War II. The couple returned to their historic brownstone in the Georgetown section of Washington in the early 1960s. They never had children but did enjoy a rather golden and extended retirement. In 1969 they bought a lovely old farmhouse in Brandon, Vermont but later moved to the college town of Middlebury. They eventually relocated to the Wake Robin retirement community in Shelbourne, where Walter kept busy with his reading and research, sessions at his drums, and his stamp albums – his mind forever keen. Six months before his death in 2008 (at the age of 97), and despite losing his beloved Mildred in June 2007, Walter wrote a life-long friend, "I am ambulatory with some walker assistance. I will be ninety seven years old next June. I am still playing the drums in our small combo, as I did at Holy Cross in the 1930's!"

Marjorie Monagan. As noted, my aunt Margie tragically lost her young husband Joseph Cetta in 1954. But she remarkably regained her equilibrium and remained vital to the family's connectedness ever since, even in the face of a second mortal tragedy. As a single mother in the 1950s and 60s, Marjorie raised her daughter Catherine Cetta with unswerving devotion, while long holding together the eclectic, multi-generational household of Monagans at 84 Euclid Avenue. She remained an academic stalwart as a Waterbury high school librarian for years, eager to help in every student's research needs and striving to whet their love of learning.

Marjorie had one more great love ahead in the person of Vincent Edward Kelly, a tall and fun-loving executive with the American Brass Company who was close friends with my uncle Andy. But by 1973 Vincent's first marriage to a Louise McElligot was failing and the couple separated that April. Quietly, he and Margie developed a new lease on life together and the pair married that August 10. They doted upon each other like a couple half their age and shined as fabulous entertainers. But alas the 58-year-old "Vinnie," as he was called, suddenly died of a brain aneurysm on May 12, 1975. This was before the couple could even celebrate their second anniversary.

Although fate was twice terrible to Marjorie, she somehow pulled herself together yet again and purchased a cottage on the shore of Lake Quassapaug in Middlebury. This cozy, rustic dwelling looking out over the gentle water and woods long served as a gathering point for family get-togethers from points near and far. Before long Margie also began paying extended visits to Naples, Florida where she had many friends, since that spot was a magnet for winter-escaping and retiring Waterburians. Eventually Margie purchased a condominium there which became her primary residence. Now 99, Marge still loves her Naples.

Through all these changes, Margie has remained an inspiring family matriarch, helping to hold the spirit of the family high through every turn of the calendar. Her greatest joys have of course been in sharing in the life of her daughter Cathy Cetta, a long-term resident of East Falmouth in Cape Cod, beginning with her days as research assistant at the famous Woods Hole Oceanography Institution. A lifelong painter in water colors and acrylics and avid gardener, she began teaching students in the marine sciences at the Cape Cod Academy where she eventually became associate head of school. Now retired, she still lives in East Falmouth with her life partner, Julie Early, an amateur pilot and administrator over the years of various private charitable trusts.

Joan Marie Monagan. Born in 1928, and the youngest of my father's generation, Joan Monagan Clinton has shared the role of matriarch extraordinaire with her big sister for years. Joan lost her beloved husband John in 2003 but her house remains the nexus of one of the more extraordinarily cohesive American families to be found in this often fractionalized age. Joan's nine children (most living close by) have all had one or more spouses/partners and produced 17 grandchildren and six great grandchildren, as listed below.

William Henry Monagan. My uncle William, the World War II gunnery officer, kept active in the U.S. Navy Reserves for years afterwards and was made a Lieutenant Commander in 1956, while still busy with his work at the Department of the Treasury and raising with his wife Dorothy their children Kathleen and Bob. The family was based for years in Silver Spring, Maryland, just outside Washington, D.C. A man of perpetual good humor and blessed with a gentle wit, William enjoyed an extraordinarily long and rather golden retirement.

Cathy Cetta on a Norwegian adventure.

Although losing his wife Dorothy in 1995, Bill was able to relish the unfolding development of his five grandchildren for years still to come. He also was long active in the Knights of Columbus and the St. Thomas Apostle Catholic Church in Washington, where he was a Eucharistic minister. He took special pleasure in Bob's daughter Colleen's young passion for Irish step dancing, while Bob himself, a Maryland insurance agent, was a fixture in the local Irish-American community, even serving as grand master of the St. Patrick's Day parades. Kathleen married a Douglass Porter and the well-travelled couple began raising their three daughters – Carolyn, Cindy, and Cathleen – in Maryland, before moving to Texas and ultimately to Durango, Colorado.

William himself lived to be 100 years old, only succumbing on July 24, 2013. He was buried with full military honors at the United States National Cemetery in Arlington, Virginia in a very moving cemetery that drew together many distant family members.

Louise Ann Monagan. The handicapped sister so lovingly looked after by my aunt Marjorie and uncle Andy succumbed in 2010, having reached the age of ninety. Following the breakup of the extended family home of Euclid Avenue in Waterbury, she had lived for yeas under the devoted care of the River Glen Health Care Center in Southbury.

The Children of Dr. Charles

Mary Elizabeth Monagan Murphy. Charles Andrew Monagan's daughter Mary Murphy lived until the age of 86, dying in 2003 only a few months after the loss of her beloved husband Richard Murphy. The couple had been married for 62 years. As noted, her sister Peggy had succumbed two decades earlier. At the time of her passing, Mary's five children were listed as follows: Mary E. Smith, Newport Beach, California; Catherine Lyons, New Castle, Maine; Richard, B. Murphy, Jr., Orleans, Mass.; Joseph M. Murphy, Takoma Park, Maryland; and William P. Murphy, East Hartland, Conn. These offspring had by then produced 11 grandchildren and five great-grandchildren, a number which has presumably since grown.

Dr. Thomas Mulry Monagan. The popular Waterbury pediatrician was also long-lived, reaching the age of 90 before his death on March 29, 2005. His 12 children and their spouses and 29 grand-children (at the moment producing 27 great-grandchildren) were a source of great joy in his retirement, but Dr. Tom became afflicted, like so many, with Alzheimer's in the end. His beloved wife Marguerite Kehoe Monagan's death preceded his by several years.

John Stephen Monagan. The former U.S. Congressman passed away in Washington, D.C. on October 23, 2005, when aged 93. Remarkably alert until the last, John had continued to live life to the full in the decades following his seven terms in congress. He had returned for many years to practicing law in Washington, while avidly pursuing his research and literary interests.

In 1988, he published a respected biography of the iconic U.S. Supreme Court justice Oliver Wendell Holms, Jr., titled **The Grand Panjandrum: Mellow Years of Justice Holmes.** This followed his 1985 biography **Horace: Priest of the Poor.** John was a particular devotee of the British novelist Anthony Powell, famous for his 12-volume Proustian series **A Dance to the Music of Time.** The two maintained a decades-long correspondence.

John was passionate about Waterbury's history and collected many of the songs and tales from the early generations of immigrants for publication and performance. One memorable recital, with the former Congressman on piano and his son Charley as the master of ceremonies, occurred at Waterbury's Mattatuck Museum in 1995. Scores of the town's old Irish-American families and many others sat rapt before his reminiscences and songs, including this author and his younger brother, Attorney Philip Monagan. In 2002, John published his wonderful memoir **A Pleasant Institution,** frequently referred to herein.

In the 1980s, John's son Charley Monagan had his own brush with politics by serving as the spokesman for Connecticut Governor William O'Neill. For 25 years he was the editor of *Connecticut Magazine.* A droll and polished writer, he is also the author of countless journalism articles and numerous books. These have included the comic **The Neurotic's Handbook** and historical novels set in Waterbury such as **Carrie Welton** and **The Easter Confession,** and non-fiction books about the city and region. Charley now lives in Southbury with his Bristol-born wife Marcia (nee Graham) with several children nearby.

John and Rosemary's next son Michael Monagan is a professional guitarist, singer, prolific song writer, and leader of a rocking Southern California band called **The Sound**. He also sometimes even performs as a soloist. His other great passion has been in working for years as a teacher and inspirer of disadvantaged children in Los Angeles, whereto he moved in 1979. Some of his most remarkable accomplishments grew out of a songwriting class he taught at the J.P. Widney High School, a magnet school in Central L.A. for students aged 13-22 who are afflicted with severe learning disabilities. From this work, beginning in 1988, Michael created a joyous, offbeat student singing ensemble, with instrumentation by himself and friends, that became a hit at major rock venues throughout Southern California for years, and lead to several CDs and the 2005 feature-length documentary: **The Kids of Widney High**. Michael and his wife Gaili Schoen, a noted film composer and pianist, have two daughters: Kylie Schoen Monagan, 30, who runs the celebrated Amali restaurant in Manhattan, and Maura, 28, who is completing advanced degree work at the University of Cambridge.

The brothers' three sisters are also all musical and world-travelled. Mary Parthenia, called "Parthy" after her great aunt, lives in Charlottesville, Virginia. A passionate photographer (with many allied artistic interests including the piano, pottery, and graphic design), she was previously married to the world known musician John McCutcheon. Their two sons together are William Grayson McCutcheon, 39, and Peter Monagan McCutcheon, 37, both residents of Brooklyn, N.Y. William is a technology engineer specializing in politics and musical performance and currently works for the Democratic National Committee. Peter is a vice president of the New York creative agency Harper+Scott and with his wife Lillian has two young children, Brady and Chloe.

Laura Monagan, born in 1957, graduated from George Washington University, with a masters from Johns Hopkins, and has long worked as a teacher in southern Maryland, close to Washington, D.C. Laura has also been long involved with both song and memoir writing. Her experiences while walking 3,000 miles across America as part of the "Great Peace March" of 1986 resulting in her book **The Unaccompanied Tour.** Her husband is Patrick Lyon, and they have a daughter named Sienna, born in 1993.

Born in 1961, the youngest sister Susie Monagan also graduated from Dartmouth and later received a masters at Cornell University in the Finger Lakes Region of New York. In 2013 she received a Fulbright Scholarship to study at the National University of Ireland in Galway. She is the director of the Smith Center for the Arts in Geneva, New York. Susie had 2 sons: Cashel Stewart, 27, an alternative energy specialist in S. Portland ME and Charlie Stewart, 24, currently serving in the Peace Corps in Zimbabwe.

My Siblings:

Stephen Jay Monagan, 1944-1981. My oldest brother Steve's colorful childhood in Bunker Hill was followed by four years at Crosby High School in Waterbury, where he was a letter man on the varsity swim team and graduated in 1962. He next gained a coveted appointment to the United States Air Force Academy, whence he graduated with the highest marks in his class in electronic engineering. On September 3, 1966, Steve married his Waterbury sweetheart Martha Morrissey from the family printing company of that name. After rigorous training, he served as an RF-4C Phantom II jet pilot during the Vietnam War. He was based for 12 months from May 1968 with the Twelfth Tactical Reconnaissance Squadron of the U.S. Air Force at Tan Son Nhut outside Saigon. The unit's primary responsibility was photographic surveillance over South and North Vietnam and Laos, and their motto was "Alone! Unarmed! Unafraid!" The squadron flew 26,000 missions between 1966-1971. Steve's plane was hit by ground fire on three missions, but he never crashed. But most of his brethren from pilot training after the Academy did not come back alive.

After Vietnam, my brother was transferred (while still in the USAF) to the originally solely Royal Air Force base in Alconbury, England as a NATO reconnaissance pilot. By now a Captain, his duties included patrolling the skies of Western Europe and probing the Soviet Union's air defenses. For two years running, he was voted the top pilot in a kind of supersonic annual NATO reconnaissance race between far flung points in Europe. But from his rural England terrestrial setting, he and Martha also resumed a steadier marital life and produced two sons – Matthew Stephen, in September 1970, and Andrew in 1973. In 1974, Steve entered advanced training under John Schoeppner at the Edwards Air Force Test Pilot School in California. After that, he served for five years as a top test pilot at Florida's Eglin Air Force Base. He also loved racing sail boats and scuba diving with Martha and found time to complete a master's in aerospace engineering at the University of Florida.

Steve's next ambition was to fly beyond the earth's limits. He thus avidly pursued the rigorous application process with the National Aeronautics and Space Administration (NASA) to be selected as an astronaut. This led to his being invited to the Johnson Space Center in Houston, Texas on several occasions in 1977 for screening and preliminary trials. In the *Space News Roundup* of September 30, a NASA publication, he was cited as being among a group of semi-finalists for space assignments in the forthcoming **Space Shuttle** program and as having already undergone intensive interviews and health and endurance tests. This must have been a terribly exciting time in his life. But in the end, that program reconfigured its recruitment process for political reasons. Nonetheless, Steve was soon made a Major back in Florida.

Capt. Stephen Monagan.

In September 1979, my brother left the U.S. Air Force to become a lead test pilot with the Calspan Corporation headquartered outside Buffalo, New York. This was a major subcontractor for NASA and the United States Air Force in testing and refining the aeronautical systems to be deployed in the most futuristic fighter and reconnaissance aircraft in the military's pipeline.

Steve's Phantom 4.

Steve's core project involved pushing to dizzying limits a very strange flying machine in the form of a "highly augmented" W.W. II B-26 bomber that had been retrofitted with such advanced computer and control systems that it could be made to mimic and probe the performance characteristics and perils of various aircraft that were otherwise still only on the drawing board. While the B-26 was climbing and diving at WW II speeds, Steve's virtual cockpit reality and instrumentation made it seem as if he were under the control of systems being tested out for radically new planes with names like the SR 71 and X-29. On weekends, Steve flew here-and-now fighter jets as a Wing Commander for the New York Air National Guard – an "air militia" nominally under the control of the Governor in Albany and not the President in Washington.

In February 1981 Stephen Jay Monagan was dispatched to Edwards Air Force Base in the Mojave desert of southern California – a place made famous in Tom Wolf's novel **The Right Stuff.** At this point, my brother was tasked with using his unique machine to help expand the training of two aviators then attending the Edwards Test Pilot School – Captain D.J. Halladay, 31, of the Canadian Air Force; and Captain Carman (Mrs.) Lucci, a 27 year-old flight engineer and Special Astronaut Candidate at NASA. On the morning of March 3, 1981, the three took off for what they presumed to be a reasonably routine test flight.

At 8,000 feet above a place called Barstow, California, either Steve or one of his trainees began a succession of what were later called "shallow diving maneuvers," meaning falcon-like swoops toward some imaginary prey. What futuristic airplane they were simulating and testing was never revealed. In any case, most of the left wing of the worn-out old bomber couldn't take it and just fell off. In a split second, Major Stephen J. Monagan and his crew were finished. So close-knit is the world of elite Air Force test pilots and their families that years after Steve died, his former pilot mentor, John Schoepner, an eventual Air Force general, married Martha. (Martha's second husband was Colonel Jim Hart, deceased). In 2022 we all met for a lunch in Sarasota, where John described my brother's last plane as being a weirdly idiosyncratic machine.

In addition to his beloved Martha (now of St. Peterburg, Florida), Steve left behind his sons Mathew Stephen, then 10 years old, and Andrew, born in 1973. Matthew, a student of this family's history and an adventurous entrepreneur, today lives in Aspen, Colorado with his wife Meghan and their three children: Honor, Stephen, and Arden. Some years earlier, he elected to change his last name back to Monaghan. Andy lives in Springhill, Florida with his wife Kate Leukart Monagan and is thriving in the house inspection business.

JAMES EDWARD MONAGAN. My second oldest brother, Jim, was a gifted student from his earliest days. He was the salutatorian of Crosby High School and winner of the Latin Prize, and went on to Georgetown University

Up in the clouds. Brother Jim and Cousin Bob Monagan parasailing at 500 feet above Florida's Gulf Coast, 2022. Meanwhile brother Phil was running an in-shore flotilla

in Washington, where he achieved the highest-possible 4.0 grade point average on offer while working at times 20 hours or more a week on the side. Jim never just learned about a subject – he *mastered* it.

While working for Telefunken in Berlin when young, Jim quickly gained fluency in German and had no need to speak any English on the job. His first marriage was to the anthropologist Alfrieta Parks, a professor at the University of Iowa in Iowa City. The couple there raised their twin daughters, Agra, now an executive with Starbucks in Seattle, and Venice, a senior counsel in a Boston investment firm – both of whom have two children. Until his retirement in 2015, Jim worked for 26 years as a senior software engineer with the Rockwell Collins Division of the Raytheon Technology Corporation in Iowa City. His special expertise was in fine-tuning the functioning of cockpit displays for commercial airline pilots. But he was also much involved with

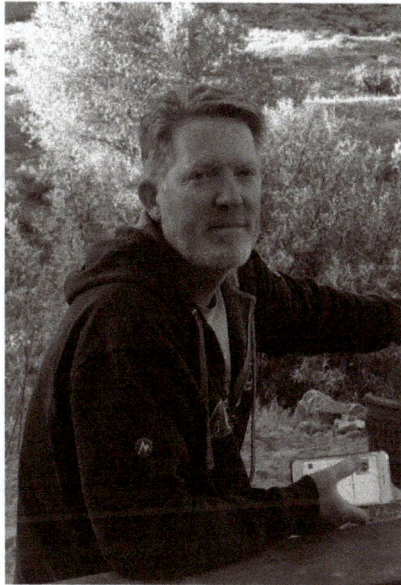

Steve's son Matthew Monaghan.

assuring that everything being generated across that vast company matched exacting federal standards in terms of critical safety issues.

Now living in Cedar Rapids with his second wife, the former Rose Marie Eggleston, Jim keeps busy in a myriad of ways, among them regular visits to his daughters and four grandchildren as well as with his wife's son Tracey Lee Eggleston and daughter Kimberly Albers and her two children. He and Rose Marie have a passion for historical tours and canoe and bicycle trips around the Midwest. Unusual for one trained in physics and computers, he writes sonnets in his spare time and of late has been perfecting his command of both Spanish and Latin. He is also an avid gardener with a prairie ecosystem in his Cedar Rapids back yard. He is also a marvel at ballroom dancing with Rose Marie.

NANCY MONAGAN ZIOMEK. Following in the footsteps of her aunts Margie and Joan, my sister Nancy, the former dispenser of absolutions in our red barn, progressed from Notre Dame to Trinity College in Washington D.C. At her first social gathering there she was asked to dance by one Thomas Ziomek, a student at Georgetown with a quietly hilarious wit, and who would become her husband in 1974. Tom hailed from Derby in the lower Naugatuck Valley and had a passion for rugby, great ethnic food and deep sea fishing. Tom went on to study law at Villanova University outside Philadelphia where Nancy joined him and began working as a secondary school teacher in the city, a role in which she had a special gift.

Tom joined the premier Philadelphia law firm of White and Williams in 1973 and became a senior partner, but never lost his deep humility and abiding love for his family and heavily Polish-American home town. He and Nancy kept a residence at Stone Harbor on the Jersey Shore, and also spent weeks every summer in Block island. Alas Tom died tragically in 2002 at the age of 55.

Tom and Nancy produced three daughters – Stephanie and Claire (who both went to Georgetown), and Audrey (Harvard). As the girls moved on, Nancy began teaching again at Rosemont College and St. Joseph's University, while

Tom sporting a decal placed by a loving daughter.

enrolling in a Ph.D. program at the nearby Widener University in Chester, Pennsylvania. In 1999, she earned her doctorate and became an assistant professor at Gwynedd Mercy University. But following the death of Tom, she moved to her beloved Block Island and resides there most of the year (when not wintering in Philadelphia's, historic district) while managing the local shellfish ecology offices of the Rhode Island Department of the Environment.

Nancy's daughter Stephanie Ziomek and her entrepreneur husband Jason Ladavac live in Villanova with their young sons – Thomas and Andrew – while Claire lives in Philadelphia. Audrey spearheads fund raising at the prestigious Lawrenceville School after previously working in adventure travel in Central America. She is married to the Honduras-born Eduardo Dueñas, a charismatic teacher in Philadelphia. The couple live in Bala Cynywyd with their twins Carl Jose and Edward Tomas.

PHILIP HARRIS MONAGAN. My younger brother Philip was born in Waterbury on September 17, 1959. His middle name refers to our mother's oldest brother Harris Innocent Hurst and her father William Harris Hurst. Phil graduated from the University of Connecticut in 1981 and next completed a law degree at the University of Miami. He early on started his own general law practice in Waterbury.

Phil was a long-time resident of Middlebury, where with his former wife Diane Ukraine Monagan, he raised his son Kevin Andrew, born on September 12, 1995, and daughter Grace Hope, born on July 16, 2000. Kevin has just graduated from the University of Minnesota, while Grace is at Notre Dame. For 30 years Phil coached and refereed in various local youth ice hockey leagues in Connecticut (while playing goalie for a weekend group at Taft). A born raconteur, and a music fan to beat the band, my younger brother is widely known throughout the Waterbury area for his professionalism and special zest for life. With his partner Julie Leahy, a radiographer, he now resides in rural Woodbury.

Your truly. As noted, this family history has been written three thousand miles from Bunker Hill in Cork, Ireland, where to I moved with my wife Jamie (nee Jane Marie Donnelly) in 2000 with our three then young children: Laura, Harris, and Owen. In the decade previous we had lived in Cornwall, Connecticut where I produced niche publications on medical breakthroughs and the diamond industry. In Ireland, my writing returned to the broader concerns of earlier years – things like humor, arts, travel, history, and

L to R, on Block Island some years back, Jim Monagan, Nancy Ziomek, Phil and David Monagan.

biography. Jamie meanwhile has long been highly successful in marketing within the performing arts world in Ireland.

Our daughter Laura has flourished with the global accountancy and consultancy firm of Price Waterhouse Cooper in its London headquarters and is married to the Australian-born Rohan Geraghty. Harris is a professional chef here in Cork, while on weekends serving as defensive captain of a sometimes champion local American football team – one of 22 in Ireland. He was recently selected as the Most Valuable Player in the league. Owen, a graduate of Trinity College in Dublin, works as a computer software engineer in New York City and is married to the Brazilian-born Anna Magliano, with whom he has traveled widely. The two share a great zest for life.

Laura, Owen and Harris when young.

APPENDIX

1. The Aughnamullen Left Behind

In nineteenth-century Ireland, it was invariably the oldest son – variously named after the grandfather or father (or in combination) – who was destined to inherit the farm and thus be generally assured of a far more stable and prosperous life ahead than awaited his brothers and sisters. A variety of records make it clear that the Monaghans of Tievaleny were headed for generations by a succession of John Monaghans. This name was repeated avidly in America, further heightening the probability that the Aughnamullen flax grower in 1796 named John Monaghan was my great-great-great-great grandfather, or even his aged father.

But note that another John Monaghan, likely his son (or even grandson), was born in Aughnamullen in 1806 (as apparent from his death record in 1891). Further, Griffith's Valuation of Ireland (the series of property surveys published in 1861) indicates that the ancestral Tievaleny farm was being worked in the late 1850s by a John Monaghan, likely the middle-aged version of the man born in 1806. This John in fact had two separate holdings in Tievaleny, although the second was likely just a piece of bog for turf cutting. A Scots-Irish resident of Castleblaney named Andrew McMath was the landlord, and he may have bought the entire townland for 117 shillings, or under 6 pounds sterling, in answer to an advertisement in the *Belfast Newsletter* of May 11, 1810. (His brother Hamilton McMath owned other great swaths of Aughnamullen.) Probably due to increasingly hefty returns from the linen markets, a certain prominent Protestant widow of Belfast named Margaret Hyndman on October 22, 1811, sold to a Robert Kerr, "gentleman" of County Down, financial speculator and dabbler in writing (and soon to marry a Russian princess), half the townlands in the area, which were to be run by a John Mitchell of one of the most notorious families County Monaghan would ever know. (As per Sandy Mitchell, the rapacious overseer of the Shirley Estate.) In any case, our John Monaghan of Aughnamullen in 1806 had a son also named John (the "4th") around 1836; and this son married an Alice Cosgrove around 1866. In 1868, they had a son John, and in the 1880s this "John the 5th" had a son named John, thus the 6th. In 1907 the latest John had yet another son named John, the 7th. The old John, the patriarch from 1806, did not die until 1891, when he was 85.

John the "4th" began managing the farm in the 1870s. He was clearly cantankerous and eager to bite back at the heavy English hand. For example, the Irish Petty Court Sessions for 1879 record that the local animal warden, John Hart, took John Monaghan to court in Ballybay on June 2 for not having a license for his dog. Perhaps because he did not bother to show up, John was fined 5 shillings and sentenced to seven days in gaol. This was an astonishing price to pay for a 33 year-old man and father of several small children – and exactly the kind of English harshness that led to Ireland's eventually successful War of Independence in 1920-1921.

By the mid-1880s, "John the 5th" had taken a lease on a piece of bogland three miles distant in a townland called Kilkit, as a source of turf for heating and possibly also of reeds to sell to thatchers. Somehow that understanding erupted into a feud with a troublesome Dowd family living nearby – not very nice neighbors. A series of lawsuits began with a case against a John Dowd for his having "unlawfully and maliciously trespassed" on said bog on July 6, 1886, and to have "made mud for turf at the same site." This was "disqualified." But a year later Ballybay was astir anew with John Monaghan's next suit against a Bernard Dowd and David Raymond for "unlawfully and maliciously cutting and carrying away a quantity of rushes" from his bog on July 14, 1887.

This turf-fighting John Monaghan's long control of the Tievaleny farm is confirmed by the Irish census of 1901. This shows the Tievaleny farm as being run by his now 65 year-old self. This farmer's son John, 28 ("the 5th), is temporarily working a separate farm within the same townland with his wife Annie. By the next Irish census in 1911, he was managing the core farm with his wife. They had two sons, a John ("the 6th) born around 1907 and his two-years-older brother Thomas. The census taker noted that the house had four rooms and four windows (making it the second largest of the 13 houses in the townland), a stable, plus two "cow houses," a dairy, a barn, a hen house, and a "figgery," which meant a small orchard.

2. The Name Issue, Continued

As much reviewed, the family has been tied up in knots for generations about the twists and turns of its own name. Then again, the first ancestor who can be confidently tracked on American soil, Owen Monaghan, had a changeable forename as well as his last. Owen is really just the way most English preferred to render it – rather than as Eoin, Eoighan, Eoghan, Eoghain (all pronounced "Owen" and common in Ireland today). It is a Celtic name, a chieftain's name, and barely belongs in English, so Owen himself may have even been a bit overly concerned with his names as well.

As noted earlier, the spellings of the surname Monaghan went through wild variations from the 1500s to the 1800s, and this hurly-burly even continued on in America in the nineteenth-century. Some of the earliest variations in the spelling of the name could be laughable – from Mongan to Mangin to Monhan, Manhegan to Manahan and Monacan, Manacan, Monnahan, Moneghan, Minihan and so on. At one early point in Andover my great-great-uncle Owen was even listed as "Monaghaghn." Amazingly, the stripped-down "Monagan" spelling was used around Lawrence, Massachusetts in the mid-1800s several times, including in apparent trial runs by Owen himself.

The early 1890s Connecticut pivoting to the "Monagan" moniker in fact seems to have been an expression of something of a larger trend within the extended family group and may have first gained momentum back in Franklin County, New York. Thus the *Malone Farmer* of Sept. 28, 1904, ran this notice soon after the death from pulmonary hemorrhage of a Mary Fenton Carroll.

> "THE PEOPLE OF THE STATE OF NEW YORK – To Katie Strader, residing at Malone, Franklin County, New York; Patrick Carroll, residence unknown if living; James Monagan, Cleveland, Ohio; George Monagan, Beatrice, Nebraska; Frank Monagan, last known address in the state of Kansas; John Monagan, last known

residence in state of Kansas; Ann Monagan, residing in Cleveland, Ohio; Deforest Monagan, residing in Oklahoma, all of full age and sound mind. And also all the heirs at law and descendants of said James Monagan, George Monagan, Frank Monagan, and John Monagan, if they or any of them be dead, by whatever name or names they may be known; constituently all the husband, wife, heirs of law and next of kin of Mary M.F. Carroll of the town of Malone in the County of Franklin..."

The notice has to do with potential claimants on the Carroll woman's estate, perhaps all related to a major lawsuit still festering after the double Rogersfield iron mining calamities of 1883.

3. A Granddaughter's Letter on "Nellie" Marks

The only two ancestors to leave Waterbury by the 1910s were the sisters Catherine and Helen, who both initially moved to Hartford. In the second case, Helen's husband Fred Marks was born there and he was obviously looking for a new lease on life after the failure of his store in Waterbury.

That couple made the move at the end of 1911 with their little daughter Marion. In 1912 they had a son named Frederick Lamont Marks, Jr. The family moved again to the New Haven area in the late 1920s. In 1929, Marion was ordained as a nun in the Sisters of Charity, an order devoted to teaching in disadvantaged areas, and she took on the name of Sister Joan Marie.

When young, her brother Fred happened onto a job installing perfectly-fitted overhead garage doors – an invention that quickly became a rage in an ever-more automobile-obsessed America. Fred would eventually create his own thriving garage door business in Hartford, and that business is still prospering to this day. With his first wife Irene Larson, Fred Lamont, Jr., had three daughters before abruptly remarrying and having a son he named Frederick Marks, 3rd, who would take over the family business in 1971. The second daughter is named Susan Marks Roberts, and I was eventually able to locate her for some lively discussions.

On December 5, 2020, Susan wrote the following letter about her grandparents, and aunt Sister Joan Marie (nee Marion), and her father. It is a wonderful recollection of a young girl's perceptions back in the mid-to late 1940s.

> Cousin David,
> When I knew my grand-parents [Fred and Helen Monagan Marks] they lived in West Haven. That was the only house that I knew. My parents lived in a house a couple of doors down from them when I was born in 1940. My grandparents' house was rented. It

was one of three similar houses on a long driveway that ran from the main road down to Long Island Sound. The houses were brown. There was an unenclosed porch across the front of the house. On the first floor was a living room, dining room, kitchen, pantry, and a back room. There was also a small room at the top of the cellar stairs. The icebox was located there. There was a big block of ice delivered periodically. There was a coal furnace. On the second floor were two bedrooms. My grandparents slept in separate rooms. I don't know why. There was a door between the rooms and their beds were close to the door. There must have been a bathroom, but I have no recollection of one.

My sister Pat [Patricia Ellen Marks Daigle, 1936-2010] and I would visit for a week at a time several times during the summer. Sometimes we visited together, but most times separately. While there we would sleep in my grandmother's bed and my grandmother would sleep downstairs in the back room. The back room had a card table on which would be set up a jigsaw puzzle. I remember my grandmother working on it with us, but I don't believe that my grandfather did.

I think that they had a good relationship, but I was nine when my grandmother died, so I don't believe that I would have been perceptive about adult relationships... On Sundays my grandfather [Fred Marks, Helen Monagans husband] would sit on the front porch. When the noon whistle blew, he and a neighbor would have a drink, though they each remained on their own porches. My younger sister, Kathy, remembers our older sister, Pat (Pat was four years older than I) telling her how devoted our grandparents were to each other. Pat included that this was even to the exclusion of their children. I'm not sure if this last thought is true, because I don't know how Pat would have been aware of the family dynamics when my father and Aunt Marion were children. Pat may have been embellishing. This reminds me that there was a third child, I believe John, but maybe not, who died in infancy. He was their first born. [She refers to the lost child possibly conceived in Ridgefield in 1906.]

My parents moved to Milford in 1941. My grandparents would frequently drive down after church for a visit. My grandmother usually had candy for us. I don't remember them staying for our midday dinner.

When I was visiting in the summer of 1949, I had a crash when riding three-on-a-bike... My grandmother took me to the doctor. I was examined. Now, whether she also had a prearranged appointment with the doctor or just used the time to talk to him about a problem she was having, I don't know. I remember that the doctor talked to her about her stools being black. I thought he said that would occur from the medicine he was giving her, but it also could have been from internal bleeding. I had to return home at that point. My grandfather told me that I had exhausted my grandmother and that's why she was sick. Though this caused psychological trauma for me (I did get over it, I think, though I still remember it), I believe that it was an indication of how upset he was. My grandmother was diagnosed with stomach cancer and went to St. Raphael's Hospital soon after where she remained until she died in November. I didn't see her again as at that time since children were not allowed to visit. After my grandmother's death my grandfather came to live with us. That Christmas he gave us leather gloves. He became quite upset when we didn't notice that they were signed from our grandmother. He said that he bought them with money that she had saved to buy our Christmas presents. It makes me sad even today to think that we hadn't noticed.

I don't recall any special interest that they shared in music or
theater. I do have a seascape that my grandmother painted in 1896
[possibly on Block Island] while she was still Helen Monagan.
I think it is very good. There was no evidence that she painted
anything else... They didn't have a piano, but we did. When my
grandfather [Frederick Lamont Marks, Sr., who died in 1954] was
living with us, he would play. He played by ear. His hands were
badly crippled by arthritis, but it didn't hinder his playing.

Aunt Marion [the first child of Helen Monagan Marks and
Fred Sr.] seemed to move quite a bit. I can't remember all the
convents she was in, but I know I visited her in Norwalk, Ansonia,
Waterbury, and West Hartford. There were probably more when I
was younger, but I remember those four because I drove to them.
I believe that West Hartford was a retirement home. That is where
Aunt Marion was living when she died.

I don't remember Aunt Marion as being particularly religious.
We never discussed religion. I had left the church when I was
about 14. I don't know how she knew, but she did. When I was
a freshman at the University of Connecticut, she had contacted
the priest there and had asked him to casually run into me. He
did contact me but he had to explain that it was at my aunt's
behest. We met a couple of times, but neither was able to convert
the other. Aunt Marion must have endured some trauma [as a
child], either physical or mental, because she remained home
and out of school for a year around the 5th or 6th grade. Aunt
Marion said that she had wanted to be a ballerina. Since the Sisters
of Mercy was a teaching order, she instead taught in the primary
grades for years. She didn't like teaching. I believe that she was
interested in music. She told me that anyone could learn to sing.
One Christmas, I think in the early '70s, Aunt Marion stayed
overnight on Christmas and spent Christmas day with me and

my children. That was a very peaceful Christmas. We didn't go to church, but we did work on a jigsaw puzzle. I saw home movies of Aunt Marion visiting us in Milford. She was in full habit at that time and had to travel with a companion [a regulation for all nuns let out of the convent for a day]. In the movies I must be 5 or younger, and I am running to her and she's picking me up and swinging me around. When we first saw the request for information, the first thing that both Kathy [Susan's sister] and I thought of was how excited Aunt Marion was when she could replace her nightgowns with pajamas. I don't remember at what point the full habit was no longer required. Aunt Marion did wear street clothes, but she always wore a short veil with them.

I'm not sure if any of this is helpful, but it was fun remembering. Please let me know if there is anything that I can clarify.

Susan

4. Cold War Monagans in Korea

My uncle Walter Edward Monagan, Jr. – a military lawyer and intelligence officer rolled into one – had been first posted to Japan following Emperor Hirohito's capitulation on August 15, 1945. Within a couple of months, he was shuffled off to Seoul in Korea as that country was being split into two along the 38th Parallel, with the northern half of the peninsula to fall under communist Soviet domination and the southern half principally under American control. Eventually, a brief measure of stability settled upon this tendentious situation, and American Army officers were allowed to have their wives brought over from the U.S.

This is the background to the first big letter home to Connecticut from Seoul, dated February 19, 1947, by Mildred Aubrey Monagan, Walter's wife. Walter was then involved in the American efforts to impose a new kind of democracy in the shattered southern half of the country, which had not known self-rule since the Japanese annexed the land in 1910. Mildred had no idea what lay ahead as she was transported thousands of miles to what most would consider a hell hole. Some young purists today may fret over certain words she chooses, but these were different times and Americans and their allies had suffered heinous atrocities in the region during the war. Ultimately, this is an intriguing and sometimes witty letter.

Seoul,
Korea
February 19, 1947

Dear Everybody,

I arrived in this bleak land on Oct. 13, after one hell of an awful 18 day trip across the northern Pacific to Yokohama, down under Kyushu, into the East China Sea then the Yellow Sea and finally the Korean port of Inchon... We ran into a terrific storm about three days out of Seattle and the thing raged for about 24 hours during which time the good ship U.S.A.T. Freeman [a 552-foot long, 9,950- ton transport ship capable of carrying 3,000 troops] jumped and rolled like a mad thing, standing at 45 degree angles, throwing dishes, chairs and passengers around like so many peas. Most of us, including members of the crew, just lay cursing and moaning while the poker and dice games among the 1500 troops stopped for the time being. From then on, I was never quite the same!

Well, D-Day finally dawned. There was terrific excitement and the usual Army confusion ... before we were finally put aboard an LCM [Landing Craft Military] for the 10 minute trip from the ship through the very shallow water into the little wooden dock at Inchon [Korea]. As each boat came in, the husbands who had gals aboard were let out of a "bull pen" and came strolling down to the edge. Such goings on; and all of this to the martial strains of an Army band. It was a beautiful, mild sunny day and the whole scene was really very colorful and rather touching... We all went directly to the train which took us to Seoul, a distance of about 20 miles which took about four hours (the engine broke down enroute).

Walter and I were quartered in the Kikui (in Seoul), a little Jap hotel [the Japanese had occupied Korea from 1910 to 1945], with mats on the floors, sliding doors and an Oriental john ('banjo" to us Far Easterners) which vaguely described, looks like an oblong pot sunk into the floor... We stayed there three weeks waiting for our house to be completed."

Mildred goes on to describe their subsequent move into a very small house, rebuilt from a Japanese officer's quarters where water from the shower taps instead came out in the kitchen sink and colored red. She describes a Peter Sellers-like cocktail party with Russian military officers who spoke no English. "We just smiled and raised our glasses inanely." Then she returns to the subject of countless domestic shortages and sometimes hilarious inconveniences and surprises: "Rice is their main diet and with this the people usually eat a native concoction called Kimchee along with it. This fragrant stuff is a combination of celery-cabbage, red peppers, garlic etc. put into crocks every Fall and allowed to ferment. It's their only vegetable during the winter, and when the servants [meaning Mildred and Walter's]) bring it from home – oh, the kitchen! But the worst experience of all is to walk into a room full of Koreans, all of whom have eaten Kimchee that day! Strong men have been known to reel and blanch. The people are now in what is called the "starving period" when the winter supply of rice is getting pretty low."

Mildred speaks of their own limited social lives. "Most of the Korean stores are little wooden shacks, thousands of them lined up on the main streets where business is transacted in the Oriental manner. All the houses in the city are up back alleys or side streets and cannot be seen except from a height. Many of them are just mud huts with thatched roofs and dirt floors. Many Americans live in Japanese houses throughout the city [meaning big ones] and it will always be a big disappointment we didn't get one!

This country has practically nothing in the line of goods. They have a few textiles, the lacquer business and some small metal manufacturing... They make a rather poor grade of silk, but the big thing here is farming. Seoul has over a million people, and I think most of them are constantly on the street. There is a mixture of dress, with most of the women still wearing the long, gay-colored draped silk or white cotton skirt and contrasting bolero jacket... They carry great heavy bundles on their heads and always a baby strapped to their backs. (We childless Americans are a mystery to them!) Many men wear bloused, padded white cotton trousers with long cotton or silk coats, also padded... It's very cold here and a number of people go around the streets with white gauze masks over their nose and mouth... Walter works under trying conditions – a cold office, no official transportation... Well, spring is coming we keep telling ourselves, and this grim place awakens, the cherry blossoms turn it into a paradise for four days, and things get a little more pleasant. The scenery is really wonderful, the whole city being surrounded by mountains; and the view from our front yard is spectacular – across the rice paddies to the river and then the snow covered mountains."

At this point, the tone abruptly shifts with Mildred's alluding to the grim tensions in the air preceding the onset of the terrible Korean War. "Occasionally we're all alerted. The men carry their guns and we don't go out after dark. The Communists get certain elements stirred up and they try to make it hot for the Americans so that we'll clear out. The damn fools don't realize that if we pulled out of here not one vehicle in this whole country could move!"

It obviously was no dream station for an American woman barely 30 years old, what with rumors rampant about a possible new war in the making. Communist agitators were constantly working at turning the population against their own government and the West, and large forces from North Korea finally invaded on June 25, 1950. When they were later pushed back by UN forces, the Chinese flooded in masses of troops on October 19 of that year. Casualties ran into the hundreds of thousands, with Seoul conquered by the Communists four times, before the situation devolved into a stalemate after fierce Allied resistance and air attacks on the Chinese. An armistice was finally signed on July 27, 1953, but the border between North and South Korea remains on tenterhooks to this day.

5. A Son's Eulogy For John Clinton

Following the death on April 6, 2003, of Joan Marie Monagan Clinton's husband John Clinton, their oldest son James delivered a moving funeral address about his remarkable, but complex father.

He noted that, despite his formidable gifts his father had his own faults, including sometimes losing his patience with the bedlam his nine kids could create in the early days. Jim recalled, "I can remember times when he would repeatedly yell at us to stop bouncing the ball, which we were doing constantly. Of course, we wouldn't stop playing, so he would eventually come running at us. In the next instant our neighbors would see several skinny Clinton boys running out of the house like they were shot out of a cannon...."

Jim fretted that for all his intense idealism, his dad kept so much emotion buried inside that it took years before father and son could deepen the connection both craved. In John Clinton's case there were unusual circumstances, as Jim pointed out.

"As I grew into adulthood, I started to think about the contrast of our family life to John's own childhood. John has one younger brother, Paul, and both of their parents were deaf. Imagine the precision, solitude, and orderliness of that world they were raised in. John loved order and precision and things like punctuality. Unfortunately, these things were rarely part of this new world that he and Joan created. There are not many people who can truly understand the personal sacrifices of John and Joan, or the chaos, noise, or the demands of such a large family... my dad understood that this was what he had to sacrifice to build a large family. It wasn't until I started having kids of my own that I felt like I was starting to figure this man out."

"John had many superlative aspects to his character. One important part of his character was that he truly believed that all men and women were created equal and deserved respect. This was not some position that he evolved into as we slowly moved toward a more politically correct society. This was something he believed in with all his heart and soul and he passed this conviction to all his children. This was not something he talked about in some lofty terms, this was a way of life for John through example."

Jim dwelt on his father's facility for developing deep knowledge about whatever interested him – from American history to world affairs and classical and even folk music – and often turning heads at parties with his great witticisms and insights. Such a long journey from an infancy when his own mother could not hear him cry. Jim described how in his father's later years he began to share more from the hidden recesses of his heart. "As smart and intelligent as John was, I believe we children finally were able to teach him something. The one single thing that sticks out most in my mind about John is how proud he was... He was proud of his family, his church, his New England roots, his beloved city of Falls Church, and his public service to our country."

A Sketch of Aughnamullen Monaghan Kin – Circa 1830

John Monaghan, holder of the Tievaleny farm, born around 1806.

Mary Monaghan, definite sister of Owen and Andrew, possibly born pre 1805. She married a neighbor named Burns, who died. During the Famine joined Owen in Andover, Massachusetts.

Owen Monaghan, great-great-great uncle born 1807-1808, and the beacon for Andrew.

Bridget Monaghan, born around 1811, married to Patrick Morran, a tenant in Ummerafree townland on the vast Shirley Estate to the south.

Edward Monaghan, later seen beside Bridget on the Shirley Estate.

Sarah Monaghan, married to a James Boyle, with son Hugh in 1827. This couple may have lived in Liverpool for some years but reappear in Tievaleny in *Griffith's Valuation* in 1861.

Andrew Monaghan, my great-great grandfather, now about eight years old.

Possible brothers **Bernard** and **Patrick Monaghan** and possible sister **Margaret Monaghan** Wilson.

Francis and Catherine Henry, with their children Terrence, Susanna, James, Ellen.

Charles Short, Elizabeth Short.

McCallans.

[The actual numbers were likely many, many times larger.]

Early Monaghans in North America and Their Progeny

Andrew Monaghan (Aug. 1, 1822-Oct. 7,1890) m. Catherine Castle (1824-Dec. 13, 1891) – Massachusetts and North Bangor, New York.

> **Edward O. Monaghan** (1844-Feb. 18, 1900) – born North Andover, Mass, died Bangor.

> **John Stephen Monagan** (Nov. 4, 1846-Nov. 1,1928) m. **Anna Nolan** (1852- Dec. 9, 1933) – b. North Andover, Mass.

>> Mary Agnes Monagan (Sept. 15, 1871-July 26, 1938) – born North Bangor, N.Y.

>> Charles Andrew (June 1, 1872-Feb. 27, 1931) m. Margaret Mulry (Dec. 31, 1885-Jan. 22, 1920) – North Bangor.

>> Katherine Elizabeth "Kate" Monagan (Apr. 27, 1874-1952?) m. George Winslow Gregg (1874-1947) – born Bristol, Connecticut.

>> William Henry Monagan (Dec. 2, 1876 – March 7, 1946) m. Elizabeth Lawlor.

>> Thomas F. Monagan (1877-Oct. 8,1881) – Bristol.

>> Helen "Nellie" Monagan (April 29, 1878-Nov. 8, 1949) m. Frederick Lamont Marks (July 26, 1879-May 19, 1954) – Bristol.

>> Anna I. Monagan (b. Bristol, June 22,1880- June 6,1907), stenographer and pianist – Bristol.

>> Walter Edward Monagan (January 10, 1882-Aug. 8, 1961) m. Mary Butler (Apr.5, 1882 -July 10, 1942) – Bristol.

>> Marguerite Bernice Monagan (Feb. 8, 1891-March 16,1932) m. Arthur Owen Nelson (1890-1948) – born Waterbury, Conn.

> **Owen Monaghan** (Apr. 8, 1847-1847) – North Andover or Lowell.

> **Elizabeth Alice Monaghan** (July 28, 1848-Apr. 29, 1849) – Salem, Mass.

> **Thomas William Monaghan** [adopted?] (1868-June 9,1917).

His children iterated in the text

Andrew's Brother Owen Monaghan

Born Lurgachamlough, Aughnamullen, Monagan (1807- Oct. 23, 1874), d. North Bangor, New York

Arrives Boston Aug. 14, 1834, settles North Andover, Mass. Marries Catherine McNamara (1817-1894) on July 20, 1939. Their children:

Elizabeth Ann Monagan (Dec. 16,1840-1920)

William Stephen Monaghan (1843-1897)

Vezina Jane Monaghan (1847-1916)

Alice Monaghan (1850-1892)

Edward Monaghan (1853-1904)

Richard Monaghan (1855-1900)

James Henry Monaghan ((1860-1885) – all Andover

See text for their marriages and progeny.

Clark – Nolan Progeny (Incomplete)

Patrick Nolan (1826-1897) m. Mary Margaret Clark (1825-1910) in Malone, New York, 1850.

> James Henry Nolan (1851-Sept. 12,1933) – born North Bangor
>
> Ann Nolan (1852-1933) m. John Stephen Monagan (1846-1928) – their offspring listed further on.
>
> Thomas Nolan (Jan. 1854-1904) m. Elizabeth Smith – marriage Bristol, Conn. 1877.
>
> George Thomas Nolan (1883-1966) m. Alice Moran (1888-1956)
>
>> Harriet Nolan (1907-1942?)
>>
>> Elizabeth Nolan (1909?) m. Martin Zucca
>>
>> George Thomas Nolan, Jr. (1912-1983) m. Olive Charlotte Hamilton (1911-2008)
>>
>>> Mary Louise Nolan (1935-)
>>>
>>> George Thomas Nolan III (1937-2021)
>>>
>>> James W. Nolan (Feb. 1, 1939-) m. (1) Virginia "Ginger" Delucia (dec. 1994), (2) Mary Ann Gregory. res Middlebury.
>>>
>>>> Jayma Nolan (Feb. 2, 1968-) div. Erik Waskiel
>>>>
>>>>> Kelsey Waskiel (Feb. 4.,1998-)
>>>>>
>>>>> Ethan Waskiel (May 18, 2002-)
>>>>
>>>> Victoria Nolan (Oct 6.1972-) m. Raymond Kasidas
>>>>
>>>>> Dylan Kasidas (April 23, 2001-)
>>>
>>> Patrick Robert (1944-) m. Judith MacCione
>>
>> James Andrew Nolan (1915-) m. Mary Martin
>>
>>> James Nolan, Jr.
>>
>> Frederick Joseph Nolan (1917-1992) m. Bernice Hackett
>>
>>> Frederick Nolan, Jr.

Alice Nolan (1922-1999) m. James Finnegan

Josephine Nolan m. Willis Frederick Nolan

Hugh Nolan (1855-)

Margaret Nolan (1856-)

Mary Nolan (1857-) m. Arthur Devlin in Bangor, N.Y. Arthur dies Waterbury 1915.

John Devlin

James Devlin

Raymond Devlin

Bertha Devlin

Leo Devlin, b. Bristol 1884

Ellen Nolan (1859-) nun?

Catherine Nolan (1862-1889) m. Thomas Miller – Bristol, Conn.

Lorena Miller (1887-1928)

Howard Joseph Miller (1889-1932)

Elizabeth Nolan (1865-) becomes "Sister Ushina"

William Henry Nolan (1867-1924)

Agnes T. Nolan (1868-1925) m. Frederick Bates in 1915, Waterbury.
Mary Ellen Nolan (1880-) m. unknown Bowen (dec.)

Albert Bowen (1899-)

Charles Monagan Descendants

Dr. Charles Andrew Monagan (1872-1931) and Margaret Mary Mulry (1885-1920)

John Stephen Monagan (Dec. 23, 1911 – Oct. 23, 2005) m. Rosemary Brady, 1949

Charles Andrew Monagan (March 8, 1950-) m. Marcia Graham

John Stephen Monagan (Sept. 17, 1985-) m. Liss Couch-Edwards

Penner Amelia Monagan (June 10, 2020-)

Matthew Graham Monagan (March 3, 1987-) m. Dhanuska Gunasekera (1991-2020), res. Brooklyn, N.Y.

Claire Bidwell Monagan (Feb. 14, 1990-) m. Peter O'Hanlon, res. Brooklyn. Son James Graham O'Hanlon (b. Aug. 31, 2022.)

Michael John Monagan (Sept. 28, 1951-) m. Gaili Schoen (Dec. 23, 1960-). Res. Santa Monica, California

Kylie Schoen Monagan (May 23, 1991-), res. Manhattan

Maura Schoen Monagan (April 25, 1993-), res. Cambridge, England

Mary Parthenia "Parthy" Monagan (March 21, 1953-) m. John McCutcheon (Aug. 14, 1952-) (div.), res. Charlottesville, Virginia

William Grayson McCutcheon (Sept. 2, 1982-), res. Brooklyn, N.Y.

Peter Monagan McCutcheon (Sept. 22, 1984-), m. Lillian Lee (1980), res. Brooklyn

Brady Wise McCutcheon (Oct. 7, 2016-)

Chloe Jade McCutcheon (July 2, 2019-)

Laura Monagan (March 4, 1957-) m. Patrick Lyon

Sienna Lyon (1993-) m. Juan Imo

Susan Monagan (Sept. 17,1961-) m. (1) Donald Travis Stewart, (2)

Richard Guttridge

Cashel Stewart

Charles Stewart

Thomas Mulry Monagan (Nov. 29, 1914-March 29, 2005) m. Marguerite Kehoe (1921-2002): progeny listed separately.

Margaret "Peggy" Monagan (June 28,1916-July 7,1983)

Family of Richard Bernard Murphy 4 Mar 1911 - 13 Jul 2003 & Mary Elizabeth Monagan Murphy 13 Dec 1917 - 12 Oct 2003

Mary Elizabeth Murphy Smith 30 Jun 1941- 13 May 2021 m. Maurice Vincent Smith 27 Aug 1941

>Margaret Mary Smith Mullally 28 May 1966 – John Mullally 4 Mar 1967 (div)

>>Mary Elizabeth Mullally 3 Jun 1991

>>Sean Maurice Mullally 21 May 1994

>>Brendan Francis Mullally 17 Jul 1997

Maurice Thomas Condon Smith 22 Dec 1967 m. Alexandra Blynn Smith Feb 1967

>>Maurice Vincent Smith II 13 Apr 2000

>>Timothy Blynn Smith 23 Nov 2003

Parthenia Ann Smith Dinora 17 Jul 1970 m. Michael James Dinora Nov 1970

>>Bridget Grace Dinora 25 Jun 2004

>>Damon Christopher Dinora 11 Oct 2006

Richard Bernard Murphy Jr. 3 Aug 1942 m. Stuart Ann Saylor Murphy 5 Feb 1942 (div)

> Anna Leah Seabury Murphy Poole 29 Mar 1967 m. Jeffrey Barnard Poole 18 Jul 1964
>
> > Fife Barnard Poole 10 Jan 2007
>
> Richard Bernard Murphy III 3 Aug 1969 m. Sarah Dabney McElroy Murphy 27 Mar 1965
>
> > Sarah Dabney Murphy 5 Jan 2002
> >
> > Stuart Allston Murphy 17 Jun 2005

m. (II) Paula Evelyn Manganero Murphy 11 May 1945 m. Roger Ostrander (div)

> Roger Vincent Ostrander III m. Katherine Holbrook Ostrander
>
> > Anne Holbrook (Brook) Ostrander 6 May 1998
> >
> > Daly Elizabeth Ostrander 1 May 2001
> >
> > Roger Vincent Ostrander IV 17 Oct 2004

Amy Ostrander Twombly 6 Nov 1971 m. Derek L. Twombly 5 Jun 1969.

> > Aidan William Twombly 18 Aug 2000
> >
> > Grayson Charles Twombly 7 Oct 2002
> >
> > Quinn Fletcher Twombly 16 Aug 2004
> >
> > Mary Claire Evelyn Twombly 29 Jan 2015

Catherine Agnes Murphy Lyons 8 Dec 1944 m. Thomas Howard Lyons 13 Aug 1944

> Maura Eileen Lyons 13 Jul 1968 m. Mark Francis Vitha 27 Jun 1970

Tara Kathleen Lyons 18 Sep 1969

Daniel John Lyons 21 Nov 1973 m. Christine Aurora Boutureira Lyons 21 Jan 1975

> Ivan Willem Lyons 9 Feb 2006

> Theodore Timothy Lyons 2 Jun 2010

Joseph Mulry Murphy 6 Jan 1951 m. Jane Dygert Hurst 15 Jan 1948 – 2 Jun 2020

> Mary Elizabeth Hurst Murphy 27 Aug 1984

> Anna Mulry Murphy 15 Oct 1987 m. Kiel Johnson 27 May 1983

>> Isla Jane Murphy 19 July 2021

William Patrick Murphy 2 Jan 1958 m. Siobhan Eileen Smith Murphy 17 Mar 1966

> Maeve Smith Murphy 11 Jan 2002 - 11 Jan 2002

> Liam Frank Murphy 16 Jun 2004

> Hannah Irene Murphy 16 Jun 2004

Charles Andrew Monagan, Jr. (Jan. 22, 1920)

Descendants of Thomas Mulry Monagan and Margaret Kehoe

1. Gretchen Monagan (Nov. 1,1943-) m. William Alan Sterling (July 2, 1943-)

Thomas Allen Sterling (1966-)

Eleanor Siobhan Sterling (1968-) m. Jon Gale (1967-)

Tatum Monagan Gale (Dec. 6, 1994-)

Sarah Sterling Gale (May 10, 1996-)

John Kehoe Sterling (Oct. 9, 1973-) m. Lindsay Katherine Lutton (Aug. 17, 1974-)

Eleanor DeNell Sterling (Aug 10, 2003-)

Riley Alexander Sterling ((Feb. 27, 2006-)

2. Ann Celeste Monagan (June 14, 1945-) m. Gerald Michael Noonan (June 8, 1945-)

John Richardson Noonan (May 19,1977-) m. Jessica Lynn Favale (May 26,1982-)

Elizabeth Monagan Noonan (Nov. 8,1978-)

3. Thomas Mulry Monagan, Jr. (July 30, 1946-) m. Debra Joan Diethelm (April 6,1949-)

Thomas Mulry Monagan III (June 10, 1971-) m. Bridget Marie Dawson (Jan. 31, 1971-)

James Martin Monagan (Oct. 21, 1972-)

Margaret Terese Monagan (Aug. 18, 1976-)

4.Barbara Ellen Monagan (Oct. 20, 1948-) m. John Jay Knox, Jr. (Dec. 10, 1947-)

John Jay Knox III (Nov. 2, 1979-) m. Sara McCullough (July 4, 1980-

Emmet Monagan Knox (Dec. 1, 1985-)

5. Christine Thomas Monagan (March 4, 1950-) m. Robert Emmet Ryan (Nov. 17, 1946-)

Elizabeth Mulry Ryan (July 4, 1981-)

Robert Emmet Ryan, Jr. (Nov. 4, 1982-) m. Rachel Calme Ryan (Apr. 12, 1983-)

Sarah Keegan Ryan (April 8,1986-) m. Gregory Michael Bales (Dec. 2, 1984-)

6. Jane DeGrove Monagan (July 5, 1951-) m. Samuel Robert Marrone (Aug. 17,1943-)

Samuel McCanner Marrone (Jan. 22, 1983-) m. Kendall Sarah Sims (Sept. 10, 1984-)

Joseph Mulry Marrone (Nov. 19, 1985-)

7. Elizabeth Deering Monagan (July 5, 1951 - twin), m. George Alban Heitz, Jr. (March 30, 1951-)

George Alban Heitz III (April 1, 1980-) m. Roxanna Trofin Heitz (Jan. 26, 1981-)

Gretchen Heitz (Apr. 22, 1982-) m. John Campbell McKeekin (May 28, 1975-)

8. Bernadette "Bunny" Katherine Monagan (Sept. 20, 1952-) m. Lloyd George Ucko (March 3, 1951-)

Christopher Charles Ucko (Nov. 30, 1977-) m. Olivia Kaplan (Apr. 24, 1980-)

Justin Alexander Ucko (Apr. 2, 1980-) m. Veronica Craun (Mar. 26, 1981-)

Martha Michelle Ucko (Feb. 26, 1983-)

9. Mary Agnes Monagan Burnett (June 4,1954-) life partner Phil Sarcione

10. Sheila Claire Monagan (Aug. 13,1955-) m. Michael Thomas Moran (Apr. 2,1954-)

Michael Thomas Moran, Jr. (Dec. 2, 1987-)

Charles Carvon Moran (Jan. 11, 1990-)

Matthew Tierney Moran (Jan. 18. 1993-)

11. Carolyn "Kiki" Monagan (June 10, 1959-) m. Paul Freed (Oct. 31,1958-)

Luke Thomas Freed (Aug. 7, 1987-)

Cassidy Kehoe Freed (Oct. 11, 1988-)

Addison Kathleen Freed (Sept. 15, 1991-)

12. Bernard Kehoe "Ben" Monagan (July 31,1962-) m. Mary Buccarelli (Dec. 31, 1965-), res. Southbury, Conn.

Mallory Katherine Monagan (Apr. 24, 1993-)

Bernard Kehoe Monagan, Jr. (July 5, 1995-)

Marguerite Barbara Monagan (June 23, 1999-)

Descendants of Helen "Nellie" Monagan (1878-1949) and Frederick Lamont Marks (1879-1954)

John Marks (1906)

Marion Marks, to be Sister Joan Marie (1909-1992)

Frederick Lamont Marks, Jr. (1911-1971) m. (1) Irene Larson

1. Patricia Ellen Marks (1936-2010) m. (1) Howard Padowitz, (2) to Rosaire Joseph Daigle

2. Susan Marks (1940-) m. (1) Frank Maisano, (2) James Roberts Dawn R. Maisano (1961-) m. Paris Sideris

    Evan Sideris

    Paris Sideris, Jr.

    Mark Maisano (1964-) m. Sandra Brown, res. Tennessee

3. Kathy Irene Marks (1948-) m. Peter Andrew Menold, res. Greensboro, N.C.

    Jennifer Menold m. Bruce G. Daley

    > Samantha Gail Daley (1998-)

    Kristy Irene Menold (1973-) m. Carl Joseph Horstkamp, res. Winston Salem, N. C.

    > Victoria Irene Horstkamp, etc. (1999-) Andrew Sterling (2002-)

    > Julia Catherine (2004-)

    > Sophia Elizabeth (2007-)

    > William Nicholas (2009-)

    > James Morgan (2012-)

    > Edmund Alexander (2014-)

    > Maximilian Leo (2016-)

    > Cecilia Rose (2019-)

Frederick Lamont Marks, Jr., m (2) Grace Platt

    Bradford William Marks, Sr.. (1943-) m. (1.) Joyce Gallio

    Bradford W. Marks, Jr. (1963-) m. Karen Cummiskey

    David S. Marks (1966-) m. Stephanie Major

        Bradford William Marks, Sr. m. (2) Judith Seraphin

Lineage of William Butler (1836-1905) – Sarah McKeon (1850-1921)

Patrick Butler, possible great-great-great grandfather (1793-1857) m. Mary or Margaret Neil (1793-1871), res. Kilkenny, Ireland

1. Michael James (1819-1869) – death Naugatuck, Connecticut

2. Anna (1820-1892) – Naugatuck.

3. Patrick Butler (1822-1864) – Naugatuck.

4. Julia ((1823-1897) – Naugatuck.

5. Margaret (Leary) Butler (1829-1882) – Naugatuck.

6. **William "Willie" Butler** (June 1836-1905) m. (1) Ellen Finnegan (1841-1872), res. Waterbury.

    Elizabeth Ann "Eliza," (Nov. 8, 1862-?)

    William Michael (Nov. 3,1864-Sept. 9, 1865)

    Julia (March 5, 1865)

    Mary (April 8, 1866-)

    Francis James (Feb. 2, 1868-)

    Julia W. (March 20, 1870-Jan. 17, 1943)

    Ellen (b. March 4, 1872), mother Ellen likely died at her childbirth

William Butler m. (2) **Sarah McKeon** (1850-1921) – her parents assumed to be Arthur and Margaret McKeon.

    William J. (1876-1930)

    George Henry (1879-1950) m. Anna Kelly (1877-?)

        Rev. George W. (1909-1989)

        James (1913-?)

        Francis J. (1910-2001)

        Edward Aloysius (1916-2003) m. Margaret Gibbons

Offspring: Katherine Perloff, John Butler, James Butler, Cary Griffin, Shannon Butler Rodefeld; at least 14 grandchildren

William "Bill" John Butler (May 27, 1918-Dec. 29. 1981) – m. Helen Conway

Joseph (1920 -)

Mary Elizabeth Butler (Jan. 11, 1882-July 10, 1942) m. Walter Edward Monagan (Jan. 10, 1882-Aug. 8,1961) – my grandparents.

Anna Louise Butler (1884-1972), decades long resident with Walter and Mary Elizabeth at 84 Euclid Avenue, Waterbury.

Augustine Butler (1891-1901)

Descendants of Walter Edward Monagan and Mary Elizabeth Butler

1. **Walter Edward Monagan, Jr.** (June 12, 1911-July 14, 2008) m. Mildred Aubrey (1913-2007)

2. **William Henry Monagan** (April 7, 1913-July 24, 2013) m. Dorothy Hewitt (July 31,1915-June 11,1995)

    Anne Kathleen Hewitt Monagan (Feb.18, 1942-) m. Douglass McDaniel Porter (April 2, 1939), res. Durango, Colorado

    Carolyn Marie Porter (Oct. 22, 1963) m. Karl Haiss, res. North Carolina

    Alexander Haiss (April 16, 2004-)

    Cynthia Louise Porter (1966) m. Frank Roe Hawkins (1966)

    Michael Douglass Hawkins (1995, Bayfield, Colorado)

    Katie Elizabeth Hawkins (1998)

    David Roe Hawkins (2000)

Cathleen Anne Porter (1969) div. Bernt Walter Kuhlmann (1951, Salzburg, Austria), Western resort developer

> Georgiana Anne Kuhlmann (1997)

> Huxley Herbert Kuhlmann (1999), male Gucci model

> Klaus William Kuhlmann (2009)

Robert Andrew Monagan (Aug. 3,1948) m. Kathleen Shuey (July 24,1952-) res. Laurel, Maryland

> Michelle Frances Monagan (Feb. 16, 1970) m. John Carty (1964), res. Annapolis, Md.

> > Laura Carty (1996-)

> > Jack Carty (1988-)

Elizabeth Jennifer Monagan (Oct. 8, 1974-) m. Neil Hemann, res. Berkley Heights, N.J.

Ava Hemann (2006)

Gretchen Hemann 2013)

Colleen Monagan (July 27,1993-)

3. **Charles Andrew Monagan** (Dec. 31, 1915-Aug. 24, 2001) m. Seena Claire Lerner Bernbach (1931-2003). His stepchildren:

> Faun Bernbach (1958-2005) m. (1) Chris Evans, (2) Peter Lucas. Marc R. Bernbach (1959-) m. Doris, res. Middlebury, Conn.

> > Abigail Bernbach

> > Rebecca Bernbach

4. **John Stephen Monagan** (March 6, 1918-Feb. 3, 1997) m. Helen Hope Hurst (Jan. 14, 1918- Nov. 22, 2003)

> **USAF Maj. Stephen John Monagan**, middle name change to "Jay," (Sept. 14, 1944-March 3, 1981) m. Martha Morrissey (1945-)

> > Matthew Stephen Monagan, later revert to "Monaghan,"

(b. June 10,1970 - Lakenheath, U.K. Royal Airforce Base) m. Margaret "Megan" Louise Behrendt (Aug. 9, 1971-) res. Aspen, Colorado

> Honor Isabella Monaghan (Jan. 20, 1996-)
>
> Stephen Behrendt Monaghan (June 11,1998-)
>
> Freya Arden Rosemary Monaghan (July 14,2006-)

Andrew John Monagan (b. May 21, 1973 – Lakenheath, U.K.)

James Edward Monagan (Nov. 21-1946-) m. (1) Alfrieda Parks, (2) Rose Marie Joyal Eggleston, res. Iowa City

Agra Parks Monagan (May 8,1977-) div. Ryan Hudson

> Tristan Hudson (2011-)
>
> Natalie Hudson (2014-)

Venice Monagan (twin, May 8,1977-) div. Christopher Maki

> Apollo Monagan Maki (2015-)
>
> Keanu Monagan Maki (2017-)

Nancy Hope Monagan (Feb. 17, 1948-) m. Thomas John Ziomek (Dec. 7, 1946- Sept. 27, 2002), res. Block Island and Philadelphia

Stephanie Ziomek (Dec. 25,1977-) m. Jason Ross Ladavac (1973-)

> Thomas Moore Ladavac (2015-)
>
> Andrew Jason Ladavac (2017-)

Claire Nolan Ziomek (Nov. 11, 1983-Aug. 1922)

Audrey McKeon Ziomek (Aug. 7, 1985-) m. Jose Eduardo Duenas (1983-)

> Edward Tomas Duenas (2017-)
>
> Carl Jose Duenas (2017, twin)

David Paul Monagan (Sept. 18, 1952-) m. Jane Marie Donnelly (June 25, 1958-), res. Cork, Ireland

Laura Elizabeth Monagan (July 6,1987-) m. Rohan Geraghty

(Sept. 27, 1981-) res. Clapham, London

Harris Hurst Monagan (Jan. 28,1990-), res. Cork

Owen Stephen Monagan (July 14, 1993-) m. Anna Magliano (Brazil), software developer, res. Manhattan

Philip Harris Monagan (Sept. 17, 1959-) div. Diane Ukraine, res. Woodbury, Conn.

Kevin Andrew Monagan (Sept. 12, 1995-), res. Minneapolis

Grace Hope Monagan (July 16, 2000-), res. Middlebury, Conn.

5. **Louise Ann Monagan** (March 27, 1920-2010)

6. **Marjorie Mary Monagan** (April 20, 1922-) m. (1) Joseph M. Cetta (1924- 1954), m. (2) Vincent Kelly (1916-1975)

Catherine Cetta (Oct. 28, 1953-) – partner Julie Early, res. Falmouth, Mass.

7. **Joan Marie Monagan** (April 2, 1928-) m. **John Brooks Clinton** (Feb. 14,1927-April 16, 2003)

(1) Maureen Ann Clinton (Feb. 7, 1950 -) div. William Hale, res. Washington, D.C.

Grace (Martha) Hale (1975-) m. Steve Sanderson

Carrie Hale (1977-) m. Barton Carroll

Donovan Carroll (Jan. 24, 2020-)

Leah Hale-Storm (Jan. 28, 1979-) m. Amaury Rolin, res. Seattle Aubere Rolin (2016-)

(2) Gail Elizabeth Clinton, M.D. (June 5, 1952-) m. Joe Teno (div.) res. Portland, Maine, psychiatrist

(3) James Clinton (Sept. 21, 1954-) m. Audrey Sue Lemon (May 5, 1954-), res. Falls Church, Virginia

Daniel Clinton (March 21, 1979-) div. Nicolle Cristina

Caroline Clinton (Aug. 12, 2013-)

Camryn Clinton (July 29, 2015-)

Kelly Clinton (Aug. 24,1985-)

Ashton Clinton (May 24,2016)

Kevin Clinton (Aug. 23, 1987-)

(4) Andrew Clinton (April 3, 1957-) m. Dorothy Hannum

Lauren Clinton (Aug. 16, 1985-) m. Robert Hawkins

Theodore "Theo" Hawkins (Nov. 6, 2017-)

Margo Clinton (April 29, 1988-)

Evan Clinton (March 21, 1991-)

(5) Paul Clinton (March 5, 1958-) m. Carmen Lazo (m. 2021), res. 802 Hillwood, Falls Church

(6) Joan Clinton (July 25, 1959-) m. Alan Beetle (div.), res. Portland, Maine

Nicole Beetle (March 9, 1990-)

Kyle Beetle (Oct. 4, 1992-)

(7) Stephen Clinton (March 9, 1962-) m. Marsha Youngblood, res. Washington, D.C.

Natalie Clinton (Nov. 23, 1989-)

Joseph Clinton (Mar. 25, 1992-)

Adelle Clinton (Aug. 26, 1994-)

Sarah Clinton (May 17, 1998-)

(8) Thomas Clinton (Oct. 11, 1964-) m. Karen Miles, res. Falls Church

Eric Clinton (Jan. 16, 1998-)

Megan Clinton (Oct. 8, 2003-)

(9) Neal Clinton (Feb.19, 1967-) m. Katie Jacomet, res. Falls Church

Abigail Clinton (July 20, 2006-)

Descendants of Bernice Monagan (1891-1932) and Arthur Owen Nelson (1890-1948) – very partial listing

Anne Marie Nelson (1916-1990) m. (1) Sullivan, (2) Kenneth Beckman Watts

> Bernice Sullivan m. (1968) Douglas Anderson

Helen Nelson (Aug. 20, 1917-June 20, 1918)

Arthur Owen Nelson, Jr. (1919-2007) m. Eileen Marie Murphy (1920-2007)

Jane Margaret Nelson (1921-1996) m. Howard Burton Gaunt

> Howard Burton Gaunt, Jr. (South Hadley, Mass.)
>
> Peter Gaunt (St. Petersburg, Fla.)
>
> Jeffrey Gaunt (St. Petersburg)
>
> June Redding Gaunt

Charles Gerant Nelson (1925-2008) m. Ann Culhane

> Charles G. Nelson, Jr. (1947-)
>
> Thomas G. Nelson (1949-)
>
> Mark A. Nelson (1950-)

The Flax Pullers,
Lillian Lucy Davidson (1879 – 1957)

FOR FURTHER READING

Ireland – Books

Ordnance Survey Memoirs 1824-1838, Vol. 40. Counties of South Ulster: Cavan, Leitrim, Louth, Monaghan, and Sligo, Patrick McWilliams.

The Menapia Quest: Two Thousand Year of the Menapii: Seafaring Gauls in Ireland, Scotland, Wales, and the Isle of Man, 216 B.C. to 1990 A.D., Norman Mongan, Herodotus Press, 1995.

Calendar of the State Papers of Ireland, Tudor Period, 1571-1575, edited by Mary O'Dowd. Surrey: Public Records Office, Kew, 2000.

Statistical Survey of the County of Monaghan, With Observations on the Means of Improvement, Sir Charles Coote, London: Graisberry & Campbell, 1801.

The Tithe Applotment Books, 1823-1837, National Archives of Ireland.

Griffith's Valuation, 1868, National Archives of Ireland.

Realities of Irish Life, W. Steuart Trench, London: Longman's, Green and Co., 1869.

History of Monaghan for Two Hundred Years: 1660-1860, Denis Carolan Rushe, Dundalk: Tempest, 1921.

At the Ford of the Birches: The History of Ballybay, Its People and Vicinity, James H. Murnane and Peader Murnane Monaghan: Murnane Brothers, 1991.

The Catholics of Ulster (good early maps), Marianne Elliott, Penguin Press, London, 2002.

Jaywalking with the Irish, David Monagan, Lonely Planet, Footscray, Australia, 2004.

A History of the Scottish People: Poverty, Income, and Wealth –1840-1940, Lectures by W.W. Knox, 2011.

Ireland Unhinged: Encounters with a Wildly Changing Country, David Monagan, Transworld Ireland, Random House, U.K., 2011; Chicago Review Press.

The Shirley Estate 1814-1906: The Development and Demise of a Landed Estate in County Monaghan. Trinity College, Dublin Ph.D. thesis, Lorraine O'Reilly, 2014.

Periodicals – Ireland

"The Linen Industry in the Parish of Aughnamullen and its Impact on the Town of Ballybay –1740-1835," Peader and James Murnane, Clogher Record, Vol. 12, No. 3, 1987, pp. 334-368.

"Assisted Emigration from the Shirley Estate, 1843-54," Patrick J. Duffy. Clogher Record. Vol. 14, No. 2, 1992, pp. 7-62.

"Eastern Ulster Origins in the Fermanagh Genealogies: O'Monaghan, the Manaig, and St. Ronan: Magarraghan, Lisgoole, and St. Aed," Donald M. Schlegel. Clogher Record, Vol. 20, No. 2, 2010, pp. 195-221.

"Orangeism in County Monaghan," Aiken McClelland, Clogher Record, Vol. 9, No. 3, 1978, pp. 383-404.

"Estate Agents in Farney: Trench and Mitchell," Lorcan Ó Mearáin, Clogher Record, Vol. 10, No. 3, 1981, pp. 405-413.

"The Lawless Sorties into County Monaghan, October 1, 1828," James Murnane, Clogher Record, Vol. 13, No. 3, 1990, pp. 146-162.

"The Cottiers of the Shirley Estate in the Civil Parish of Donaghmoyne," Theo McMahon & Maire O'Neill, Clogher Record, Vol. 20, No.2, 2010, pp. 243-286.

"A Poitin Affair Near Ballybay in 1797," Thomas J. Barron, Clogher Record, Vol. 8, No. 2, 1974, pp. 182-193.

"Patterns of Land Ownership in Gaelic Monaghan in the Late Sixteenth Century," Patrick Duffy, Clogher Record, Vol. 11, No. 3, 1981, pp. 304-323.

"Castleblaney Rent Book, 1777," Peader Livingstone, Clogher Record, Vol. 10, No. 3, 1981, pp. 414-418.

"A People Set Apart: The County Monaghan Settlers of Prince Edward Island," Brendan O'Grady, Clogher Record, Vol. 12, No. 1, 1985, pp. 23-44.

The Breakley Collection, "Isaiah Breakley of Greenvale Mills," (Huguenot who first forged Aughnamullen's linen industry) by Kenneth C. Breakley and Marilyn J. Breakley, 2004.

NEW WORLD – BOOKS

Exiles and Islanders: The Irish Settlers of Prince Edward Island, Brendan O'Grady, Montreal: McGill-Queen's University, 2004.

Erin's Sons: Irish Arrivals in Atlantic Canada 1751-1898, Vol. III, by Terence Punch, 2008.

The History of Lawrence, with Portraits and Biographical Sketches [to 1880], H.A. Wadsworth, Lawrence: Hammon Reed, 1880.

Lawrence Yesterday and Today (1845-1918), Maurice B. Dorgan, Lawrence: Dick and Trumpold, 1918.

History of the City of Lawrence, J.F.C. Hayes, Massachusetts: E.D. Green, 1868.

Historical Sketches of Franklin County and Its Several Towns, Frederick J. Seaver, Albany, New York, 1918.

DeBeers Maps, Franklin County, New York, 1876.

The Town and City of Waterbury, Connecticut from the Aboriginal Period to Eighteen Hundred and Ninety Five, Joseph Anderson, New Haven, 1896.

The Brass Industry in the United States: A Study of the Origin and the Development of the Brass Industry in the Naugatuck Valley and its Subsequent Extension over the Nation. William C. Lathrop, Mount Carmel, Conn. (As lovingly rebound for the Kennedy High School Library in Waterbury in 1963 by my aunt Marjorie (Monagan) Cetta Kelly, the school librarian).

The Development of the Brass Industry of Connecticut, William Gilbert Lathrop, New Haven: Yale University Press, 1936.

A Pleasant Institution: Key C-Major, John S. Monagan, Lanham, Maryland: University Press of America, 2002.

Waterbury: A Region Reborn, Charles Monagan. Chatsworth, California, Windsor Publications.

Waterbury 1890-1930 (Postcard History Series), John Wiehn and Mark Heiss, Charleston: Arcadia Publishing, 2003.

A Brief History of Waterbury, Edith Reynolds & John Murray, Charleston: The History Press, 2009.

Waterbury Irish: From the Emerald Isle to the Brass City, Janet Maher with John Wiehn, Charleston: The History Press, 2015.

Connecticut Icons, Charles Monagan, Guilford: Globe Pequot Press, 2007.

The Easter Confession, Charles Monagan, 2020.

See Ticonderoga Sentinel from February 20, 1840, onwards, regarding George Gregg.

OTHER SOURCES

This work has been informed by countless hours of review of primary governmental, maritime, and church records in Ireland, Scotland, Canada, England, and the United States. Also central to the search has been the review of thousands of historic newspaper articles, scores of which have been specifically referenced in the text – but thousands not. A vast compendium of American newspapers reaching from the late 1700s to 1963 can be accessed free of charge on the U.S. Library of Congress website *Chronicling America*. But a far more exhaustive and international on-line archive has been cross-searched innumerable times via the paid-to-access *Newspapers.Com*.

Certain American states provide tremendous free portals for accessing their history with material reaching far beyond what can be found in *Chronicling America*. Exceptionally bountiful is the site *Historic New York Newspapers*, which allows one to comb through old Franklin County records with tremendous specificity, thoroughness, and ease. The *Malone Palladium* was of singular importance in this research. Rhode Island's more limited web portal was nonetheless helpful. Prince Edward Island, Canada, must be commended for providing wonderful free access to its historic newspapers.

But for some mendacious reason, the wealthy U.S. states of Massachusetts and Connecticut fall low on the list in providing and maintaining digitally available records for their citizens' understanding and tracking of their history. Worse, two singularly important newspapers regarding this family's past – the *Waterbury Republican-American* and *Boston Globe* – appear to have deliberately closeted their great troves of history from public access, apparently wishing to merchandize them at greater profitability at some later point. Thus, many references to the Monagans, Butlers, and Nolans of Waterbury or Bristol were drawn from the *Waterbury Democrat* and *Hartford Courant*. As historic a moment as was the November 6, 1960, appearance of the next American president John F. Kennedy before Waterbury's Green, with my cousin Congressman John Monagan at his side, the Waterbury Republican still blocks public online access to its coverage of that night. Why?

Also extremely important have been the innumerable census records cited within this text, both at the national and alternating five-year state levels in the U.S. My research has hugely drawn on the vast data bases with countless primary records assembled by the free *Familysearch.Org* website, and much more so by the constantly expanding *Ancestry.Com* with all its near instantly available DNA test comparisons to many millions of others. Many suggested and real genealogical links have been carefully cross-checked through Ancestry.Com's global DNA library, which is a wonder of our times.

In terms of old-fashioned, hand-hewn veracity, what the State of Massachusetts does absolutely excel at is in the maintaining and making easily available vital personal records from the 19th century – many crucial facts here derive from the devotion of the unnamed individuals behind this beautiful legacy. Another great boost has come from the Irish government's funding of an exhaustive digitalization of what remains of the country's baptismal, marital, and death records at the local church level – which is all the more important since half the nation's historic records went up in a fire at Dublin's Four Courts in 1922. But most of the County Monaghan Catholic church records were lost long earlier.

The Public Record Office of Northern Ireland (PRONI) data bases have also led to important revelations. The British National Archives have been further useful regarding certain specific issues. Among the most important data bases in Ireland are the Tithe Applotment books and Griffith's Valuation of Ireland. Undoubtedly, significant new sources will become available within even the next few years, helping this family story and countless others to unfold further. Obviously, I have by no means covered the full A to Z of this family's past here. So I can only wish future researchers much joy and revelation in bettering me.

ACKNOWLEDGMENTS

This history has come about thanks to the contributions of many family members, beginning of course with the insights provided by my late parents, John and Hope Monagan. My familial fascination was further fed by my aunt Margie Monagan Kelly, a skilled research librarian, and my uncle Walter Monagan, that world-travelled lawyer with a restless, inquiring mind. This interest was later powerfully amplified by the detailed recollections passed along by the former Congressman John S. Monagan as he was developing his 2002 memoir, *A Pleasant Institution – Key in C. Minor.*

An endless stream of new questions and fascinations arose as this project evolved, with any number of them first very thoughtfully reviewed with my wife Jamie. My siblings – Jim, Nancy, and Phil – had their own takes on an older Waterbury and contributed much to this story.

Numerous cousins have also splendidly helped. From Falmouth, Massachusetts, Cathy Cetta has been vital in both reviewing important questions with her now 100-year-old mother, my aunt Margie, as well as in expanding my understanding of Waterbury's older Italian-immigrant ways. Special gratitude is also due to my Virginia cousin James Clinton, the oldest son of Joan Monagan Clinton, now 94. Jim went as far as to conduct extensive, formal oral history interviews with his mother, who has been so vital in holding the family collective together, and a guiding star in my life. My cousin Bob Monagan provided important material about his father William who lived to be 100, as well as added information about my uncle Walter who only made it to 97. At the eleventh hour important contact was also made with his niece Carolyn Marie Porter, who lives in the North Carolina highlands and is a passionate genealogist herself. Stay tuned for a more definitive version of this family history from Carolyn in a few years.

Several children of the former Congressman Monagan have also heartily contributed. Michael Monagan in California has been a source of invaluable contacts and steady encouragement. His maternal first cousin, Andrew Pierce, a formidable researcher and generous spirit, has shared several vitally important tips regarding the early Monaghans in the Massachusetts mills towns. Charley Monagan, the Connecticut writer and Michael's older brother, has provided an impressive font of knowledge on not only his extended family but the Naugatuck Valley's wider history. Special thanks are also owed to their sister Parthy Monagan of Charlottesville, Virginia who spent many hours in curating and making book-ready most of the earliest historical photos surviving within this family.

It has been a joy to connect with descendants of Helen Monagan Marks – a long lost family line – through the legacy of her son Frederick Lamont, Jr. Susan Marks Roberts and her niece Kristy Horstkamp have generously led this dialogue. Susan's recollections about her aunt Marion, the magic child of that generation, born in 1908 and a future nun, are a particular treasure. It has also been uplifting to connect with Joe Murphy, a long-standing professor of religion at Georgetown University, and son of Mary Monagan and her husband Dick Murphy.

This project has also particularly benefited from the warm support of two of the numerous daughters of Thomas and Margie Monagan – Gretchen Monagan Sterling in Vermont, and Jane Monagan Marrone in Darien, Connecticut. Seeing as their parents were iconic figures in town and had 12 children (who observed Waterbury in widely prismatic ways), their take on an earlier life in the "Brass City" is priceless.

From the Nolan side of the family – Anna Nolan having been the wife of my great-grandfather John Stephen Monagan – James W. Nolan, my uncle Andy's friend at the Waterbury Elks Club, is owed special thanks for his discerning memories and fine photographs. He recently lost his brother George to the global Covid pandemic. Back in the day, cousin Jim was a tireless campaign worker for Congressman Monagan, underlining how our families remained so tightly interlinked for more than one hundred years.

Finally, I must thank and credit my children Laura, Harris, and Owen – as well as all the others of their generation for that essential starting point in any book – a target audience. It is up to the next generation to keep this incredible story of human achievement growing. There is so much of which to be proud.

And finally with very special thanks to my wife Jamie, a beacon of curiosity and adventure in my life.

Purling, New York, July 1987. Front: Grandmother Kathleen Donnelly holding our newly Christened daughter Laura Elizabeth Monagan. Rear: the author holding his niece Audrey Ziomek, DM's father-in-law Bill Donnelly, Hope Monagan, Andy and Seena Monagan, Tom Ziomek, Jake Monagan, Nancy Monagan Ziomek and her daughter Stephanie.

www.ingramcontent.com/pod-product-compliance
Lightning Source LLC
Chambersburg PA
CBHW071938260326
41914CB00004B/672